The Rough Guide
History of the

USA

Rough Guides online

www.rough

D0232121

credits

Rough Guides series editor: Mark Ellingham
Text editor: Olivia Swift
Production: Katie Pringle and Julia Bovis
Design: Henry Iles
Cartography: Katie Lloyd-Jones
Proofreading: Derek Wilde
Picture research: Amanda Russell

publishing information

This edition published November 2003 by
Rough Guides Ltd, 80 Strand, London WC2R ORL

distributed by the Penguin group

Penguin Books Ltd, 80 Strand, London WC2R ORL
Penguin Putnam, Inc., 375 Hudson Street, New York 10014, USA
Penguin Books Australia Ltd, 487 Maroondah Highway, PO Box 257,
Ringwood, Victoria 3134, Australia
Penguin Books Canada Ltd, 10 Alcorn Avenue,
Toronto, Ontario, Canada M4V 1E4
Penguin Books (NZ) Ltd, 182–190 Wairau Road,
Auckland 10, New Zealand

Typeset to an original design by Henry Iles

Printed in Spain by Graphy Cems

© Greg Ward, 2003
432 pages includes index

A catalogue record for this book is available from the British Library.
ISBN 1-85828-777-4

The Rough Guide
History of the

USA

by Greg Ward

series editor
Justin Wintle

acknowledgements

Thanks, as ever, from the bottom of my heart, to Samantha Cook, for her unfailing love, inspiration and encouragement during what (quite apart from the writing of this book) was a difficult year, and also to my mother. I'd also like to thank Olivia Swift, for her informed and constructive editing; Jonathan Buckley, for showing faith and making it all possible; Justin Wintle, for his invariably helpful suggestions and improvements; Peter Yapp, for his early involvement in the project; my brother Michael, for some supportive advice and the loan of several invaluable books; the Church Street Bookshop; and various friends who challenged my own ideas and contributed their own, including Jim Cook, John Eglin, Rob Humphreys and Robert Jones.

contents

introduction

The **United States of America** has existed as a political entity for little more than two centuries, and at its current size for considerably less than that. To that extent, the United States remains a young country; its history is shorter than those of almost all of its peers, and can readily be cast in terms of an infant nation finding its feet, grappling with internal tensions and turmoil as it grows at a tempestuous rate, and finally reaching maturity as the pre-eminent global military, economic, and in many respects cultural, superpower. In another sense, however, the history of the United States is of course no shorter than that of anywhere else. It stretches back long before North America held any states, united or otherwise, or even any colonies, while the peoples that have shaped its destiny can trace their stories back way before their separate arrivals in the 'New World'. Even in more recent times, although the 'United States' itself first came into being on the East Coast in the eighteenth century, the other regions that it ultimately came to incorporate were not simply waiting to be swept into the national saga; their own histories were already well under way.

In hindsight, that the US now extends across North America from the Atlantic to the Pacific might seem inevitable. To the so-called 'founding fathers' who declared its independence in 1776, fearful that their own untested republic of thirteen states might prove too large and disparate to survive, it was much less so. They had little idea what lay west beyond the mountains – might a single river flow right across the continent? Might an impassable mountain range block all westward traffic ?

Kauai

Oahu

Maui

HAWAII
1959

Big Island

0   50 miles

RUSSIA

USA

ALASKA
1959

CANADA

0   200 miles

C A N A

Seattle

WASHINGTON
1889

OREGON
1859

IDAHO
1890

MONTANA
1889

NORTH DAKOTA
1889

WYOMING
1890

SOUTH DAKOTA
1889

San Francisco

NEVADA
1864

Salt Lake City

UTAH
1896

NEBRASKA
1867

Denver

COLORADO
1876

CALIFORNIA
1850

Los Angeles

ARIZONA
1912

Santa Fe

KANSAS
1861

OKLAHOMA
1907

NEW MEXICO
1912

TEXAS
1845

San Antonio

MEXICO

	Louisiana Purchase 1803
	Ceded by Spain 1819
	Texas annexed 1845
	Oregon Territory established 1846
	Ceded by Mexico 1848
	Bought from Mexico 1854
	Bought from Russia 1867
	Annexed 1898

THE GROWTH OF THE UNITED STATES

D A

MINNESOTA 1858

WISCONSIN 1848

MICHIGAN 1837

Montréal

MAINE 1820

VERMONT 1791

NEW HAMPSHIRE 1788

Boston

NEW YORK 1788

MASSACHUSETTS 1788

RHODE ISLAND 1790

IOWA 1846

Chicago

Detroit

New York City

CONNECTICUT 1788

PENNSYLVANIA 1787

NEW JERSEY 1787

ILLINOIS 1818

INDIANA 1816

OHIO 1803

DELAWARE 1787

St Louis

WEST VIRGINIA 1863

VIRGINIA 1788

MARYLAND 1788

MISSOURI 1821

KENTUCKY 1792

TENNESSEE 1796

NORTH CAROLINA 1789

ARKANSAS 1836

Memphis

SOUTH CAROLINA 1789

MISSISSIPPI 1817

ALABAMA 1819

Atlanta

GEORGIA 1788

Charleston

LOUISIANA 1812

Savannah

New Orleans

FLORIDA 1845

N

0   200 miles

The date of statehood is given for each state.

America was not the '**virgin continent**' that European settlers liked to imagine; it had not been for perhaps 14,000 years. Archeologists still debate the exact process by which it was peopled, and speculate that some humans may have arrived before the first major influx of migrants spread into North America on foot from Asia around 12,000 BC. Since that time, it had been home to hundreds of different tribal groups, living in utterly distinct ways and speaking mutually unintelligible languages.

Physical geography was of course a major influence on the development of differing cultures. Topographical features that divided the continent into distinct regions, and made the dissemination of ideas more difficult, included the **mountain** ranges like the Appalachians in the east, the Sierra Nevada in the west, and the Rockies nearer the centre; the **deserts** that cut off what became Texas and the Southwest from the great civilizations that emerged further south, in Mexico and beyond; and the vast trackless expanse of the **Great Plains**. As America's indigenous plants and animals didn't lend themselves to domestication, **agriculture** came late, and only to certain regions, such as the Atlantic seaboard and the river valleys of the Southwest. Elsewhere, Native Americans hunted in the woodlands of the Southeast, fished the Pacific, or stalked the giant herds of buffalo on foot, out on the plains.

Although the **Spanish** were the first Europeans to explore North America, and set up early permanent settlements from Florida to the Southwest, the **British** colonies of the East Coast turned out to be the most prosperous and most enduring. Having first fought to ensure their survival, with British help, against both native peoples such as the Algonquians and Iroquois, and their French allies, the colonies subsequently broke with the mother country and won their independence in the Revolutionary War. The **Constitution** under which they established themselves as the **United States** ranks among the greatest achievements of the Enlightenment. With its intricate system of checks and balances – and with the protection for individual citizens afforded by its first ten amendments, the **Bill of Rights** – it has proved robust and flexible enough to guide American political discourse, and remain the basis of government, for more than two centuries. Its impact upon the rest of the world has been incalculable, from the French Revolution onwards. However, for all its lofty sentiments, the Constitution failed adequately to address the status of two integral ingredients in the American melting pot: the **Native Americans**, as yet still dominant across most of North America, and the **slaves**, imported as labourers from Africa.

During its first century, spared any significant military threat from its neighbours, and too far across the Atlantic to be in any danger from the European powers, the United States was free to fulfil what it came to see as its '**Manifest Destiny**', overcoming native resistance to conquer the entire continent. Even as it did so, however, internal ructions over slavery threatened to tear it apart. It took a devastating **Civil War** to forge North and South into a genuine union, and to free the slaves, while another century passed before the slaves' descendants finally became citizens in any meaningful sense.

By the time its modern boundaries were fixed, at the end of the nineteenth century, the United States was playing an increasingly prominent role on the world stage. Imperialist adventures in Cuba and the Philippines were followed by massive interventions in two world wars, and then embroilment in countless regional conflicts, most notably in Korea and Vietnam, against the real or perceived threat of global communism. To this day, however, it's still possible to count foreign incursions against US territory on the fingers of one hand. The British in 1812 threatened New Orleans and burned Washington, DC; the Mexicans invaded Texas in 1836 and 1846, though neither time did they actually set foot on American soil; and the Japanese attacked Pearl Harbor in 1941. Throw in a cross-border raid by Pancho Villa in 1916, and that's about it. That helps to explain why the appalling events of **September 11, 2001**, came as such a great shock to the nation. As the twenty-first century opens, the United States finds itself in a world grown abruptly less familiar, the master of unprecedented military might yet searching for some elusive new strategy that will ensure the security it has for so long taken for granted.

list of maps

1
First peoples, first encounters

To 1564

The first definitely dated trace of human beings in the Americas stems from just 14,000 years ago, when the true pioneers of North America, nomadic hunter-gatherers from Siberia, first reached what's now **Alaska**. Thanks to the last ice age, when sea levels were three hundred feet lower than in the modern Bering Strait, a **'land-bridge'** – actually a vast plain, measuring six hundred miles north to south – connected Eurasia to America.

At that time, Alaska effectively formed part of Asia rather than North America, being separated by impenetrable glacier fields from Canada and points south. Much like an air lock, the region has 'opened' in different directions at different times; migrants reaching it from the west, oblivious to the fact that they were leaving Asia, would at first have found their way blocked to the east. Several generations might have passed, and the connection back towards Asia been severed, before an eastward passage appeared. Crucially, that cold period of 'quarantine' may have served to eliminate microbes adapted to more temperate climates. The settlers were thus stripped of their immunity to many of the endemic diseases of the 'Old World', with fatal consequences for their descendants when such diseases were ultimately introduced by European invaders. When thawing ice did clear a route into North America, it was not along the Pacific coast but via a corridor that led east of the Rockies and out onto the Great Plains.

This migration was almost certainly spurred not by the impulse to explore what in itself cannot have seemed very promising territory, but by the urge to continue to pursue the large mammal species, and especially **mammoth**, that had already been harried to extinction throughout almost all of Eurasia. A huge bonanza awaited the hunters, when they finally encountered America's own indigenous '**megafauna**', such as mammoths, mastodons, giant ground sloths and enormous long-horned bison, all of which had evolved without fear of, or protection against, human predation.

Within a thousand years, both North and South America were filled with a total of ten million people. Although that sounds like a phenomenal rate of spread, only a small group of original human settlers need have been responsible. To achieve that impact, it would have taken a band of just one hundred individuals to enter the continent, and then advance a mere eight miles per year, with a population growth of 1.1 percent each year. The mass extinction of the American megafauna coincides so exactly with the advent of humans that humans must surely have been responsible, eliminating the giant beasts in each locality in one fell swoop, before pressing on in search of the next kill.

Quite apart from its ecological impact, the consequences of the elimination of large land mammals were legion. It precluded future American civilizations from domesticating any of the major animal species that were crucial to Old World economies. Without cattle, horses, sheep or goats, or significant equivalents, they lacked the resources used elsewhere in the world to supply food and clothing to large settlements, provide draught power to haul ploughs or wheeled vehicles, or increase mobility and the potential for conquest. What's more, most of the human diseases later introduced from the rest of the world evolved in association with domesticated animals; the first Americans developed neither immunity to such diseases, nor any indigenous diseases of their own that might have attacked the invaders.

At least three distinct waves of **migrants** arrived via Alaska, each of whom went on to settle in, and adapt to, a more marginal environment than its predecessors. The second, five thousand years on, were the '**Nadene**' or Athapascans – the ancestors of the Haida of the Northwest, and also the Navajo and Apache of the Southwest – while the third, another two thousand years later, found their niche in the frozen Arctic north and became the **Aleuts** and the **Inuits**.

The most highly developed and centralized civilizations in the prehistoric Americas appeared in Mexico, where the emergence of the Olmec around 1200 BC was followed by such cultures as the Maya and the Aztec, and in Peru, home to successive peoples from the Chavín to the Inca. In North America, by contrast, although regional centres rose and declined, and cultural traits came to be shared by the inhabitants of considerable areas, no equivalent states came into being. From the Algonquian farmers of what's now New England, via the hunters of the Southeastern woodlands and the Pueblo peoples of the Southwest, to the Chumash and the Makah along the Pacific coast, who lived by catching fish, otters and even whales, individual peoples adapted successfully to local conditions. None, however, was as expansionist or as technologically advanced as their Meso-American counterparts.

Leaving aside the **Vikings**, who probably reached the Newfoundland coast at much the same time as the Inuit, and stayed for a far shorter period, the crucial moment of contact with the rest of the world came when **Christopher Columbus** reached the Bahamas in 1492. Estimates of the total indigenous population of the Americas at that time vary widely. Although serious suggestions for North America range between two and twelve million, an acceptable median figure would be around fifty million people in the Americas as a whole, with five million of those in North America, speaking around four hundred different languages.

The impetus that spurred Columbus and other early voyagers to cross the Atlantic was not the desire to discover new lands but to establish direct trading routes to Cathay (China) and the Indies. Existing trade networks required long and expensive overland travel, and used so many middlemen along the way, especially in Islamic territories, that commodity prices were pushed to prohibitive levels. Thus when the Portuguese managed to reach India via the southern tip of Africa, they were at first content to leave the transatlantic discoveries to Spain. For seventy or so years, the primary goal of North American navigators – and the reason the eastern American coastline was swiftly mapped – remained the hope that a Northwest Passage to China might yet be found.

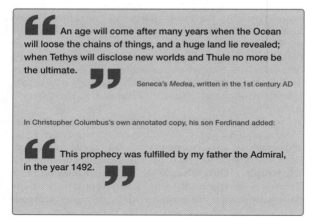

An age will come after many years when the Ocean will loose the chains of things, and a huge land lie revealed; when Tethys will disclose new worlds and Thule no more be the ultimate.

Seneca's *Medea*, written in the 1st century AD

In Christopher Columbus's own annotated copy, his son Ferdinand added:

This prophecy was fulfilled by my father the Admiral, in the year 1492.

Obliged to satisfy their sponsors back home, expedition leaders ruthlessly exploited any opportunity for profit that came their way. At first, if nothing else of value was found, they'd either carry so-called 'Indians' to Europe as slaves, or set them to work on plantations cleared from their former lands. When colossal riches were indeed obtained, thanks to the Spanish plundering of the Aztec and Inca empires, would-be *conquistadores* soon dreamed that further golden cities might lie hidden in North America. Though exploration by both land and sea proved unsuccessful in those terms, a steady stream of less spectacular discoveries – whether new foodstuffs such as potatoes, or access to the cod fisheries of the northern Atlantic – was soon boosting economies throughout Europe.

Even before any permanent European colonies were established in North America, the impact on its native population was devastating. The pattern swiftly emerged that almost all 'Indians' were affected by the immediate onslaught of epidemic diseases. Typically, as for example in the wake of de Soto's expedition to the Southeast of the future United States in 1540, around half would die within the first decade of contact. One consequence was that, in the absence of humans, lands that were previously populated and farmed were swiftly reclaimed by forest and wildlife. Notions of North America as a virgin continent, or as an unspoiled natural wilderness, were spurious from the start.

c.60 million BC Two mighty primeval islands collide, creating **North America** as a single landmass, and throwing up the Rocky Mountains. From then on, further collisions, combined with the advance and retreat of ocean water levels and polar icecaps, create intermittent opportunities for species to migrate to and from North America, via Eurasia along both eastern and western routes, and also via South America.

c.5 million BC The major topographical features of North America have taken shape, including the Great Plains and the Grand Canyon.

c.2.8 million BC The Panamanian isthmus rises, establishing a permanent link between North and South America, and thus sending warm water currents north along the west coast of North America.

c.1.7 million BC The first **mammoths** reach North America – the Columbian mammoth, later followed by the smaller woolly mammoth.

c.400,000 BC The first bison-like creatures reach North America.

c.16,000 BC Ice Age reduces sea levels by approximately 120 metres, creating the **Beringia** land-bridge.

c.12,000 BC The first **humans** arrive in northeastern Siberia, probably in pursuit of the 'megafauna' of large mammal species that were driven to extinction throughout Eurasia around this period, quite possibly due to over-hunting. Over the next millennium, humans, mammoths, elks, buffalo and bears alike continue to migrate eastwards into Alaska, where they may initially have found their route southeast towards North America proper blocked by glaciers.

c.11,200 BC The earliest uncontested date for a human presence in what's now the United States. Fluted spear points from the **Clovis** culture, originally identified when excavated with mammoth bones from a site in Clovis, New Mexico, have been found in all the lower 48 states.

c.10,900 BC Clovis spear points cease to be made, at much the same time as the North American megafauna becomes extinct; human predation is almost certainly responsible. In addition to mammoths and ground sloths, casualties include horses, which evolved in North America around

45 million years ago, and migrated into Asia and Africa from around 25 million years ago, but now die out. These large-scale extinctions allow other species, including some of those that arrived with humans, to fill vacant ecological niches. **Folsom** spear points, suitable for killing buffalo and even more deftly manufactured, appear in what's now New Mexico.

c.10,200 BC Folsom spear points disappear, probably because humans are now hunting buffalo by mass drive-hunts rather than individual spearing. This in turn suggests that the buffalo were evolving into their modern form, which differs from their ancestors by congregating in enormous herds and having shorter horns.

c.10,000 BC By now humans are firmly established throughout both North and South America.

c.7200 BC A hunter dies beside the Columbia River; his skeleton, discovered in 1996, is now known as '**Kennewick Man**'.

c.7000 BC The **Nadene** group of humans, the ancestors of the Haida of the Northwest, and the Navajo and Apache of the Southwest, enter North America via Alaska.

c.5000 BC The people who became the **Aleuts** and the **Inuits** form the last wave of humans to reach North America via Alaska. Either they or the Nadenes are thought to have introduced the bow and arrow, which had long been known in Eurasia.

The first sign of agriculture in the Americas: squash is domesticated in Mexico, and maize in Panama.

c.2500 BC Agriculture makes its appearance in North America: pumpkins and gourds arrive from the south, to be cultivated alongside poor-quality indigenous grasses such as sumpweed and goosefoot.

Kennewick Man

Academic debate over the origins of human settlement in the Americas exploded into fierce public controversy following the discovery in July 1996 of a 9000-year-old skeleton in the Columbia River near Kennewick, Washington. Embedded in the pelvis of the so-called **Kennewick Man**, a stone spear point – familiar to archeologists as a Cascade projectile point – testified to a non-fatal wound received thirty years before he died at the age of around 50.

Under the Native American Protection and Repatriation Act of 1990, tribes who show a cultural affiliation with human remains can demand their return and deny scientists further access. The five peoples who duly did so – the Umatilla, Colville, Wanapum, Nez Perce and Yakama – were opposed by archeologists who argued that the extreme age of the find rendered such claims absurd. There were further suggestions that the remains showed Caucasoid or Polynesian traits, and were thus not 'Native American' at all. Several court rulings later, the scientists currently have the upper hand, and Kennewick Man is in a laboratory rather than in the ground. However, although definitive results have yet to be published, it now seems that the remains are consistent with the theory that humans first arrived in the Americas from central Asia, via Siberia and Alaska.

While that hypothesis accounts for the mass peopling of the continent, it does not preclude other, conceivably earlier, small-scale influxes. Some scientists feel that the role of boats has long been underestimated, and suggest that Asian voyagers may have followed the shoreline around the northern Pacific; even when the 'land-bridge' is closed, the longest open-water crossing necessary to reach Alaska is just three miles. Use of inshore craft would also help to explain quite how quickly humans seem to have reached the southernmost tip of South America.

c.1500 BC Maize and squash are now being grown in the Southwest and Midwest.

c.1200 BC **Olmec** culture, characterized by the carving of giant stone heads and the development of the first writing system in the Americas, emerges along Mexico's Gulf Coast. It will endure for around a thousand years.

c.900 BC A new civilization arises in the Andes, centred on Chávin de Huántar.

c.700 BC The **Adena** people of the Ohio Valley begin to construct large burial mounds.

The Aleuts of Alaska acquire the skill of making pottery from Siberia.

c.500 BC Zapotecs erect pyramids at Monte Alban in southern Mexico.

New strains of maize, more suited to a cooler climate and shorter growing season, are developed along the Rio Grande; agriculture expands rapidly thereafter.

c.150 BC The city of **Teotihuacán**, just north of the Valley of Mexico and dominated by giant pyramids, holds a population of 200,000.

c.100 BC The **Basketmakers** of the Southwest herald the start of the Pueblo-Hohokam cultural tradition.

c.250 AD Polynesian seafarers reach the previously uninhabited islands of **Hawaii**, the furthest extent of the so-called 'Polynesian Triangle' that covers the southern Pacific Ocean. The distribution of the sweet potato throughout the Pacific appears to prove that Polynesians sailed at least once as far as South America.

400 AD The **Hopewell** peoples, mound-building successors to the Adena in the Eastern woodlands, fade out of sight.

900 AD **Mississippian** settlements, characterized by city-like conglomerations of earthen mounds, appear throughout the Southeast, especially east and south of the Mississippi and Ohio valleys.

The Mound Builders

The major question for the first archeologists who attempted to understand North American prehistory was how to explain the thousands of earthen mounds scattered across the continent. In 1804, for example, Lewis and Clark encountered the ruins of **Cahokia**, at the confluence of the Mississippi and Missouri rivers. It seemed unthinkable that the ancestors of what were seen as degraded 'red Indians' were capable of such achievements. Instead the myth of the **Mound Builders** was born. This vanished civilization was assumed to be of white European origin, descended perhaps from Irish monks or Viking seafarers, or conceivably a lost tribe of Israel, who had been violently displaced by savage Indians.

A thirteen-year enquiry by the Smithsonian, published in 1894, finally proved that native peoples were indeed responsible, and a century of further investigations have fleshed out the detail. Although no single group created all the mysterious monuments, the phenomenon clearly centred on the **Ohio Valley**, in the so-called Eastern Woodlands. It's first identifiable around 700 BC, when the **Adena** people – the earliest North American users of tobacco – began to construct large burial mounds. Around 100 BC, they gave way to the **Hopewell** culture, which as well as greatly expanding their long-distance trading networks and erecting ever more elaborate burial mounds, also created such complex earthworks as Ohio's 1250-foot-long Great Serpent Mound.

The Hopewell declined after 400 AD, to be replaced by the **Mississippian** culture, which spread throughout the Southeast by 900 AD. Combining agriculture in river valleys with hunting and fishing, they sustained large cities such as Cahokia itself – a complex of mounds and pyramids with up to forty thousand inhabitants – and Moundville in Alabama. Many Mississippian sites endured into the sixteenth century, when the slaughter and pestilence brought by de Soto's 1540s expedition sounded their death knell.

986 AD The Viking **Eirik the Red**, outlawed from Iceland, settles in Greenland; **Bjarni Herjolfsson**, attempting to visit the new colonies, becomes lost in fog and eventually sights America.

1001–02 Leif Eiriksson – also known as Leif the Lucky – buys Bjarni's ship and sails from Greenland to establish **Vinland**, where he spends a single winter, probably at L'Anse aux Meadows in northern Newfoundland. Climatic conditions may well have been much better than they are today, though it remains unclear what were the 'grapes' that gave Vinland its name.

1004–05 Leif's brother Thorvald returns to Vinland. Exploring the coast, he kills eight **Skraelings** or 'wretches' – probably Inuit, newcomers to the area around this time – and is then killed by a larger group of Skraelings.

The Great Serpent Mound, a Hopewell culture site in the Ohio Valley

1010–13 Thorfinn Karlsefni, together with sixty men and five women, voyages to Vinland. During the winter, his wife Gudrid bears a son, Snorri. Trading relationships with the Skraelings soon deteriorate into war, and after another winter Karlsefni returns to Greenland. The following year, Eirik's daughter organizes another expedition, which dissolves amid bloody feuding and further Skraeling attacks. Although the Greenland colony will endure until the late fifteenth century, there's no definite evidence of further voyages to Vinland.

The Mexican connection

No North American civilization ever rivalled the wealth and sophistication of the great cultures of ancient Mexico. Nonetheless, Mexican influences undoubtedly filtered north. In the Southwest, the gradual shift from a hunter-gatherer existence to a village-based way of life was triggered by the arrival of three crops first domesticated in Mexico. Both maize and squash were present by 1000 BC. Beans followed around 200 BC, completing a 'trinity' that provides a complete protein source. Add pottery, again introduced from Mexico, around 200 AD, and the stage was set for the **Ancestral Puebloans**.

WERNER FORMAN/CORBIS

First emerging as 'Basketmakers' around 100 BC, the Ancestral Puebloans spread

Bowl created around 1100 AD by the Mimbres people of what's now New Mexico

1050–1250 The Mississippian walled city of **Cahokia**, near modern St Louis, is now the equal in size of any city in Europe. Centring on a huge pyramid, it holds around a hundred additional mounds and temples, and a population estimated at up to forty thousand.

1325 The previously obscure **Aztecs** migrate to the Valley of Mexico from somewhere to the north and found their capital Tenochtitlán.

1430 Prince Henry the Navigator of Portugal establishes

throughout the Southwest by 700 AD. Over the next five centuries, they established countless village communities or 'pueblos', and were responsible for such impressive monuments as the 'cliff palaces' of Mesa Verde. Their civilization reached its apogee in **Chaco Canyon**, in northern New Mexico, between 1050 AD and 1125 AD. This ceremonial centre, whose multi-storey pueblos could hold up to twenty thousand people, was intimately linked to the south. Locally mined turquoise, its most valuable commodity, was traded from hand to hand down into the heart of Mexico; ninety percent of the turquoise found in Tenochtitlán was of Southwestern origin. In return came parrots and macaws from southern Mexico, and, quite possibly, an early form of the *kachina* religion, which in adapted form still persists among the Hopi, Zuni and other modern descendants of the Ancestral Puebloans. Some argue that Chacoan civilization collapsed after succumbing to human sacrifice, and strong echoes have been found in the *kachina* religion of Aztec deities such as Tlaloc, the god of rain, and Quetzalcoatl, the plumed serpent, who brought both rain and corn. For the Aztec preoccupation with death and blood, however, Southwestern peoples substituted an obsessive focus on rain.

himself at Sagres, and sends successive expeditions further down the African coast. At some point, probably once it becomes clear that it is possible to sail south of the Equator and return, the overt goal of these voyages becomes to find a route to the Indies. The young Christopher Columbus will take part in at least one such trip later in the century.

1469 The marriage of Queen Isabella of Castile and Prince Ferdinand of Aragon creates **Spain**.

1483 After a five-year guerrilla war, the Spanish conquer the indigenous people of **Grand Canary**, and set about converting the Canary Islands into sugar plantations. The process became a template for Spanish actions in the Americas.

1488 **Bartholomeu Dias** rounds the Cape of Good Hope, at the southernmost tip of Africa, and thus opens up a Portuguese sea route to India.

Cliff Palace, built by Ancestral Puebloans at Mesa Verde, southwest Colorado, around 1200 AD

1492 The fall of Granada marks the final defeat of the Moors in Spain. Ferdinand and Isabella immediately dispatch **Christopher Columbus** across the Atlantic. He sails from Palos on 3 August, with ninety men in three caravels, calls at the Canaries in early September, and makes landfall on a small island in the Bahamas, which he names **San Salvador**, on 12 October. He calls the **Taino** people he finds there 'indios'. His explorations take him on to other islands, including first **Cuba**, and then **Hispaniola**, where he finally encounters gold. After one of his ships runs aground on Christmas Day, he establishes the settlement of La Navidad, then sails for home; he reaches Lisbon on 4 March and Palos on 15 March, announcing that he has reached the Indies.

1493 Within two months of Columbus's return, **Pope Alexander VI**, who was born a Spaniard, issues papal bulls that grant the Spanish exclusive possession of all lands to the south and west towards India, not held by a Christian prince on Christmas Day 1492, beyond a line one hundred leagues west of the Azores and Cape Verde Islands.

On 25 September, Columbus sails again from Cadiz, this time with seventeen ships and at least 1200 sailors and prospective colonists. They reach **Dominica** on 3 November, then cruise the Caribbean. Returning to Hispaniola, Columbus finds that La Navidad has been destroyed, and founds **Isabella**, which becomes the base for a bloody campaign of conquest and genocide. Jamaica and southern Cuba are also visited before Columbus eventually returns to Cadiz in June 1496. By now the lack of any evidence that he has reached either the Indies or Cathay is leading to great scepticism.

1494 Spain and Portugal sign the **Treaty of Tordesillas**, which moves the previously decreed north–south boundary line to 370 leagues west of the Azores, and grants the Portuguese all lands to the east.

Christopher Columbus (1451–1506)

Despite the claims of other cities, there's little doubt that **Cristoforo Colombo**, or Christopher Columbus, was born in **Genoa** in 1451. His earliest maritime experience came with the Genoese fleet, but after swimming ashore following a naval battle in 1476, he made his home in **Lisbon**. He subsequently sailed in Portuguese ships both down the coast of Africa and, debatably, north to Iceland.

During the early 1480s, Columbus started to seek sponsorship for his '**Enterprise of the Indies**'. Far from being unique in realizing the earth to be round, he differed from other navigators mainly in his drastic underestimate of its size. Intricate calculations, based on sources ranging from Marco Polo to the Bible, persuaded him that Japan lay 2400 miles west of the Canaries, as opposed to the actual 11,000 miles, and that he could therefore sail westwards from Europe to the Indies. Turned down by Portugal, England and France, he made his base in Seville, Spain, where Queen Isabella kept him hanging on for several years.

Only following the fall of Granada in 1492 did Ferdinand and Isabella make Columbus an admiral, and dispatch him 'to discover and acquire certain islands and mainlands in the Ocean Sea'. Though his first voyage, which took him to the Bahamas, Cuba and Hispaniola, convinced popular opinion that he had reached the Indies, doubts crept in after he returned from a second, longer, trip in 1496 without any concrete proof. On his third voyage he did at least reach the mainland of South America – he never set foot in North America – but both that and the fourth disintegrated amid great personal suffering. He died at Valladolid in 1506, wealthy by contemporary standards but convinced he had been cheated of his due reward, and by now believing that he had reached the eastern tip of the Malay peninsula.

1497 Commissioned by Henry VII of England after failing to attract support in Spain and Portugal, the Genoese-born **John Cabot** sails from Bristol in search of the island of Hy-Brasil. Crossing the north Atlantic in just 33 days, he reaches the northern tip of **Newfoundland** – just five miles from Leif Eiriksson's settlement – on 24 June, sails the length of the Newfoundland coast until 20 July, and returns to Bristol in August. He reports his discovery as being an island just off the coast of Cathay.

1498 On his third voyage, **Columbus** discovers Trinidad and reaches South America at the mouth of the Orinoco. Back at Hispaniola, the colony is in such disarray that a judge sent from Spain arrests Columbus and his two brothers and sends them home in disgrace in 1500. Columbus is later released and honoured, but never recovers his full authority. From now on, several Spanish adventurers, often spurred by unauthorized perusals of Columbus's maps and reports, embark on quasi-piratical expeditions to South America and the Caribbean.

John Cabot sails on a second voyage with five ships, but never returns, and is presumably lost at sea. His son Sebastian later claims that they cruised down the North American coast as far south as Delaware, and thus establishes in retrospect a pretext for England's claim to North America, but there's no evidence that this ever took place.

1499 **Vasco da Gama** of Portugal sails into Lisbon, completing the first return voyage to India.

1500 Pedro Álvares Cabral of Portugal, en route to India with thirteen ships, sails sufficiently far west to sight Brazil on 22 April, which he takes possession of under the name Ilha da Vera Cruz. Under the Treaty of Tordesillas, the new land, which is soon realized to be more than a mere island, belongs to Portugal; some thus argue that the Portuguese may have known of its existence when the treaty was signed.

From now on, expeditions by Portuguese and English voyagers will map the coast of Newfoundland, with hopes of finding a Northwest Passage to China. By 1506, **fishermen** from those countries, and also northern France and Spain, are sailing to Newfoundland waters for cod. Soon this becomes a large-scale industry, with ships making two voyages to the Grand Bank each year.

1502 Columbus, on his fourth voyage, still expects to find a route beyond Cuba to the Indies. After sailing along the Central American coast from Honduras to Panama, he's shipwrecked on Jamaica, where he remains for a year before managing to return to Spain in November 1504.

1504 The Florentine **Amerigo Vespucci** writes home to a friend, describing in exaggerated terms his role in two naval expeditions – one to Hispaniola with the Spaniard Alonso de Ojeda in 1499, and one along the coast of Brazil with the Portuguese captain Gonçalho Coelho in 1501. From his statement that he has found 'what we may rightly call a New World . . . a continent more densely peopled and abounding in animals than our Europe or Asia or Africa', the geographer Martin Waldseemüller derives his 1507 suggestion that the lands be called **America**, and duly marks the new name on his ground-

> **❝** They do not have arms, and they are all naked, and of no skill in arms, and so very cowardly that a thousand would not stand against three [armed Spaniards]. And so they are fit to be ordered about and made to work, plant, and do everything else that may be needed, and build towns and be taught our customs, and to go about clothed. **❞**
>
> Christopher Columbus, of the Taino of the Caribbean, 1492

breaking map. It originally applies only to the southern continent.

1513 Ponce de León, the governor of Puerto Rico, ostensibly in search of an island named Bimini that's said to hold the Fountain of Youth, encounters **Florida**, which he names 'Pascua florida', or Floral Passover. Sailing south along its eastern shore, he rounds the tip, traces the Keys, and explores the west coast.

Vasco Núñez de Balboa crosses the Isthmus of Panama and sights the Pacific Ocean on 25 September.

1517 Don Diego Velázquez, governor of Cuba, sends **Francisco Hernández de Córdoba** to explore the **Yucatán**, where he reports seeing fine cities and great wealth, and he also has to fight pitched battles to survive.

1518 Slaves are imported from West Africa to Hispaniola for first time.

Velázquez now sends **Juan de Grijalba** to the Yucatán; as he sails north along the coast of Mexico, he comes to the attention of the Aztec ruler **Moctezuma**. Meanwhile **Alonso Álvarez de Pineda** sails west from Florida around the Gulf of Mexico, explores the mouth of the **Mississippi**, and touches on Texas before being killed in Mexico. Between them, these voyages finally establish that there is no westward sea route to the Indies.

1519 The Portuguese navigator **Ferdinand Magellan** sets sail, commanding a Spanish expedition that discovers a route around the southern tip of South America, via the strait that bears his name, in 1520, and completes the first circumnavigation of the world in 1522. Magellan himself, however, dies in the Philippines in 1521.

Hernán Cortés lands in Mexico with six hundred men, and on his own initiative, making skilful use of Indian allies and exploiting Moctezuma's fatalistic belief that Cortés may be the returning deity Quetzalcoatl, succeeds in taking control of **Tenochtitlán**. In the next two years, dissension among the Spaniards and the emergence of a new Aztec ruler, Cuauhtémoc, leads to further bloody fighting, but by 1521 the Aztec empire has been overthrown.

1521 Ponce de León returns to Florida, and this time attempts to establish a trading colony, at the mouth of the Caloosahatchee River near modern Fort Myers. Ferocious resistance from local 'Indians' drives the would-be settlers away, and Ponce de León dies of an arrow wound.

1524 The Italian **Giovanni da Verrazzano**, despatched by the French king François I, sets out to explore the still unknown gap between Newfoundland and Florida. Making landfall at Cape Fear, in what's now North Carolina, on 1 March, he sails south as far as modern Charleston and then turns north. Although unable to find a gap in the narrow Outer Banks, he believes he's sighted the Pacific Ocean on the far side. He misses both the Chesapeake and Delaware bays, but describes New York Bay and the Hudson River, and names Rhode Island. His encounters with native peoples are generally friendly until he reaches **Maine**, which he characterizes as the 'Land of Bad People' thanks to the behaviour of the **Abenaki**, who 'used all signs of discourtesy and disdain, such as exhibiting their bare behinds and laughing immoderately'. He sails home from Newfoundland in June, having established the French claim to North America.

1526 **Luís Vasquez de Ayllón** of Spain sails with five hundred followers from Hispaniola and attempts to establish a settlement alongside the Cape Fear River on the Carolina coast. However, thanks to disease and a lack of native co-operation, San Miguel de Guadalupe is abandoned within a year.

1528 **Pánfilo de Narváez**, one of the *conquistadores* who defeated the Aztecs, lands with six hundred settlers at

Florida's Tampa Bay, marches north into the region known as Appalachee, and then builds makeshift rafts near Tallahassee in the hope of sailing to Mexico, only to be shipwrecked on the Texas coast.

1532 Francisco Pizarro lands in Peru with an even smaller force than Cortés, but by similar tactics, including kidnapping their leader Atahualpa, succeeds in overthrowing the Inca empire within two years.

1534 In two successive voyages **Jacques Cartier** of St-Malo explores Newfoundland and the Gulf of St Lawrence for France, in the hope of finding the Northwest Passage. Local Hurons guide him up the St Lawrence Seaway into the region they call **Canada**, where he reaches modern **Montreal**, the site of the Huron village of Hochelaga, on 2 October, 1535.

1535 Hernán Cortés sails north along the Pacific coast of Mexico as far as **Baja California**.

1536 Following several years of wandering westwards from Galveston Island on the Texas coast, during which they encountered peripheral settlements affiliated with the Pueblo peoples of the Southwest, **Álvar Núñez Cabeza de Vaca** and three other survivors of Narváez's 1528 expedition finally reach a Spanish outpost in the Mexican state of Sonora. Their tales, enhanced by rumours, encourage the notion that further lands of great wealth might lie to the north.

1539 Esteban, a black Moorish slave who was one of Cabeza de Vaca's former companions, guides a party into the Southwest. Racing ahead of his nominal leader, the Franciscan Fray Marcos de Niza, Esteban is killed at the **Zuni** pueblo of Hawikkuh in what's now New Mexico. De Niza turns back, but conflates the six Zuni villages with the legendary Seven Cities of Antilla, to create a new myth about the **Seven Cities of Cíbola**.

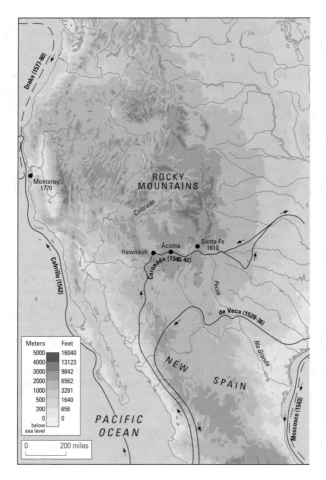

Drake (1577-80)

ROCKY
MOUNTAINS

Monterey
1770

Colorado

Cabrillo (1542)

Ácoma
Hawikkuh   Santa Fe
1610

Coronado (1540-42)

Pecos

de Vaca (1528-36)

Rio Grande

Meters	Feet
5000	16040
4000	13123
3000	9842
2000	6562
1000	3281
500	1640
200	656
0	0
below sea level	

NEW

SPAIN

Moscoso (1543)

PACIFIC
OCEAN

0   200 miles

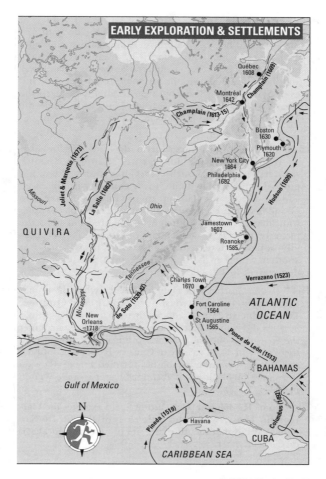

EARLY EXPLORATION & SETTLEMENTS

Québec 1608

Montréal 1642

Champlain (1698)

Champlain (1613-15)

Boston 1630

Plymouth 1620

New York City 1664

Philadelphia 1682

Hudson (1609)

Joliet & Marquette (1673)

La Salle (1682)

Missouri

Ohio

QUIVIRA

Jamestown 1607

Roanoke 1585

Tennessee

Charles Town 1670

Verrazano (1523)

de Soto (1539-42)

Mississippi

New Orleans 1718

Fort Caroline 1564

St Augustine 1565

ATLANTIC OCEAN

Ponce de León (1513)

BAHAMAS

Columbus (1492)

Gulf of Mexico

N

Pineda (1519)

Havana

CUBA

CARIBBEAN SEA

Hernando de Soto, governor of Cuba and veteran of Pizarro's conquest of the Inca, lands in **Florida** with 573 men and 220 horses. In a brutish campaign that combines deliberate slaughter with genocide by disease, he spends the ensuing years exploring north as far as the Savannah River and the Blue Ridge Mountains, south to Mobile Bay, and even crossing the Mississippi near Memphis to reach the Ozarks and Oklahoma. A year after his death beside the Mississippi in June 1542, 311 survivors manage to return to Mexico.

1540 Francisco Vásquez Coronado leads a major *entrada* (expedition), including three hundred Spanish soldiers, into the Southwest. They fight and win a pitched battle at Hawikkuh, make contact with the Hopi and see the Grand Canyon, then winter along the Rio Grande, where their relations with the Pueblo peoples soon degenerate into outright war. Lured out onto the plains by tales of the golden city of Quivira, they eventually concede defeat somewhere in Kansas, and after another winter in New Mexico return to Mexico City despondent in 1542.

1541 Jacques Cartier sails again to Canada, where he founds the settlement of Charlesbourg Royal near **Quebec**. Largely due to Huron attacks, it is abandoned within a year. As the colonists return home in 1542, they encounter the Sieur de Roberval, who was originally due to sail with them as François I's viceroy of Canada. Roberval continues to Quebec, where he establishes fortified France-Roy on the same site, but it too is abandoned after a single winter, in 1543.

1542 Juan Rodríguez Cabrillo of Spain explores the **California** coast, where he fails to spot the future San Francisco Bay, but identifies the site of modern San Diego on 27 September.

1550s Hundreds of European vessels are now descending each year on the Grand Bank fisheries of Newfoundland. The French especially begin to establish temporary camps along the shoreline where cod are cured in the sun, and develop a lucrative sideline in trading with local Indians, obtaining furs in return for knives, hatchets and beads.

1555 English curiosity about America is stimulated by Richard Eden's translation of Peter Martyr's *Decades of the Newe World*.

1562 Jean Ribault of France establishes a short-lived colony on Port Royal Sound in Florida.

John Hawkins of England delivers a cargo of slaves from Africa to Hispaniola. On a repeat voyage in 1564–65, he returns home via Florida and Newfoundland, in an early prototype for the 'Triangular Trade' on which the slave trade will come to be based.

1564 René de Laudonnière of France founds **Fort Caroline** on the St Johns River in Florida.

2
The colonial era

1565–1763

In the two hundred years after the **Spanish** founded North America's first permanent foreign settlement, at **St Augustine** in Florida, the colonial population grew to around two million people. Several European nations, including the **French** and the **Dutch** as well as the Spanish, launched competing colonial ventures, and settlers flocked in from many other countries besides. However, it was the **British** (at first, English) possessions along the Atlantic seaboard that came to dominate – which explains, of course, why the traditional approach to US history remains so Anglo-centric to this day.

To account for the fact that 350,000 immigrants came to North America from the British Isles during the seventeenth century alone – when fewer than 250 French families migrated to Canada – it's necessary to understand both why they wanted to leave Europe, and why they chose specific destinations in America. **Religion** was undoubtedly a major motivation, with the Puritans of Massachusetts – responsible for the **Great Migration** of the 1630s – merely the most prominent among those who sought the freedom to establish new idealized societies in a new world. Unlike the French and Spanish, the Protestant British allowed religious dissenters to join and for that matter lead their colonies, and even sanctioned Maryland as a Catholic colony. Rather than seeing them as literally fleeing persecution, it makes more sense to regard the colonists as pursuing religious opportunity. After all, the Puritans established their own Commonwealth in England in the middle of the seventeenth century, while the Board of Trade in London declared in 1750 that 'toleration and a free exercise of religion . . . should ever be held sacred in his Majesty's Colonies'. Thus French Huguenots fled to the Carolinas, not Canada, while thousands of German Protestants found refuge in Pennsylvania and Delaware.

Economic factors, too, played a significant role; only half of the pioneers on the *Mayflower* were Puritans, the rest were simply hoping to better their prospects. A one-way journey across the world seems less unthinkable when times are hard back home, and in seventeenth-century England around half of the peasantry had lost the ability to farm during the previous hundred years, due to the enclosure of formerly common lands. That said, many early colonists hoped to find instant riches to match those gained by the Spanish in Mexico, and lacked the experience or even the inclination to make a success of the mundane reality of subsistence farming. Six out of every seven new arrivals at Jamestown, for example, died within their first year. In their wake, however, came thousands more, for whom the plentiful availability of agricultural land represented a far greater hope of advancement than anything that overcrowded and war-torn Europe had to offer. It also has to be acknowledged that less desirable elements streamed in too: transported criminals, most obviously, but also those wishing to escape debts, the law, failed marriages and other such vicissitudes.

Each of the various colonies took on distinct characteristics, influenced in part by differences in climate and terrain. The **New England** colonies, where the pattern of settlement was for individual settlers to carve out their own small farms, tended to attract free men and families who could afford to pay their own passage to America, and who were steeled by their faith for the sheer hard work required. Further south, and especially in **Virginia** and the **Carolinas**, it swiftly became clear that the most suitable way to raise crops such as **tobacco** was on large plantations. Only the very poorest of English immigrants were prepared to come to America to work for others, however, and even they arrived as indentured servants, expecting to be granted their own lands after perhaps three years. As a result, the southern colonies soon became dependent on **slavery**. Their reliance on exports made them especially vulnerable to boom-and-bust cycles, while the white population enjoyed a significantly less equal distribution of wealth than did their neighbours to the north.

That the colonies eventually outgrew their relationship with Britain should not obscure the benefits that they originally derived from it. Even if it was motivated largely by the desire for simple profit in the case of the private joint-stock companies that funded them, or by customs revenues in the case of the British government itself, the English and subsequently British colonies typically maintained their involvement with the home country to a much greater extent than did their rivals. As time went by, both the French and the Spanish ventures in North America were effectively colonies of colonies – of Canada and Mexico respectively – rather than being sustained and enabled to grow by investment and migration from Europe.

Even in nurturing their colonies, however, the British also restricted them. The concentration of settlements along the coast made control from overseas much easier. It was not in British interests to allow free-for-all expansion into the interior, so in many ways the presence of **Indians** along the frontier was a useful restraint, deterring would-be pioneers and runaway slaves alike from attempting to move westwards. That doesn't mean the British – with the honourable exception of William Penn's **Pennsylvania** – were benign in their attitude towards Indians, or cultivated Indian alliances to the same extent as the French. Especially in the early years, however, when Indians vastly outnumbered the colonists, it was simpler to play different tribes off against each other – after all, the so-called Indians had no collective sense of themselves as Indians – than to embark on expensive military campaigns, and to wait for them to die off from the inevitable epidemics.

In the crudest terms, the survival of the British colonies was secured by force of arms, and the willingness to ship large military expeditions across the Atlantic. The expulsion of the Dutch from New York in the seventeenth century served as a prelude to the global imperial wars of the eighteenth. In 1763, the **Treaty of Paris** confirmed the final defeat of the French and their Indian allies in North America. Ironically, it also ensured that the fourteen colonies that remained after a century of expansion and amalgamation no longer needed British protection.

1565 Pedro Menéndez de Avilés founds San Augustín – **St Augustine** – in Spanish Florida, forty miles south of French Fort Caroline. Two days later Jean Ribault sets off to destroy the new colony, but loses his ships in a storm; a week after that Menéndez attacks Fort Caroline by land, massacres the French, and renames the fort San Mateo.

1568 French forces recapture San Mateo, with Indian assistance, and massacre the Spanish.

1576 **Martin Frobisher** of England, seeking the Northwest Passage, reaches Frobisher Bay and the Hudson Strait. After finding 'fool's gold', he returns during the two following years, to no profit.

1579 Having rounded Cape Horn and sailed up the west coast of the Americas, **Francis Drake** claims what is probably Drake's Bay, not far north of San Francisco Bay, for England as **New Albion**. California is generally believed to be an island.

1580 A Spanish naval victory ends French aspirations in Florida.

1584 An expedition sponsored by **Sir Walter Raleigh** names the location of his planned colony **Virginia**.

1585 Raleigh's first colonists settle on **Roanoke Island**, only to sail home to England with Drake in 1586 after he attacks St Augustine.

1587 A second party settles on Roanoke Island, which is destined to become known as the 'Lost Colony' after the island is found to be deserted in 1590.

1590 Richard Hakluyt publishes the first volume of his *Principall Navigations, Voiages and Discoveries of the English Nation*, which promotes English interest in colonial ventures.

John White's 1587 map showing the ill-fated Roanoke colony

Roanoke – the 'Lost Colony'

According to popular myth, the first English attempt to settle in North America – Sir Walter Raleigh's **Roanoke** – remains an unsolved mystery, in which the 'Lost Colony' disappeared without trace.

Sir Walter never visited North America. Queen Elizabeth granted his half-brother, Sir Humphrey Gilbert, the original patent to establish a colony, but he died following an abortive landfall in Newfoundland in 1583. Raleigh took over, and directed subsequent explorations further south. A 1584 expedition pinpointed Roanoke Island, hidden from Spanish view behind the Outer Banks of North Carolina, and named the region **Virginia**, in honour of the Virgin Queen.

Ralph Lane's party of 1585 sailed home with Sir Francis Drake the following year, having failed to find gold. In 1587, 117 more colonists set off, intending to farm a more fertile site beside Chesapeake Bay, but fearing Spanish attack the ships that carried them dumped them at Roanoke once again. Their leader, **John White**, who went home to fetch supplies a month later, was prevented by war with Spain from returning until 1590. Though he found Roanoke abandoned, he was reassured by the absence of the agreed distress signal, a carved Maltese cross, while the word '**Croatoan**' inscribed on a tree seemed a clear message that the colonists had moved south to the island of Croatoan. However, threatened by both the Spanish and by hurricanes, White's ships refused to take him there.

There the story usually ends, with the colonists never seen again. In fact, several reports reached Jamestown during the next decade of English settlers being dispersed as slaves among the tribes of North Carolina. Rather than admit their inability to rescue their fellow countrymen, and thus expose a vulnerability that might deter prospective settlers or investors, the Jamestown colonists seem simply to have written their predecessors out of history.

> **"** [P]eople began to die very fast, and many in short space . . . . The disease also was so strange that they neither knew what it was, nor how to cure it; the like by report of the oldest man in the country never happened before, time out of mind. **"**
>
> Report from the Roanoke colonists, 1587

1598 The French found a fur-trading settlement on Sable Island in the region they call **Acadia**. During the next decade, similar outposts are established on the St Croix River and at Port Royal, and at **Tadoussac** near the mouth of the St Lawrence. None survives for very long, in part because unauthorized traders ignore the official monopoly.

Juan de Oñate crosses the Rio Grande to colonize **New Mexico** for Spain.

1602 Bartholomew Gosnold of England lands at New Bedford, and also names Cape Cod and Martha's Vineyard.

1603 Samuel de Champlain of France explores the St Lawrence River.

1604 The English sign a peace treaty with Spain.

1606 James I charters the **London Company**, to settle between 34° and 41° North, which sends out 120 colonists under Christopher Newport, and the **Plymouth Company**, to settle between 38° and 45° North, which launches two unsuccessful expeditions.

1607 Newport's group founds **Jamestown**, in swampy terrain sixty miles up the James River from the Chesapeake Bay, where the coastal plain already holds 25,000 Algonquian. Attempting to kidnap their chief, Powhatan,

A plan of an idealized Native American settlement in Virginia, drawn by John White in 1587

Captain **John Smith** is taken prisoner, only to be 'rescued' by Powhatan's daughter **Pocahontas** in an elaborate ceremony that he mistakes for a potential execution. After 66 out of 104 colonists die within the first nine months, Smith insists the settlers clear and plant fields to ensure their survival. That makes him so unpopular that he's forced to return to England in 1609.

The Plymouth Company lands settlers on the Kennebec River in what's now **Maine**, but the settlement is abandoned in 1608.

1608 De Champlain founds a small French trading post at **Quebec**. In each of the next two years, with Huron and Algonquian allies, he travels up the Richelieu River and fights against the Mohawk beside what will become Lake Champlain. This bloody introduction to firearms incurs the lasting enmity of the Iroquois.

1609 The London Company receives a new charter as the **Virginia Company**, vesting government of the colony in a council that has the power to appoint its own officers. Of 220 Jamestown colonists, 160 die during the '**starving time**' of 1609–10.

The **Dutch** send **Henry Hudson** to find the Northwest Passage. He coasts from New England to Virginia, and sails up the **Hudson River** as far as Albany.

1610 **Santa Fe** is founded as the capital of New Mexico.

1613 **Pocahontas** is captured by the Jamestown colonists. She subsequently converts to Christianity and marries planter **John Rolfe**.

1614 The **Dutch** found **Fort Nassau**, later relocated as Fort Orange, near Albany, and supply guns to the Iroquois to ensure their co-operation.

The Spanish in the Southwest: New Mexico

In 1598, **Don Juan de Oñate** advanced north along the Rio Grande to establish the colony of **New Mexico**, encompassing modern New Mexico and Arizona, plus parts of Utah, Colorado, Nevada and California. The fiercest resistance, at Ácoma Pueblo, was subdued by an artillery onslaught in which eight hundred Acomans died. Oñate was recalled in disgrace for his cruelty, but the colony endured, establishing its capital, **Santa Fe**, in 1610.

Their dreams of wealth dashed by the realization that New Mexico was the end of the road, lacking access to the ocean or rich neighbours for trade or plunder, the colonists appropriated Pueblo farmlands and enslaved their inhabitants. Despite deploring violence, Franciscan missionaries insisted the Pueblos convert to Catholicism. Tensions culminated in the **Pueblo Revolt** of 1680, when the Pueblos united with the Navajo and Apache to drive the Spaniards out. As the native alliance fragmented, the Spanish returned to retake Santa Fe in 1693.

New Mexico was always a peripheral part of the Spanish empire, more a buffer zone to shield Mexico than a viable economic entity, and its colonists little more than subsistence farmers. When the French colony of **Louisiana** appeared to the east, the Spanish set up missions in the new province of **Texas**, and armed clashes occurred along the frontier. French guns enabled the Comanche, Ute and Apache to raid for crops and livestock along the Rio Grande. Hispanic ranchers, inadequately supplied from Mexico, could only offer minimal resistance with bows and arrows.

Once Louisiana proved unprofitable, Louis XV simply gave it to Spain in 1762. Determined to resist encroachment by the infant United States, Carlos III placed the region under direct control from Spain in 1776. However, too few settlers moved in to make any difference, and in 1802 he handed Louisiana back to Napoleon.

Captain John Smith maps the northeast coast, and names **New England**.

De Champlain reaches Lake Nipissing and Lake Huron, establishing a route by which French fur traders can reach the interior. French missionary work begins with the arrival of four Recollet friars.

1616 John Rolfe's experiments with growing **tobacco** give the Jamestown colonists a cash crop to trade with England.

1619 The governor of Virginia, George Yeardley, replaces martial law with representative government – the **House of Burgesses**, comprising two elected burgesses from each of the colony's eleven plantations, holds its first annual meeting. Also, twenty African **slaves** arrive on a Dutch ship.

1620 The *Mayflower*, carrying around a hundred colonists drawn from a group of dissident Puritans who had originally left Scrooby in East Anglia for Holland in 1607, reaches Cape Cod on 9 November. Since, as they may have intended, this lies beyond the jurisdiction of the Virginia colony, the so-called **Pilgrims** agree under the **Mayflower Compact** to be governed by leaders of their own choosing, then move on to settle at **Plymouth** in late December.

> " Though there be Fish in the Sea, and Foules in the ayre, and Beasts in the woods, their bounds are so large, they are so wilde, and we so weake and ignorant, we cannot much trouble them. "
>
> Captain John Smith, founder of Jamestown, 1607

Squanto and the Pilgrims

When the Pilgrims founded Plymouth, the site's former inhabitants – the **Patuxet**, overwhelmed by smallpox in 1617 – still lay unburied. In March 1621, however, a solitary survivor appeared; and he spoke perfect English. The enigmatic **Squanto** epitomizes the complex relationship between colonists and Native Americans.

Carried to England by Captain Weymouth in 1605, Squanto had returned with John Smith in 1614, but was immediately re-captured by a Captain Hunt, 'a wretched man that cares not what mischiefs he doth for his own profit'. Sold into slavery at Malaga, Squanto escaped to **London**, where he lived with John Slaney, a Cornhill merchant. He returned home in 1619, only to find his entire tribe had perished.

Before he threw in his lot with the Pilgrims, Squanto was an advisor to the Wampanoag 'sachem' (chief) **Massasoit**. Governor William Bradford hailed him as 'a special instrumente sent of God for their good beyond their expectation'. The colonists had been stealing food, but Squanto 'directed them how to set their corne, where to take fish', and other such skills.

Although it was largely thanks to Squanto that the Pilgrims could celebrate the first **Thanksgiving**, his interpreting abilities allowed him to occupy a powerful and ambiguous space between the English and the local tribes. He 'plaid his owne game by putting ye Indians in fear', negotiating treaties while threatening each with the violence of the other. Indeed, in presenting himself as 'Squanto', he adopted the name of a malevolent devil-like entity. He told the Wampanoag that the Pilgrims controlled the plague, which the English echoed by saying their 'God . . . hath it in store, and can send it at His pleasure to the destruction of His and our enemies'. His sudden death in November 1622 ended his extraordinary role in the emergence of New England.

1622 The **Council for New England** – the new name for the reorganized Virginia Company – grants the new colony of **Maine** to Sir Ferdinando Gorges, Captain John Mason, and their partners.

Now led by **Opechancanough**, the Algonquians kill almost a third of the Jamestown colonists in a surprise uprising; the English in turn poison 250 Indians during supposed peace negotiations in 1623.

1624 Weakened by ongoing debt and Indian strife, the Virginia Company goes bankrupt. James I takes control of Virginia as a **royal colony**, with a Crown-appointed governor; despite his personal loathing of tobacco, he's keen to secure the tax revenues, which rapidly amount to a quarter of all English customs revenues.

An English colony is founded on the **Caribbean** island of St Christopher, to be followed by similar ventures on Barbados, Nevis, Montserrat and Antigua.

Dutch settlers disperse along the Hudson and Delaware rivers.

1625 **New Amsterdam**, on Manhattan Island, is established as the principal town and port of the Dutch colony.

James I is succeeded by **Charles I**.

> ❝ [The Indians] died on heapes, as they lay in their houses; and the living, that were able to shift for themselves, would runne away and let them dy . . . and the bones and skulls upon their severall places of their habitations made such a spectacle after my coming into those partes, that as I travailed in the Forrest, nere the Massachusetts [Bay], it seemed to mee a new found Golgotha. ❞
>
> Colonist in New England, 1620s

1629 A group of wealthy Puritans receives a royal charter as the **Massachusetts Bay Company**. Taking advantage of a loophole in the charter, which fails to specify a location for the company's annual meeting, they subsequently relocate to New England and establish their own government. Their official seal depicts an Indian speaking the words 'Come over and help us.'

The official 1629 seal of the Massachusetts Bay Company

Charles I also grants Sir John Heath the territory between 31° and 36° North, which is to be called **Carolina**. No plans are made for settlement.

Maine is divided in two at the Piscataqua River, with Sir Ferdinando Gorges retaining the name of Maine to the north, and Captain Mason being assigned **New Hampshire** to the south.

1630 Heralding the start of the **Great Migration**, around a thousand Puritan settlers arrive in Massachusetts in seventeen ships. Their first elected governor, **John Winthrop**, establishes **Boston** on the Indian site of Shawmut, and the **General Court**, originally consisting of just twelve 'freemen' or shareholders, meets for the first time. Over the next fourteen years, the court progressively transforms itself into a representative body of two houses, which includes deputies from new towns such as Salem, Dorchester, Mystic and Lynn.

1634 Granted twelve million acres by Charles I to create the colony of **Maryland**, named after Charles's queen, the Catholic Lord Baltimore founds St Mary's City at the mouth of the Potomac. His policy of religious toleration turns out to attract more Protestant dissidents than Catholics, but the ready availability of good land for growing tobacco means that the colony is swiftly successful.

1635 The English Laud Commission attempts to revoke the charter of the Massachusetts Bay Company, but the colony carries on regardless.

Settlers from Massachusetts move into the Connecticut River Valley.

1636 The preacher Roger Williams, banished from Massachusetts after advocating Indian land rights and the separation of church and state, establishes the city of **Providence**, with democratic government and freedom of worship. He eventually obtains a charter for the colony of **Rhode Island** in 1644.

Massachusetts' General Court sets up a college to train Puritan ministers. Following a bequest of money and books from John **Harvard** in 1639, the college takes his name.

> **“** Colonies degenerate assuredly when the colonists imitate and embrace the habits, customs and practices of the natives. There is no better way to remedy this evil than to do away with and destroy completely the habits and practices of the natives. **”**
>
> Sir William Herbert, "colonial promoter"

1637 After the **Pequot** tribe refuse to pay tribute to the newly declared colony of **Connecticut**, they are massacred in the Mystic River Valley by a combined English, Narragansett and Mohegan force.

1638 **Anne Hutchinson**, who in the three years since she arrived in Massachusetts from England has been leading prayer meetings at her home in Boston, is charged with acting more 'as a Husband than a Wife and a Preacher than a Hearer', and expelled from Massachusetts. She settles in Rhode Island.

On Long Island Sound, on the borders of Connecticut, John Davenport and Theophilus Eaton found the rigorously Puritan colony of **New Haven**.

The colony of **New Sweden** – dominated at first by Dutchmen like **Peter Minuit**, keen to circumvent the Dutch West India Company – sets up Fort Christina on the Delaware, on the site of modern Wilmington.

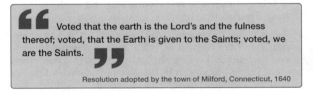

> ❝ Voted that the earth is the Lord's and the fulness thereof; voted, that the Earth is given to the Saints; voted, we are the Saints. ❞
>
> Resolution adopted by the town of Milford, Connecticut, 1640

1642 Paul de Maisonneuve founds **Montreal**.

1643 Representatives of Connecticut, New Haven, Plymouth and Massachusetts meet in Boston to form a defensive confederation as the **United Colonies of New England**.

1644 **Opechancanough** leads the Algonquians in another surprise attack on Jamestown, but by now the ten thousand colonists can better survive four hundred losses. Extensive reprisals culminate in the capture and murder of Opechan-canough in 1646, and the demise of the Algonquians as a significant threat.

1649 At the end of the English Civil War, King Charles I is **executed**, and the Puritan **Commonwealth** is established.

1651 The first **Navigation Act** decrees that all trade between England and its colonies must be in English ships.

1653 Massachusetts annexes the isolated settlements of Maine.

1654 The first Jews reach North America, arriving at New Amsterdam after being expelled from Brazil.

1655 Intimidated by a Dutch force under **Peter Stuyvesant**, the inhabitants of New Sweden – most of whom are by now Swedes or Finns – capitulate and join New Netherland.

1660 The monarchy is **restored** in England, in the shape of King **Charles II**.

The second **Navigation Act** requires that at least three-quarters of the crew of any ship trading between England and its colonies be English, and that certain 'enumerated commodities' produced in the colonies, such as sugar and tobacco, can only be shipped to England.

The first Bible is printed in North America, translated by John Eliot into Algonquian.

1663 The **Staple Act** requires that any products exported from Europe to the English colonies must be shipped via England.

1664 King Charles II dispatches an English naval expedition to conquer New Netherland; the Dutch surrender New Amsterdam in the face of its unexpected arrival, and formally cede the entire colony in a treaty of 1667. They briefly recapture some of their possessions in 1673, but English rule of **New York** is permanently re-established within a year. Fort Orange becomes Albany, while New Amsterdam is **New York City**.

Charles II grants the region from the Hudson to the Delaware to his brother, James Duke of York, as the proprietary colony of **New Jersey**. James in turn awards it to Lord Berkeley and Sir George Carteret, who subsequently sell part as East Jersey to Scottish investors, and the rest as West Jersey to a Quaker consortium.

1665 Fearing annexation by New York, New Haven unites with Connecticut.

1670 The **Hudson's Bay Company** is formed in London, and receives a monopoly of trade in the Hudson's Bay basin.

Two hundred settlers from Barbados found **Carolina**, a new colony belonging to a group of English aristocrats, the **Lords Proprietor**. Its capital, **Charles Town**, will become Charleston in 1783.

1672 The Royal African Company is granted a monopoly on slave trading to the English colonies.

1673 Another **Navigation Act** imposes duties on trade between the colonies in sugar, tobacco and other products.

1675 The so-called 'King Philip' – Metacom, the son of Massasoit who first negotiated with the Pilgrims – leads the Indians of New England in **King Philip's War** against the English. Indian attacks destroy twelve of the region's ninety towns, and kill around 1 in 16 of all colonists. Using Indian allies, and adopting guerrilla tactics, the colonists fight back in 1676, and extinguish all potential for future resistance.

The start of the slave trade

The North American **slave trade** had humble beginnings. On 20 August, 1619, John Rolfe at Jamestown noted: 'There came in a Dutch man-of-warre that sold us 20 negars'. By that time, however, a million African slaves had already been imported to the Americas as a whole. Indeed only five percent of slaves – perhaps 400,000 out of the eight million or so taken from Africa – were ever carried straight to North America.

While those first few may have been indentured servants rather than slaves, slavery rapidly became institutionalized. The Virginian colonists, after years of poverty, starvation and even cannibalism, had just discovered the potential of **tobacco** as a cash crop, while still remaining reluctant to farm. To entice new settlers from England, any immigrant who survived three years could claim fifty acres of land. A labour force that could be obliged to work for life without pay – and even held a resale value – seemed heaven-sent.

The blueprint was established on the **sugar** plantations of the Caribbean, where the British colonies – an integral part of the same imperial enterprise, even if they now seem distinct because they never joined the United States – were far more profitable than their North American equivalents. Asserting that blacks were 'an heathenish, brutish and an uncertaine, dangerous kinde of people', Barbados adopted a **slave code** in 1661 that spread to North America after Barbadian settlers established the colony of Carolina in 1670.

By the Revolutionary era, forty percent of the population of Maryland and Virginia, compared to a mere two percent in New England, were slaves. Despite that disparity, however, in a very real sense all the North American colonies depended on slavery. New Englanders grew food to supply the Caribbean, and participated in the '**Triangular Trade**', in which rum and guns were exchanged for slaves in West Africa, to be traded for sugar in the West Indies.

1676 Virginia frontiersmen, arguing for aggression against neighbouring Indians to allow rapid expansion, as opposed to an expensive and ineffective policy of defensive containment, rise under Nathaniel Bacon. As well as attacking Indians, **Bacon's Rebellion** burns Jamestown and drives out Governor Berkeley. It fizzles out after Bacon dies of dysentery, but Charles II dismisses Berkeley as an 'old fool', and sends in Sir Herbert Jeffreys as a new military governor. After Jeffreys dies in turn in 1678, the old guard of Virginia planters reassert control, chastened into cultivating popular support by reducing taxes and presenting themselves as champions against royal interference.

1680 **New Hampshire** receives a royal charter.

The Spanish are driven out of New Mexico by the **Pueblo Revolt**.

Protestant Huguenots, fleeing France and denied the right to settle in French colonies, arrive at Charles Town. Ten thousand eventually settle in the English colonies.

1682 The first Quaker settlers arrive in William Penn's **Pennsylvania**, and found **Philadelphia**.

Reaching the mouth of the Mississippi, a French nobleman, the **Sieur de la Salle**, claims the valley for France as **Louisiana**.

1683 The Duke of York approves the **Charter of Liberties**, conceding a combined legislative assembly for New York, Maine, Nantucket and Martha's Vineyard – though he will later repudiate it as king.

1684 The charter of Massachusetts is annulled following disputes with the Crown.

1685 Charles II dies and is succeeded by his brother, James II.

The coming of horses

There were no **horses** in the Americas in 1492. Although the horse evolved in North America 45 million years ago, it had been extinct – thanks to humans – for 13,000 years. The only domesticated animals were the dog, used by certain tribes to drag their belongings across the plains, and the turkey, raised for its feathers in the Southwest.

Reintroduced by the **Spanish**, significant quantities of horses first reached the **Southwest** around 1600. Within ten years of the foundation of New Mexico, the **Navajo** and **Apache** were raiding Spanish and Pueblo settlements along the Rio Grande for their horse herds. When the Spanish were driven out by the Pueblo Revolt of 1680, the animals they left behind were dispersed by trade and warfare. Horses rapidly spread across Texas, and also up the western Rockies to reach the Shoshone and Flathead of the Northwest. They then infiltrated the Great Plains from both south and west. At that time, the region supported a small population of sedentary farmers, who planted riverside fields and hunted buffalo on foot. With the odd exception, like the **Crow** on the Missouri, few such peoples abandoned their old lifestyle. Instead former hunter-gatherers, from marginal territories, seized on the new possibilities and became nomadic 'Horse Indians'.

At first, tribes such as the **Comanche**, **Sioux** and **Blackfoot** contented themselves with far-ranging buffalo-hunting expeditions, and traded with the farmers. In time, however, as they became more populous and more aggressive – and acquired firearms – they violently displaced their predecessors, and indulged in semi-permanent warfare. Their much romanticized culture was undoubtedly dynamic, but it was also fundamentally unstable, and dependent on trade with Europeans for the necessities of life. In due course, they were in turn driven from the plains by mounted US cavalry, and their place taken by the **cowboys**, before new technologies superseded the horse altogether.

Sailing straight from France with a military expedition, **de la Salle** fails to spot the mouth of the Mississippi, and lands at Matagordo Bay in Texas, where he builds Fort Louis. The colony soon founders, while de la Salle is killed by his men in 1687 as he attempts to lead them overland to Canada.

1686 Seeking to assert royal control, James II merges all eight northern colonies, including New York and East and West Jersey, into the **Dominion of New England**. The new governor, Sir Edmund Andros, rapidly provokes opposition by raising taxes and replacing Puritan officials with Anglicans.

1688 In the **Glorious Revolution**, the Dutch William Prince of Orange takes the English throne from James II, and establishes joint rule with his wife Mary Stuart.

1689 News of the Glorious Revolution prompts uprisings throughout the Dominion; Andros is overthrown by rebels in Boston, as are his representatives in New York and Maryland. Following complex negotiations with the new king, the Dominion is dissolved.

1691 Failing to obtain a renewal of its original charter, **Massachusetts** becomes a **royal colony**, into which the Plymouth colony is subsumed. Though an elected assembly controls taxes, the royal governor – initially Sir William Phips – can veto all legislation. Religious toleration is extended to all Protestants, marking an end to Puritan domination. Rhode Island and Connecticut regain their autonomy.

Settlements along the Albemarle Sound, founded during the 1650s as offshoots of Virginia, are granted recognition as **North Carolina**, which thus creates the matching colony of **South Carolina**.

1692 Sir Edmund Andros is appointed governor of Virginia.

Eighteen supposed **witches** are executed in **Salem**, Massachusetts.

The Puritans

Although the New England colonies gave religious dissenters the opportunity to live according to their beliefs, the original colonists abhorred notions of toleration or pluralism. Not that they were a homogenous group; although bracketed together as **Puritans**, they incorporated many shades of belief. Their roots lay in sixteenth-century England. Charging that the English Reformation had not gone far enough, Puritans aimed to 'purify' Protestantism by ridding the Anglican church of all traces of Catholic doctrine, and rejected both bishops and monarchy in favour of self-governance by congregations.

The Pilgrims who settled in Plymouth in 1620 were **Separatists**, who saw their destiny as entirely apart from the Church of England. Of greater significance was the founding in 1630 of the **Massachusetts Bay Colony**. The leader of these 'Non-Separating Congregationalists', **John Winthrop**, proclaimed that New England would be 'a refuge for manye, whome [God] meant to save out of the general destruction', and that as a 'City on a Hill' it might serve as a model for a true reformation of England itself.

A corollary of the Puritan self-image as the chosen of God was that setbacks reflected God's displeasure, and were thus perhaps the work of the devil or his agents. Such fears culminated in the **Salem witch trials** of 1692, when a group of girls accused hundreds of women of being witches. Eighteen were tried and hanged before church authorities withdrew their support, after accusations reached as high as the governor's wife. While that's often seen as marking the end of the Puritan experiment, it has to be acknowledged that the increasing economic prosperity of New England represented a fulfilment of Puritan aspirations rather than a decline in values, and that Puritan concepts of morality, duty, thrift and industry have continued to influence American society ever since.

1693 Virginia founds the College of William and Mary.

Spaniards under Don Diego de Vargas **recapture Santa Fe** and re-establish New Mexico.

1696 A new **Navigation Act** reaffirms its predecessors, voids any laws passed by colonial assemblies that run counter to those acts, and elevates colonial customs commissioners to the same level as English customs officers.

1697 The French seize the trading posts of the Hudson's Bay Company, which they will hold until 1714.

1698 The **Wool Act** forbids colonists to export wool and woollen cloth to England, or to trade it between different colonies.

The Royal African Company loses its monopoly on **slave trading**; entrepreneurs are soon bringing slaves to the Americas in ever-greater numbers.

The long-peripheral settlement at **Jamestown** is abandoned following a fire.

1701 **Yale College** is founded in Saybrook, Connecticut, by Cotton Mather among others, as a counterbalance to the perceived liberalism of Harvard. It will move to New Haven in 1745.

Having made peace with the Iroquois, the French under **Antoine de Cadillac** found a fortified trading post at **Detroit**, to control the junction of lakes Erie and Huron.

1702 Queen Anne comes to the throne in England. **Queen Anne's War**, the North American and Caribbean component of the wider conflict known in Europe as the **War of the Spanish Succession**, pits the French and Spanish against the English, with the Iroquois remaining neutral. Hostilities begin with an unsuccessful expedition from Carolina against San Augustín in Spanish Florida.

East and West Jersey are reunited to become the royal colony of **New Jersey**.

1704 Allied French and Indian forces attack widely throughout New England, notably capturing the family of the minister John Williams in Deerfield, Connecticut.

Delaware breaks off as a separate, non-Quaker, colony from Pennsylvania.

1706 In *The Good Old Way*, **Cotton Mather** bemoans the decline in Puritan influence in the colonies.

1707 The **Act of Union** combines England, Scotland and Wales into the United Kingdom of **Great Britain**.

1708 French and Indians combine to capture the British settlement of **St John's** in Newfoundland.

1709 A Quaker meeting house is built in Boston.

1710 A naval expedition from New England, supported by British ships and marines, captures **Port Royal** in French Acadia. A further land and sea operation the following year, however, fails to take Quebec and Montreal.

1711 The **Tuscarora** of North Carolina, whose lands are being occupied by German and Swiss immigrants, attack plantations and kill two hundred settlers. In response, Captain James Moore leads an expedition from South Carolina, in which several Indian tribes including the Yamasee participate, and which in 1713 destroys the main Tuscarora settlement and sells hundreds of captives into slavery. The survivors migrate north to join what thus become the Six Nations of the Iroquois.

1712 Twenty-five blacks and two Indians stage a slave revolt in **New York City**; after killing nine whites, they are captured and executed.

William Penn and the Quakers

The **Quakers** first emerged during the English Civil War, rejecting both spiritual and social hierarchies, and proclaiming that men and women alike should be free to pursue the 'inner light' of religious revelation. They called themselves the **Friends of God**; their nickname derived from one member's comment that they quaked before the power of God. That this pacifist and radically tolerant group, despite persecution in New England, established a large and thriving North American colony was due to the somewhat paradoxical sponsorship of one of England's wealthiest aristocrats.

William Penn, the son of an admiral who had prospered under both the Puritan Commonwealth and the restored King Charles II, converted to Quakerism during the 1660s. On his father's death in 1680, Charles settled a debt by granting the young Penn 45,000 square miles west of the Delaware River to settle as **Pennsylvania**, named by Charles himself after the admiral.

While Penn promoted the new lands as 'a Free Colony for all Mankind that should go hither', he admitted that 'though I desire to extend religious freedom, yet I want some recompense for my trouble'. The Quakers he shipped across the Atlantic in their thousands joined English, Dutch and Swedish settlers who were already there, and were in turn joined by non-conformists from all over Europe, attracted by cheap land prices as well as religious freedom. Lasting peace with the Indians, and respect for native land rights, meant that displaced Native Americans also flocked in.

Penn spent just four years in the colony, and ended up in a debtors' prison in London. Pennsylvania flourished, however, its fertile soil proving ideal for European farming methods and crops. **Philadelphia** – the City of Brotherly Love – held ten thousand people by 1700, and soon overtook Boston to become the most important city in North America.

1713 Under the **Treaty of Utrecht**, Acadia becomes the British colony of **Nova Scotia**, but few British settlers choose to join the many French who remain, and the French are still a powerful presence on Cape Breton Island.

1715 A **Yamasee** revolt in South Carolina is swiftly repressed, this time with help from the Cherokee and even the Tuscarora. The defeated Yamasee retreat into Spanish Florida.

1716 Seeking to encourage colonial expansion, Virginia governor Alexander Spotswood, accompanied by the 'Knights of the Golden Horseshoe', leads an expedition up the James River, over the Blue Ridge Mountains, and into the **Shenandoah Valley**.

1718 The foundation of **New Orleans** by the **Sieur de Bienville** moves the focus of French Louisiana away from Gulf Coast settlements such as Mobile and Biloxi.

The British parliament allows for felons convicted of capital offences to be sent to the colonies instead. Many end up as disruptive presences on the tobacco plantations of Virginia and Maryland.

1719 The assembly of **South Carolina** revolts, seeking direct rule from England to provide better defence against the Indians and Spanish. Both North and South Carolina become **royal colonies**, a status that will be sealed in 1729 when the Crown buys out the Lords Proprietor.

1728 The Massachusetts legislature disputes the governor's demand for a fixed salary, on the grounds that Magna Carta entitles it to make decisions on public taxation and expenditure.

The Danish mariner **Vitus Bering**, leading a Russian expedition, names and explores the Bering Sea, but fails to see the Alaskan coast in the fog.

The Iroquois

At the time of European contact, northeastern North America was inhabited by two principal native groups. The **Iroquoians**, centred around Lake Ontario and the St Lawrence, were surrounded, to the south and west and along the Atlantic coast, by the **Algonquians**. As the French penetrated the Great Lakes, they established an alliance with the **Huron**, an aberrant Iroquoian group affiliated with the Algonquians. That swiftly threw them into conflict with the **Five Nation Iroquois**, five previously warring tribes – the Seneca, Cayuga, Onondaga, Oneida and Mohawk, all in what's now upstate New York – who had been persuaded a century earlier to form a Great League of Peace and Power by a Mohawk visionary, Dekanawida, and his disciple Hiawatha.

Though never a single unified entity – fifty chiefs maintained individual autonomy – the Great League enabled the Iroquois during the seventeenth century to establish control from Maine to Michigan, and from the St Lawrence to Tennessee. Using guns bought from Dutch settlers along the Hudson Valley, they fought unceasingly against the French and their Algonquian allies. Keeping their numbers up by adopting prisoners of war, they eventually incorporated almost every Iroquoian tribe.

Joined by the Tuscarora of North Carolina in 1722, the **Six Nations** spent the eighteenth century charting an independent course between the French and the British. During negotiations with the colonists in 1744, an Onondaga chief, unimpressed by the squabbling representatives of Pennsylvania, Virginia and Maryland, recommended 'by your observing the same methods our wise forefathers have taken, you will acquire fresh strength and power'. Ultimately, however, their decision to side with the British in the Revolutionary War led to their eclipse; in 1779, **George Washington** ordered that Iroquois country be not 'merely overrun but destroyed', and a punitive expedition into western New York eliminated the Iroquois as a military force.

1729 Provoked by a French plan to replace one of their villages with a tobacco plantation, the **Natchez** Indians rise on the Mississippi. Joined by African slaves, they kill 250 colonists, before the French and their Choctaw allies crush the rebellion.

Benjamin Franklin takes over the fledgling *Pennsylvania Gazette*. Three years later, he publishes the first edition of *Poor Richard's Almanack*.

1730 North America's first **synagogue** is constructed, on Mill Street in New York.

1733 General James Oglethorpe, granted a 21-year charter, establishes the colony of **Georgia**, interposed as a buffer between Spanish Florida and the Carolinas, and lays out its capital, **Savannah**. It's intended as a slave-free colony, where free migrants drawn from Britain's urban poor can work their own small land-holdings, but by 1751 the migrants will be 'stark Mad after Negroes', and Georgia will be taken under royal control, slavery permitted, and the land turned over to rice and indigo plantations.

The **Molasses Act**, designed to protect sugar planters in the British West Indies, imposes heavy duties on the importation of sugar and its byproducts to North America from French and Dutch Caribbean possessions.

1735 Peter Zenger, whose *New York Weekly Journal* has featured articles hostile to Governor William Cosby, is acquitted on charges of seditious libel, after a trial that helps to establish the freedom of the press.

1736 English preacher **John Wesley** makes an extended visit to Savannah, Georgia.

1737 Reverend **Jonathan Edwards** publishes *A Faithful Narrative of the Surprizing Work of God*, describing recent religious revivals in and around the Connecticut Valley. It will inspire the English evangelical preacher **George**

Whitefield to tour the American colonies between 1739 and 1741, and help to spark a widespread upsurge in religious fervour, among conservatives and radicals alike, known as the **Great Awakening**.

1739 England and Spain embark on the **War of Jenkins' Ear**, sparked by Spanish reprisals against British smugglers who have been evading Spain's restrictions on trade with its colonies. The British capture Porto Bello in Panama, but assaults on San Augustín, Florida (1740), and Cartagena, Columbia (1741), both fail, as does a Spanish naval expedition against Georgia and South Carolina.

In September, a **slave revolt** on the Stono River near Charles Town is suppressed; the rebels are hunted down and beheaded.

1740 The **Plantation Act** entitles foreign-born (Protestant) colonists to claim British citizenship, and thus own land in North America.

1741 Vitus Bering leads another Russian expedition to the Northwest, which this time lands in **Alaska** to be greeted by hostile Tlingit; Bering dies on the way home.

1743 Quaker **John Woolman** preaches against slavery in New Jersey.

Benjamin Franklin helps to set up the American Philosophical Society.

1744 As the French come to the aid of the Spanish, **King George's War**, known in Europe as the War of the Austrian Succession, breaks out. French and Indian raiding parties attack all along the New England frontier.

1745 Following French attacks on Nova Scotia, a New England expedition under Massachusetts governor William Shirley, with British naval support, captures the largest town in New France, **Louisburg** on Cape Breton Island.

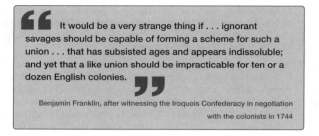

It would be a very strange thing if . . . ignorant savages should be capable of forming a scheme for such a union . . . that has subsisted ages and appears indissoluble; and yet that a like union should be impracticable for ten or a dozen English colonies.

Benjamin Franklin, after witnessing the Iroquois Confederacy in negotiation with the colonists in 1744

1748 In the **Treaty of Aix-la-Chapelle**, the British exchange Louisburg for Madras in India, and thus end the war with no increase in colonial territory.

With traders from both Virginia and Pennsylvania working as far westward as the Mississippi, a Virginian party establishes the first permanent settlement west of the Alleghenies, at **Draper's Meadow** on the Greenbrier River.

1749 In a bid to bolster the British colonial presence in **Nova Scotia**, 2500 settlers from England found **Halifax**.

Virginians and British partners are granted a royal charter for the **Ohio Company**.

France erects Fort Rouillé on the site of modern **Toronto**, builds another post at Niagara, and fortifies Detroit.

1750 Christopher Gist explores for the Ohio Company as far as the falls of the Ohio. A trading station is subsequently built at Wills's Creek, close to the newly named **Cumberland Gap**.

Jonathan Mayhew, preaching in Boston, celebrates the centenary of the execution of Charles I; John Adams will later call this 'the opening gun of the Revolution'.

1753 Benjamin Franklin establishes the first **penny post**, in Philadelphia.

1754 In June, at the **Albany Congress**, representatives of all the New England colonies, as well as New York, Pennsylvania, and Maryland, meet with the Iroquois Six Nations to discuss defence against the French. They also consider, but reject, Benjamin Franklin's **Plan of Union**, a proposal that the Crown should appoint a President-General of the United Colonies, while colonial assemblies would choose a 48-member Grand Council, to suggest laws that would be subject to Crown approval.

In response to the French construction of Fort Duquesne, on the site of modern **Pittsburgh**, Virginian troops are dispatched under the command of **George Washington** to drive them out. After Washington's encampment, Fort Necessity, is attacked, he surrenders on 4 July, but is allowed to return home.

1755 News of Washington's defeat helps to trigger the **French and Indian War**, known in Europe as the **Seven Years' War**. British forces take two French outposts in Nova Scotia, but General Edward Braddock's expedition is all but destroyed by a French/Indian ambush near Fort Duquesne. George Washington engineers a safe retreat for the survivors. Over the next two years, Indian raids along the frontier send colonial expansion into reverse, while the French destroy British forts on Lake Ontario, and on Lake George in what's now upstate New York.

1758 Under a vigorous new prime minister, **William Pitt the Elder**, the British are able to launch vastly superior forces against the French, while the British navy dominates the Atlantic. The French abandon Fort Duquesne, and a British fleet captures Louisburg, thus allowing an advance up the St Lawrence River.

The French in North America

The **French** colonies in North America failed to grow at anything like the rate of their British rivals. Although a chain of French settlements extended far into the Great Lakes region during the seventeenth century, only along the **St Lawrence Valley** did significant numbers of French families settle and farm. What lay beyond were primarily trading posts, staffed by soldiers and indentured servants who returned home when their tours of duty were over. Indians brought in furs from an even wider area, to exchange for manufactured goods, and especially weapons. Individual tribes developed such close economic ties with the French that they gladly lent them their military muscle, but that was at the cost of endless inter-tribal warfare, notably against the Iroquois. Few migrants were attracted to this cold and perilous frontier, particularly since French colonies refused to accept religious dissidents.

In 1673, Jacques Marquette and Louis Jolet canoed down the Mississippi as far as the Arkansas. The ill-defined territories through which they passed were named **Louisiana**, in honour of Louis XIV; a new capital, **New Orleans**, was established in 1718. The slave-based plantation colony that grew up along the Mississippi did not, however, flourish, and served largely for its nuisance value in preventing British expansion.

The so-called **Seven Years'** or **French and Indian War** broke out in 1755, after British troops under the young George Washington attempted to drive the French out of the Ohio River Valley. The British went on to conquer all of Canada, expelling French settlers from Acadia in Nova Scotia in 1755 (they fled to Louisiana, to become the Cajuns). In forcing the **surrender of Quebec** in 1759, General Wolfe brought the war to a close. The French subsequently ceded Louisiana to the Spanish rather than let it fall to the British, and thereby put an end to their involvement in the continent.

1759 The British General **James Wolfe** lays siege to **Quebec**, commanded by General Montcalm. Both men die in battle on the Plains of Abraham, where British victory forces Quebec to **surrender** on 18 September. On his deathbed, Montcalm remarks: 'I console myself that in my defeat and in her conquest, England will find a tomb.'

The **Cherokee** fight back in South Carolina against settlers who are encroaching on their lands and hunting 'scalps' for bounty, but are forced to capitulate within two years by British and colonial troops.

1760 The French win a second battle on the Plains of Abraham, and lay siege to the British in turn, but following the arrival of British reinforcements **Montreal** surrenders on 8 September, ending the French colonial adventure in North America. Benjamin Franklin is moved to celebrate 'not merely as I am a colonist, but as I am a Briton'.

George III comes to the throne in England.

1762 The **Spanish** declare war on the British, only to lose both Manila and Havana, while the British also capture the French Caribbean possessions of Guadeloupe, Martinique, Grenada, St Lucia and St Vincent.

1763 Under the **Treaty of Paris**, France cedes to Britain Acadia, Canada, Cape Breton, and all Louisiana east of the Mississippi, except for New Orleans, which together with the rest of Louisiana it separately grants to Spain. France does, however, retain some fishing rights off Newfoundland, and also regains certain Caribbean islands. Britain restores Havana to Spain, in exchange for Florida. The Mississippi now becomes the border between the British and the Spanish.

A series of distinct Indian uprisings captures all but three of the outposts in the Great Lakes and the Ohio Valley that the British have just taken from the French. Together they're characterized as **Pontiac's Rebellion**, although the Ottawa chief Pontiac, who is unsuccessful in his assault on Detroit, only enjoys limited local authority. One by one, the Indian tribes make peace, and allow the British to return to the forts; the king attempts to establish a lasting frontier by forbidding further colonial settlement west of the **Proclamation Line** along the Appalachians, but pioneers continue to venture westwards.

3
Revolution and independence

1764–89

With hindsight, it might seem inevitable that the American colonies fought for and won their **independence** from Britain. In 1763, however, when British rule in North America appeared to have been consolidated for the foreseeable future, no one expected it to happen. And yet a mere thirteen years later, the Declaration of Independence was signed. Even acknowledging the ineptitude and insensitivity of the British government, such a precipitous decline in the trans-Atlantic relationship takes a lot of explaining.

Tracing the political events of those years – and specifically, the various taxes and customs duties imposed by the British parliament – there's often a nagging sense that they *coincided* with a growing alienation in the colonies, or at least gave it a convenient focus, rather than actually *causing* it. Much of the most commonly cited catalogue of colonial grievances centres on the merchants of Boston. Although their interests almost by definition ran counter to those of the British, they seldom occupied a particularly elevated moral position. Certainly they resented the imposition of duties, but they were equally infuriated by attempts to suppress their lucrative, large-scale smuggling operations. But were the concerns of mercantile New England really shared on the frontiers of western Pennsylvania, or the plantations of South Carolina?

In reality, for the **Revolutionary War** to break out, the

different colonies didn't need to have identical complaints against the British. For that matter, to depict the struggle for independence simply as the process by which British colonists rejected their mother country is to forget that well over a third of the colonists were of German descent, while almost a fifth of the population were African slaves, whose interests were scarcely represented by either side. Most of the eventual leaders of the campaign – the '**Founding Fathers**' of the United States – were drawn from the colonies' wealthiest elite, and when they first expressed their dissatisfaction with Britain advocated neither independence nor revolution. Instead, men such as George Washington originally saw their goal as being to restore liberties that had been eroded rather than to claim new ones. It was the growing realization that their brethren in Britain did not see them as equals, as expressed above all in the British preparedness to impose **taxation** without political **representation**, that propelled them towards the break. Furthermore, with the diminished need for defence against French or Indian attack, the continuing British military presence in North America cast Britain in the role of an **occupying power** – and the British insistence that the Americans should pay for the privilege hardly helped.

One by one, as American dissidents and demagogues confronted the flaws in the colonial relationship from their different perspectives – whether Samuel Adams in Boston, Patrick Henry in Virginia, or even Benjamin Franklin in London – they were pushed by logic and pulled by rhetoric towards the conclusion that the relationship was no longer viable. Sympathetic Britons also offered their support and served further to radicalize the debate, with Thomas Paine even crossing the Atlantic to write his fiery *Common Sense*.

When war came, American victory was by no means assured. One major factor was **George Washington**'s success in creating the Continental Army in 1775, and then managing to keep it in the field for eight years, despite the lack of a national infrastructure up to the job of recruiting, financing or administering it. With the exception of his desperate last-ditch crossing of the Delaware to attack Trenton in 1776, his tactics for much of that period consisted of retreating and avoiding confrontation. As the years went by, it became clear that the longer the Americans could avoid losing an all-out battle, the more likely it was that the British would overextend their lines as they advanced through the vast and unfamiliar continent; thus Burgoyne's triumphant progress along the Hudson in 1777 ended within months with his humiliating surrender at **Saratoga**.

For as long as the war endured, many colonists continued to oppose independence; perhaps a third, in John Adams's estimate, remained loyal to Britain. In the South the factions for and against secession were evenly enough matched to fight what amounted to a civil war, while in New York the Loyalists were a majority. By the time it was all over, a total of around 100,000 Loyalists had left the new nation, for Canada or Europe.

Ultimately, the intervention of the **French** – once the nascent Congress had managed to convince both itself and the major powers that it could form meaningful alliances – was decisive. French naval power thwarted the British ability to carry troops at will along the Atlantic coast, and when General Cornwallis surrendered at **Yorktown**, in what turned out to be the culminating engagement of the war, Frenchmen outnumbered Americans in the forces that surrounded him by almost three to one.

With the war won, the victors were faced with a baffling conundrum. For the new nation to survive and prosper, it could not remain obliged to obtain the consent of individual states to raise money, and subject in all measures to the veto of any one of them. And yet the arguments advanced as reasons to separate from Britain served equally well to argue against the thirteen colonies joining to form a single union. Why should Massachusetts or Virginia submit once more to a far-off centralized government with the authority to override their own legislatures and discipline their citizens? That circle was squared to sufficient mutual satisfaction by the devising of a **Constitution** that kept the executive, the legislature and the judiciary separate, each able to collaborate with but not control the rest. A perceived need to be able to counter potential anarchy or violence from the dispossessed persuaded many of the 'Founding Fathers' – as resistant as ever to the notion of a genuine popular revolution – to stomach the creation of a strong central government, while the abolitionists among them decided to tolerate slavery as a necessary evil. The Republic was born.

1764 When Prime Minister **George Grenville** pushes through the **American Revenue ('Sugar') Act**, the British parliament moves beyond the regulation of trade with the colonies to an explicit attempt to raise revenue from them, to help service the large war debt and support a standing army in North America. Hoping to reduce smuggling, the act halves the duty on sugar-related imports from the French and Dutch Caribbean, but places new duties on imports of textiles, coffee, wine, refined sugar and indigo. Customs agents are granted swingeing powers of search and seizure, with offenders to be tried in non-jury vice-admiralty courts.

The **Currency Act** forbids the colonies to print their own paper money; as it has already been banned in New England, the greatest impact is on **Virginia**, where existing currency depreciates alarmingly.

The cry of '**no taxation without representation**', first heard after the Molasses Act of 1733, is raised by **James**

Otis in Massachusetts, while Boston and New York adopt a 'non-importation' policy towards dutiable British goods.

On the western Pennsylvania frontier, the **Paxton Boys**, who feel that the colony's Quaker-influenced assembly is failing to protect them, massacre the Conestoga Indians as scapegoats, and march east to pursue Christianized Indians who have taken refuge in Philadelphia. In February, Benjamin Franklin persuades them to make a formal protest rather than to fight, and they achieve improved representation in the assembly.

1765 In March, parliament authorizes the first direct tax on the colonies. The **Stamp Act** requires a revenue stamp to be affixed to all legal documents and printed matter – newspapers, insurance policies, deeds, leases and even dice and playing cards. All payments have to be in sterling, and again vice-admiralty courts will try offenders.

In May, **Patrick Henry** persuades Virginia's House of Burgesses to adopt the **Virginia Resolutions**, which state that they have 'the only sole and exclusive right and power to lay taxes and impositions on the inhabitants of this colony'. The Massachusetts Assembly takes a similar stance, and violent opposition co-ordinated by the '**Sons of Liberty**' intimidates all stamp agents into resigning. Nine colonies send representatives to October's **Stamp Act Congress** in New York City, which issues a Declaration of Rights and Grievances petitioning for the repeal of all the recent acts. When the Stamp Act finally becomes law on November 1, it is almost universally boycotted, with even the courts suspending operations. Meanwhile, the non-importation campaign spreads.

The **Quartering Act** obliges the colonies to provide lodging and supplies for British troops. Fears that a standing British army may become an oppressive occupying force – 'a rod and Check over us' – are heightened as troops move

> **"** It is inconsistent with the spirit of the common law and of the essential fundamental principles of the British constitution that we should be subject to any tax imposed by the British Parliament; because we are not represented in that assembly in any sense. **"**
>
> John Adams, 1765

from the frontier to the Atlantic cities, and the guns of Fort George are redirected to face towards New York City rather than out to sea. Even those soldiers who remain in the west seem intended to prevent further expansion rather than to protect existing settlements.

1766 Grenville having fallen from power, for unrelated reasons, **William Pitt the Elder** denounces the Stamp Act as 'impolitic, arbitrary, oppressive, and unconstitutional'; it is **repealed** in March. However, the simultaneous **Declaratory Act** echoes similar legislation applying to Ireland by asserting parliament's authority to make laws binding the American colonists 'in all cases whatsoever'. Duties on molasses are subsequently reduced, but all colonial exports to Europe are now required to clear through British ports.

In December, the New York assembly – which celebrates the demise of the Stamp Act by voting funds for statues of Pitt and George III – is suspended by parliament for refusing to comply with the Quartering Act.

1767 With Pitt incapacitated by mental distress, Chancellor of the Exchequer **Charles Townshend** capitalizes on the widely held misconception, which he may well not share, that the colonists are prepared to accept 'external' taxation on trade as opposed to 'internal' taxes within the colonies. The so-called **Townshend Acts** impose duties on imports of paper, paint, glass, lead and tea; set up a Board of Customs Commissioners in Boston; and reorganize vice-admiralty courts at Halifax, Boston, Philadelphia and Charleston. New revenues are intended to pay governors and other officers, freeing them from dependence on the colonial assemblies. Townshend then dies, and **Lord North** takes control.

John Dickinson's *Letters of a Pennsylvania Farmer* concede parliament's right to regulate trade, but deny its right to tax for revenue.

Charles Mason and Jeremiah Dixon fix the border between Pennsylvania and Maryland: as the **Mason–Dixon line**, it becomes the shorthand term for the boundary between slave and free states.

1768 On refusing to withdraw a **Circular Letter**, drafted by Samuel Adams and James Otis, that urges other colonies to join in resisting the Townshend Acts, the Massachusetts Assembly is dissolved. In June, customs officers in Boston who have impounded **John Hancock**'s ship, the *Liberty*, are confronted by an angry mob. They call for protection, and two regiments of British troops arrive in September.

In the treaties of **Fort Stanwix** and **Hard Labor**, the Iroquois and Cherokee concede further lands along the Ohio.

1769 In May, the Virginia assembly asserts that only Virginians have a right to tax Virginians, and condemns other British legislation. Other colonies follow suit.

Father Junípero Serra establishes Spain's first mission on the west coast, at San Diego de Alcala.

1770 After the British government **repeals the Townshend Acts** in March – only retaining the duties on tea, to save face – and promises to lay no new taxes on the colonies, the non-importation movement collapses. However, January sees street fighting between the Sons of Liberty and British 'redcoats' on Golden Hill in New York, while on March 5, in the so-called **Boston Massacre**, sentries outside Boston's Custom House fire on a mob that's taunting them. Passions in Massachusetts are inflamed by the deaths of five colonists, including former slave Crispus Attucks.

The **Treaty of Lochaber** with the Cherokee allows for further westward expansion; Benjamin Franklin among others advances plans for a new colony of **Vandalia**, in modern West Virginia and eastern Kentucky

1771 Governor William Tryon of North Carolina wins the Battle of **Alamance** against backcountry outlaws known as **Regulators** who have been administering vigilante justice and refusing to pay taxes, in protest against their lack of protection by, and representation in, the colonial assembly. Casualties are light, but six Regulators are executed for treason. The incident highlights deep-seated sectional differences.

1772 A crowd from **Providence**, Rhode Island, boards and burns the customs schooner *Gaspee*, after it runs aground in Narragansett Bay in June. Even moderates are alarmed when the subsequent commission of inquiry is given authority to ship the culprits to England for trial, so no witnesses come forward.

The news that the governor and judges of Massachusetts are to be paid from customs revenues prompts Samuel Adams and James Otis to form a **Committee of Correspondence** in Boston. Similar committees spring up throughout the colonies, to keep abreast of developments and discuss responses.

1773 In April, parliament passes the **Tea Act**, a bid to restore the fortunes of the ailing **East India Company** by allowing it to sell its glut of tea in America. Colonial merchants and smugglers are infuriated; although tea is now much cheaper, colonists refuse to countenance the hated import duty. On December 16, thousands of protesters gather in Boston when Governor Hutchinson of Massachusetts demands that three tea ships – in one of which his sons have invested – be allowed to unload their cargoes, and pay the duties. Immediately afterwards, in the **Boston Tea Party**, two hundred colonists loosely disguise themselves as 'Mohawks' under the direction of Samuel Adams, board the vessels, and tip several thousand pounds' worth of tea into the sea.

Letters to British ministers from Governor Thomas Hutchinson and his lieutenant governor, Andrew Oliver, obtained by Benjamin Franklin, are published in Boston. They appear to show that prompting from America explains the 'obnoxious' policy of Great Britain, and the Massachusetts Assembly petitions for Hutchinson's removal.

1774 Under pressure from George III, who declares 'the colonists must either submit or triumph', parliament singles out Massachusetts for punishment. The **Coercive Acts** close Boston's port until tea duties are paid and the East India Company is compensated; transfer any trials for riot or revenue obstruction that might result in the death penalty to London; annul the colony's charter by introducing a

> 66 The crisis is arrived when we must assert our rights, or submit to every imposition, that can be heaped upon us, til custom and use shall make us as tame and abject slaves, as the blacks we rule over with such arbitrary sway. 99
>
> George Washington, as he set off for the First Continental Congress of September 1774

military governor, and making other officials subject to royal appointment; and renew the expired Quartering Act. Together with the **Quebec Act**, which extends the boundaries of Canada south to the Ohio and west to the Mississippi – a region to which several Atlantic colonies have claims – and reaffirms French civil law and Catholicism, the package becomes known as the **Intolerable Acts**.

Virginia's **House of Burgesses** is dissolved for having voted for a day of 'Fasting, Humiliation and Prayer' in support of Massachusetts, and further 'tea parties' take place in New York City, Maryland and New Jersey.

On September 5, delegates from twelve colonies – excluding Georgia, Quebec and Nova Scotia – gather for the **First Continental Congress** in Philadelphia. None explicitly advocates independence, and a 'Plan of Union' devised by Joseph Galloway of Pennsylvania, which proposes home rule for the colonies under the British Crown and parliament, is defeated by a single vote. Instead Congress adopts John Adams's **Declaration of Rights and Grievances**, which appeals to the British people to 'permit us to be as free as yourselves, and we shall ever esteem a union with you', but threatens that 'we will never submit to be hewers of wood or drawers of water'. Its course of action is embodied in a **Continental Association** that will boycott British goods and close off international trade, including the slave trade.

Meanwhile, on September 1, Massachusetts' new military governor, **General Thomas Gage**, seizes the Provincial Powder House outside Boston. The following week, a meeting in Suffolk County denounces Gage and advocates armed resistance. Paul Revere carries these **Suffolk Resolves** to Philadelphia, where Congress endorses them.

Benjamin Franklin (1706–90)

Even by his contemporaries, **Benjamin Franklin** came to be seen as a larger-than-life character – the self-taught philosopher-scientist who was the archetypal plain-spoken American frontiersman and yet embodied the wit, sophistication and thirst for knowledge of the Enlightenment. That romantic image tends to obscure his crucial role as both politician and diplomat at so many pivotal moments in the struggle for independence. Franklin proposed the Plan of Union at the Albany Congress of 1754; was a member of the five-man committee that drafted the Declaration of Independence; put forward the Articles of Confederation in 1777; negotiated the 1778 treaty that brought France into the Revolutionary War and the 1782 treaty that ended it; and at the age of 81 first hosted, and then cajoled into near-unanimity, the Constitutional Convention.

Born in Boston as the tenth and last son among seventeen children, Franklin ventured as far as London before he was 20. He made his fortune in Philadelphia as a printer and journalist, publishing *Poor Richard's Almanack*, packed with his own pithy maxims – such as 'deny Self for Self's sake', and 'sin is not hurtful because it is forbidden but it is forbidden because it is hurtful' – and the *Pennsylvanian Gazette*. Wealthy enough to retire at 42, he then devoted himself to science – famous for his kite-flying experiments with electricity, he invented the lightning rod and various domestic stoves and chimneys – and to public service.

When he first represented Pennsylvania in London, in 1757, it was to advocate that Pennsylvania should be taken from the Penn family, and made a royal colony. His conversion to the cause of independence came in 1772 – by which time he was also representing Georgia, New Jersey and Massachusetts – with the realization that Massachusetts Governor Thomas Hutchinson was conniving with the British government to suppress the liberties of the colonists. Thereafter he worked tirelessly to devise a framework for the new nation, and to establish its presence on the world stage, spending almost the entire decade of his 70s as its (much-feted) ambassador to France before returning to Philadelphia for his final years.

Benjamin Franklin Drawing Electricity from the Sky, a portrait by Benjamin West, 1816

1775 In February, parliament considers two '**conciliation plans**'. It rejects Lord Chatham's, to recognize the Colonial Congress and acknowledge the colonists' right to assent to all taxation, but accepts Lord North's, which would 'forbear' taxing any colony that finances its own defence, judiciary and administration. However, it declares Massachusetts to be in rebellion, and under the **New England Restraining Act** it forbids the colonies to fish in the North Atlantic, or to trade with anywhere but Britain and the West Indies.

What will become known as the **Revolutionary War** begins in April. Instructed from London to thwart the colonists' military preparations, General Gage despatches 750 soldiers from Boston to confiscate munitions being held at **Concord**, twenty miles northwest. At dawn on April 18, on **Lexington Green**, they encounter seventy Massachusetts militiamen – known as **Minute Men** because they could assemble so quickly – who have been forewarned by Paul Revere. Eight militiamen are killed after an anonymous person fires the '**shot heard round the world**'. The British continue to Concord, where they fail to find the armaments, and are then harried as they retreat towards Boston; 273 redcoats die, and the rest barely escape surrender. Boston is subsequently besieged by a 10,000-strong patriot army.

Sailing from Britain with reinforcements, generals **William Howe**, **Henry Clinton** and **John Burgoyne** reach Boston on May 25. On June 17, Gage launches Howe's men in a frontal attack on the colonists' fortifications on **Bunker Hill**, facing the city. Despite great casualties, the British prevail, but Boston remains encircled.

In May, the **Second Continental Congress** assembles in Philadelphia. Delegates include **Benjamin Franklin** and **Thomas Jefferson** as well as representatives from Georgia. At first it seems that the southern colonies may not find common cause with the more radical north, but following an appeal from Massachusetts, Congress agrees in June to take charge of the forces outside Boston. In a deliberate choice of a general from outside New England, **George Washington** of Virginia is named as commander in chief. Reaching Boston on July 2, he assumes control of the new **Continental Army**. The **Navy** will be created in November.

Congress agrees a **Declaration of the Causes for Taking Up Arms** in early July, proclaiming its readiness to fight against 'voluntary slavery', but falls short of declaring independence. As the search for compromise continues, the '**Olive Branch Petition**' to the king professes loyalty and asks for a suspension of hostilities. Ignoring it, George III proclaims America to be in rebellion on August 23, branding the colonists as 'open and avowed enemies'.

Meanwhile, in May, Benedict Arnold and Ethan Allen's Green Mountain Boys capture **Fort Ticonderoga** and Crown Point on Lake Champlain, and Arnold moves on to take but then abandon St John's, eighty miles north. Richard Montgomery's small force occupies **Montreal** on November 13, but Montgomery dies as he and Arnold are heavily defeated at Quebec on December 31.

Lord Dunmure, the governor of Virginia, alienates planters by offering freedom to slaves who support the British. His Loyal Ethiopian Regiment is defeated by Virginians and North Carolinans at **Great Bridge** on December 11.

The **Transylvania Company** buys lands between the Kentucky and Cumberland rivers from the Cherokee, and a party under **Daniel Boone** cuts the Wilderness Road to provide access via the Cumberland Gap. A delegation from Transylvania is not, however, recognized by Congress in 1776, and it becomes part of Virginia.

> **"** Gentlemen may cry peace, peace, but there is no peace. The war is actually begun! The next gale that sweeps from the north will bring to our ears the clash of resounding arms! Our brethren are already in the field! Why stand we here idle?. . . I know not what course others may take, but as for me, give me liberty, or give me death. **"**
>
> Patrick Henry, to resistance leaders in Richmond, Virginia, on March 23, 1775, three weeks before "the shot heard around the world"

1776 In January, **Thomas Paine**, who has moved to Philadelphia from England in 1774, publishes the pamphlet *Common Sense*, which sells around 150,000 copies. Its sustained polemic against hereditary privilege, as embodied in the 'royal brute' George III, and angry, exuberant advocacy of American independence, inspires many thousands to think the unthinkable. Adam Smith's very different *Wealth of Nations*, which appears in March, strikes a chord with American merchants.

North Carolina's Loyalists are defeated at **Moore's Creek** on February 27. In March, the Americans storm and capture **Dorchester Heights**, overlooking British positions in Boston, and install cannon hauled overland from Fort Ticonderoga. In return for not burning the city, General Howe is allowed to withdraw, and on March 17 nine thousand soldiers sail for Halifax. Once Boston is reoccupied, Washington decamps with his army for **New York**, anticipated as the next British target.

The Second Continental Congress opens American ports to all non-British shipping in April, and looks for foreign alliances, especially with France and Spain. On July 4, the **Declaration of Independence** finally rationalizes its

Thomas Jefferson's draft of the Declaration of Independence, with handwritten amendments by Benjamin Franklin and John Adams

The Declaration of Independence

Although in early 1776 some delegates still hoped for reconciliation with Britain, and even George Washington opposed secession, by spring the groundswell in Congress towards **independence** was becoming, in John Adams's words, 'a Torrent'. The foreign alliances essential to win the war could only be formed if America became a sovereign nation – even if the thorny issue of how individual colonies that had yet to establish their own state governments and constitutions could consent to such a union had yet to be settled.

On June 7, seven of the thirteen colonies represented in Congress voted for **Thomas Jefferson**, John Adams, Benjamin Franklin, Roger Sherman and Robert Livingston to prepare a proclamation. Adams insisted that Jefferson should do the job: 'first, you are a Virginian . . . second, I am obnoxious, suspected and unpopular . . . third, you can write ten times better than I can'.

Jefferson's draft was amended both in committee, and by Congress in the two-day debate before it was approved as the **Declaration of Independence** on July 4. While the most notorious 'lost' section, blaming George III for the 'execrable commerce' in slaves, was not the ringing denunciation of slavery that legend might suggest, its deletion was due to pressure from South Carolina and Georgia, 'whose reflections', as Jefferson put it, 'were not yet matured to the full abhorrence of that traffic'.

As Adams later petulantly insisted, and Jefferson modestly acknowledged, the Declaration was not so much a work of stunning originality as a distillation of prevalent, much-debated ideas. One especially significant controversy centred on whether for Jefferson to champion 'Life, Liberty, and the pursuit of Happiness' as 'unalienable Rights' represented a change in emphasis from John Locke's 'life, liberty, and property', towards a notion of a common, collective pursuit of happiness, or whether 'happiness' and 'property' should be regarded as synonymous. In a nation where 'property' was in turn to become a code word for 'slaves', that proved to be a very pregnant debate.

status as the de facto government. As many members feel that they are signing 'our own death warrants', the names of the signatories are kept secret for several months to prevent reprisals.

A British land and sea attack on **Charleston**, led by General Clinton and **Lord Cornwallis**, is repelled on June 28, but that same month, faced by a British advance on Montreal, Congress decides to abandon the Canadian campaign. Benedict Arnold retreats to Fort Ticonderoga.

General Howe duly sails from Halifax to the waters off New York in June. He's joined in July by his brother, Admiral Lord **Richard Howe**, bringing reinforcements from Europe, and in August by Clinton and Cornwallis, creating a combined force of over thirty thousand men. David Bushnell's hand-cranked *Turtle*, the first-ever **submarine**, manoeuvres itself beneath the British flagship *Eagle*, but fails to attach a bomb. The British land first on Staten Island and then Long Island, before launching a devastating assault on **Brooklyn Heights** on August 27. Under cover of fog, Washington manages to withdraw to Manhattan. Fruitless peace negotiations ensue, before the British occupy New York in September.

Washington is in almost continuous retreat all through the autumn, across New Jersey and Delaware and into Pennsylvania, while Congress flees Philadelphia for Baltimore. Washington's army disintegrates to barely six thousand men, most of whose service is due to expire at the end of the year. He therefore stakes all by **crossing the Delaware** to make a successful surprise attack on the British camp at **Trenton**, New Jersey, on December 26, in which a thousand German mercenaries are taken prisoner.

Also in December, Benjamin Franklin lands in France as American ambassador.

The Franciscan friars **Domínguez** and **Escalante** set off from Santa Fe in July hoping to establish a route to the Spanish mission at Monterey, California. Deterred by the sight of snow-capped mountains in what's now southwest Utah, they turn back defeated.

1777 At the start of the year, as Washington pledges his own money to keep his army together, Lord Cornwallis assembles eight thousand men at **Princeton** and advances on Trenton. On January 3, however, the Americans outflank him, capture Princeton, and drive the British back towards New Brunswick. With all but easternmost New Jersey now cleared of the enemy, Washington establishes his winter quarters close to **Morristown**. Howe, meanwhile, is enjoying the winter in New York, and deceived by reports of Washington's strength makes no moves against him.

In England, **General Burgoyne** wins approval for a **three-pronged attack** to isolate New England and cut the colonies in two. He will lead one army south from Quebec to Lake Champlain and down the Hudson; Howe will move up the Hudson to meet him at Albany; and a third force will travel up the St Lawrence, land at Oswego to capture Fort Stanwix, then advance through the Mohawk Valley.

Burgoyne duly lands at Quebec on May 6, and captures **Fort Ticonderoga** on July 6. At first the American defeat appears calamitous, but as the overconfident Burgoyne presses onwards his lines become drastically overextended, while American militiamen flock to the region. Burgoyne sustains heavy casualties when a bid to seize American supplies in **Bennington** fails on August 16, while a separate British force abandons its siege of Fort Stanwix on August 22.

In the absence of explicit orders, and assuming Burgoyne will succeed without him, Howe turns his attentions

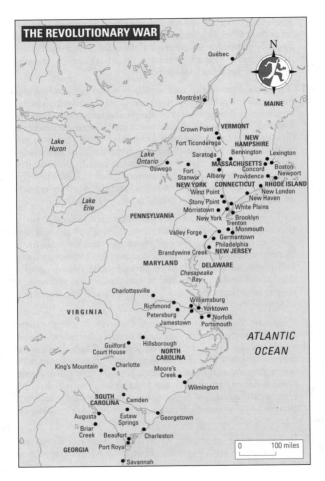

THE REVOLUTIONARY WAR

Québec

Montréal

MAINE

N

Lake Huron

Crown Point
Fort Ticonderoga
VERMONT
NEW HAMPSHIRE

Lake Ontario

Saratoga
Bennington
Lexington

Oswego
Fort Stanwix
MASSACHUSETTS
Concord
Boston
Newport

NEW YORK
Albany
Providence
CONNECTICUT **RHODE ISLAND**

West Point
New London
New Haven

Stony Point
White Plains

PENNSYLVANIA
Morristown
New York
Brooklyn
Trenton
Monmouth

Valley Forge
Germantown

Brandywine Creek
Philadelphia
NEW JERSEY

MARYLAND
DELAWARE

Chesapeake Bay

Charlottesville

Williamsburg

Richmond
Yorktown

VIRGINIA
Petersburg
Norfolk

Jamestown
Portsmouth

ATLANTIC OCEAN

Guilford Court House
Hillsborough

NORTH CAROLINA

King's Mountain
Charlotte

Moore's Creek

Wilmington

SOUTH CAROLINA
Camden

Augusta
Eutaw Springs
Georgetown

Briar Creek

Beaufort
Charleston

GEORGIA
Port Royal

Savannah

Lake Erie

0   100 miles

southwards instead. Landing an army south of Philadelphia, he defeats Washington at **Brandywine Creek** on September 11. The British **occupation of Philadelphia** on September 27 is confirmed by a further victory at **Germantown** on October 4.

Burgoyne meanwhile continues to head for Albany, but suffers further attrition in two bloody confrontations, at Freeman's Farm on September 19 and Bemis Heights on October 7. Now hugely outnumbered, he **surrenders** to **General Horatio Gates** at nearby **Saratoga** on October 17. His 5700 men are at first to be allowed to return to England on condition they play no further part in the war, but when the Americans appreciate they will simply be deployed elsewhere, thus allowing other soldiers to take their place, a pretext is found to detain them in New England.

Congress retreats first to Lancaster and then to York, while, as the British secure control of the Delaware, Washington takes up quarters at **Valley Forge**, on the Schuylkill River twenty miles northwest of Philadelphia. Almost a quarter of Washington's eleven thousand men die from hunger or disease in the ensuing severe winter, and a further thousand desert. However, stirrings and suggestions that Washington should be replaced as commander by the victorious Gates come to nothing.

On November 17, Congress creates the **United States of America**, by adopting the **Articles of Confederation**. The new **Continental Congress** cannot raise money directly, only request it from states; each state has a single vote, and all must consent to any change. The Articles are sent to the states for ratification, which takes until 1781. Spurred by the news of Saratoga, Louis XVI of **France** recognizes US independence in December; the **Marquis de Lafayette**, who arrives on his own initiative during the summer, is by now a major-general in the Continental Army.

> **Small islands, not capable of protecting themselves, are the proper objects for kingdoms to take under their care; but there is something very absurd in supposing a continent to be perpetually governed by an island.**
>
> Thomas Paine, *Common Sense*, 1776

1778 France and the United States sign a treaty on February 6 in which France pledges support during the war, and both agree not to conclude separate peace agreements with Britain. An alarmed Lord North persuades parliament to repeal the Tea and Coercive acts, and to despatch peace commissioners to America, but Congress rejects these overtures and unanimously ratifies the treaty in June.

Hearing that a French fleet has sailed for North America, **General Sir Henry Clinton**, who has replaced Howe in Philadelphia, fears that the Delaware will be blockaded. He evacuates the city – whereupon Congress returns to it – and falls back towards New York, harassed by Washington. In an attack on Clinton's column at **Monmouth** on June 28, General Charles Lee fails to follow Washington's orders and squanders the chance of a decisive victory. The retreating British board transports to New York, while Washington crosses the Hudson in pursuit.

By the end of July, the British are penned within New York City, and the battle lines are back as they were in the summer of 1776. There's hope that the arrival of the French fleet, commanded by the **Comte d'Estaing**, may break the deadlock, but the deep-keeled French men-of-war prove unable to reach New York. They then fail to support American troops in a combined land and sea attack on Newport in early August, after being scattered by a sudden storm. After that fiasco creates ill feeling between the French and the Americans, d'Estaing sails to the Caribbean, where he fails to retake the French island of **St Lucia**, captured by a British detachment.

A further reversal comes when a surprise British assault overwhelms **Savannah** on December 29.

Elsewhere, **John Paul Jones** raids Whitehaven on the northwest coast of Britain in April, then captures the British sloop *Drake* off the north coast of Ireland. On the western frontier, Loyalists and Iroquois conduct bloody raids in upcountry New York and Pennsylvania, while the American General George Rogers Clark captures Cahokia in May and Kaskaskia on July 4, both on the Mississippi River, and Vincennes on the Wabash on July 28. A British counter-attack recaptures Vincennes in December.

1779 By taking Fort Sunbury and **Augusta** in Georgia in January, the British trigger what's effectively a civil war across the South. Repelled in both South Carolina and Georgia in February, the British nonetheless defeat the Americans at **Briar Creek** on the Savannah River in March and move towards Charleston in May, before being forced back on Savannah. On May 10 British ships take and fire both **Portsmouth** and **Norfolk** in Virginia. In September, d'Estaing arrives with his fleet to besiege

> ❝ Should America succeed . . . the West Indies must follow them; Ireland would soon follow the plan and be a separate State . . . then this Island would be reduced to itself, and soon would be a poor Island indeed. ❞
>
> George III, June 11, 1779

Savannah, but a combined French–American onslaught fails in October, and d'Estaing returns to the Caribbean.

Further north, at the end of May, General Clinton attempts to draw Washington into battle. A British expedition seizes uncompleted forts at **Stony Point** and **Verplanck's Point**, guarding a crucial ferry crossing on either side of the Hudson, but the arrival of American reinforcements deters them from continuing the twelve miles upstream to West Point. An American counter-attack recaptures Stony Point on July 15, while a similar operation led by Major Henry 'Light-Horse Harry' Lee – the father of Robert E. Lee (see p.172) – devastates **Paulus Hook**, the last major British outpost in New Jersey, on August 19. Meanwhile, on Clinton's orders, Governor Tryon of New York ravages the Connecticut shore of Long Island Sound.

In the west, General Clark advances once again up the Ohio and Wabash rivers, and forces the British lieutenant governor of Detroit, Henry Hamilton, to surrender at **Vincennes** on February 25. General John Sullivan's summer campaign against the Iroquois in western New York diminishes the threat along the frontier still further.

On September 23, at **Flamborough Head** off the northeast coast of England, John Paul Jones fights a pitched naval battle during which he loses his own *Bonhomme Richard* in capturing HMS *Serapis*, and utters the immortal words 'I have not yet begun to fight !'

Spain enters the war in June, albeit without recognizing US independence, and spurred by French promises of aid in recapturing Florida and Gibraltar. Spanish forces take **Baton Rouge** and **Natchez** in September.

By December Clinton has decided to concentrate British campaigning on the South. Having evacuated Rhode Island in October, but leaving a garrison in New York –

John Trumbull's portrait of George Washington

George Washington (1732–99)

George Washington, who commanded the army that secured American independence, presided over the convention that framed its constitution, and served as its first president, was born beside the Potomac River in Westmoreland County, Virginia, on February 22, 1732. His family were middling planters, and his father's death when George was 11 meant he received a meagre education by the standards of his peers. After training as a surveyor, however, he amassed a reasonable fortune, along with considerable knowledge of Virginia's western frontier. Thus he was chosen in 1753 to deliver a note warning the French to stop fortifying the forks of the Ohio River (near modern Pittsburgh), and in 1754 to lead a Virginian militia to drive them out. Although he was forced to surrender after some initial success, and then ignominiously defeated when he returned with General Braddock's British soldiers the next year, he established his reputation as a military leader.

After years spent hunting, farming and serving in the Virginia legislature, Washington was therefore summoned to lead the **Continental Army** in 1775. Despite his show of indifference, he was passionately committed to the role; refusing to accept a salary, he even subsidized the army himself. Other than his legendary crossing of the Delaware to attack Trenton in December 1776, he won few tactical victories, but his grasp on overall strategy, together with his ability to organize, discipline and inspire his men, were crucial to victory.

A further retirement was followed by the call to serve once again, when he was unanimously elected as **president** in 1789. The office had been devised with him in mind, and he in turn treated it and the nation with scrupulous respect, avowing that 'Many things which appear of little importance of themselves at the beginning may have great and durable consequences from their having been established at the commencement of a new general government.' Deliberately positioning himself above the fray, both of factionalism at home and of entanglement abroad, he became the living emblem of his country, making his death in 1799 a national tragedy.

and with Washington ensconced for the winter at Morristown – he sails for Charleston with 7500 men on December 26.

The British **Captain James Cook**, who in 1778 has become the first non-Polynesian to reach **Hawaii**, is killed at Kealakekua Bay when he returns to the islands in February.

1780 Having resisted British land and sea operations since February, **Charleston surrenders** on May 12; 5400 Americans are taken prisoner. Clinton sails for New York in July, instructing Lord Cornwallis, in control of South Carolina and Georgia, to press northwards. Assigned by Congress to oppose him, General Gates advances impetuously into South Carolina and is heavily defeated at **Camden** on August 16. On October 7, however, irregular patriot forces overwhelm a British battalion attempting to enter North Carolina at **King's Mountain**. Gates has meanwhile retreated to Charlotte, where he's replaced as southern commander by **General Nathanael Greene**.

In the north, Washington endures another grim winter. Even when the thaw makes movement possible, both sides restrict themselves to occasional forays. Another French fleet, under the **Comte de Rochambeau**, reaches Newport on July 10, but no joint operations are devised.

In September, the capture of a British spy reveals that **Benedict Arnold**, now commander at **West Point**, has been negotiating to betray it to the British. After the handover is thwarted by Washington's opportune arrival, Arnold escapes to become a British brigadier general.

1781 In January, Washington responds firmly but relatively sympathetically to mutinies in Pennsylvania and New Jersey, when American soldiers protest that they are being kept in the army for longer than the three years for which they feel they agreed to enlist.

Alarmed by the depreciation of its paper currency, Congress attempts to co-ordinate fiscal policy by appointing Robert Morris as Superintendent of Finance in February. The **Bank of America** is chartered by the end of year, while subsidies from France and The Netherlands help to promote a return to specie money.

The **Articles of Confederation** are ratified in March. Now officially 'The United States in Congress Assembled', with Samuel Huntington as its president, Congress authorizes a commission consisting of John Adams, John Jay, Benjamin Franklin, Henry Laurens and Thomas Jefferson to conduct any peace negotiations. Terms can only be agreed with French approval.

Both sides recognize the South as the crucial theatre of war. Following various British forays, **Lord Cornwallis** attempts to secure **Virginia** in April. After two months of constant harassment from Lafayette, and without fighting a major battle, he falls back on the coast in order to maintain communications with New York. He heads first to Portsmouth and then ensconces himself at **Yorktown** on the Virginia peninsula. Meanwhile, in the **Carolinas**, General Greene cuts off and captures a succession of British-held forts and cities. His decisive victory at **Eutaw Springs** on September 8 narrows British control to Charleston and its vicinity.

Washington spends the spring contemplating schemes for his forces, based at West Point, to combine with Rochambeau's to attack New York City. News in June that **Admiral de Grasse** will soon be arriving with a French fleet from the West Indies spurs Rochambeau to leave Newport and link up with Washington at White Plains in July. Bluffing that they're about to besiege New York, in late August both armies suddenly march south instead, covering two hundred miles in fifteen days. Washington crosses the Delaware once more on September 1, and reaches Philadelphia the next day.

De Grasse arrives in the Chesapeake Bay on August 30, two days after the British Admiral Graves, who thinks he is chasing the French, turns up in New York having failed to find them. A combined British fleet then sails south from New York, only to be defeated by the much larger French fleet in an offshore naval battle that starts on September 5. Under cover of that conflict, three thousand French troops land at Jamestown, while thousands more are ferried to the Chesapeake from Newport.

With the British fleet driven off, Cornwallis is surrounded by both land and sea. The American and French lay siege to Yorktown on September 18, and a sustained bombardment forces the **surrender** of its garrison of 7247 soldiers and 840 sailors on October 18. Five days later, a British expedition from New York sails into the Chesapeake, too late to bring relief. To Washington, who, with the British still holding New York City and Charleston, anticipates another year of war, Cornwallis's surrender is 'an interesting event that may be productive of much good'; Lord North, receiving the news in London, cries 'Oh God! It is over! It is all over!'

1782 Both the British army and its Loyalist supporters have already begun to leave North America when the British parliament votes in February not to continue waging the war. Although Sir Guy Carleton, who replaces Clinton as British commander in April, continues to occupy New York, the British successively evacuate Wilmington, Savannah and Charleston.

After **Lord North** resigns as prime minister in March, his successor Lord Rockingham authorizes talks with the American peace mission, which open in Paris in April. The three active peace commissioners – Jay, Adams and Franklin – eventually decide to disregard their instructions to consult with the French, and sign a provisional treaty on November 30.

Thomas Jefferson (1743–1826)

President Kennedy once hailed a group of Nobel Prize winners as the greatest concentration of brain power the White House had ever seen, 'except when **Thomas Jefferson** dined alone'. Choosing to overlook his eight years as president, Jefferson himself commemorated three achievements on his tombstone: his authorship of the **Declaration of Independence** (which only became common knowledge during the nineteenth century); his drafting of Virginia's **Statute of Religious Freedom**, the basis for the First Amendment; and his founding of the **University of Virginia**.

Born into an elite Virginian family on April 13, 1743, Jefferson trained as a lawyer, and was a member of Virginia's House of Burgesses before attending the Continental Congress. Though he was reticent in debate, his writing skills led to his drafting of the Declaration of Independence (see p.77). During the Revolutionary War, he served as governor of Virginia, then spent five years as ambassador to **France** after his wife died in childbirth. Appalled by the corruption of Europe, he welcomed the **French Revolution**, observing that 'the tree of liberty' needs to be 'watered with the blood of tyrants'. On a more private level, he also flirted with an English artist, Maria Cosway, and had the first of several children by his household slave Sally Hemings, his former wife's half-sister.

Absent when the Constitution was created, Jefferson took some convincing of its merits when he returned to become Washington's **Secretary of State**, and strongly advocated the need for the **Bill of Rights**. His opposition to the business-oriented policies of Alexander Hamilton led directly to the emergence of the country's first political parties. Subsequently, as **president** from 1801 onwards, he failed to realize his vision of the new nation as an agrarian republic – he believed 'those who labor in the earth are the chosen people of God' – deploring the growth and industrialization of its cities, and the rampant spreading of slave plantations, despite owning a plantation himself. He died at his beloved Virginia home, **Monticello**, on the fiftieth anniversary of the Declaration of Independence.

1783 Britain makes preliminary peace with France and Spain in January. The provisional treaty is ratified in April and signed as the **Treaty of Paris** on September 3. Britain acknowledges not only US independence but also American control west to the Mississippi and north to the Great Lakes. The Americans retain fishing rights off Canada, and agree that Congress will 'earnestly recommend' states to return lands confiscated from Loyalists. Spain recovers Florida.

Grievances in the Continental Army, encamped all this time at **Newburgh**, New York, come to a head in January with protests over pay, and again in March, when disgruntled officers appear to threaten a coup d'état unless the states yield more power to Congress. Washington defuses the situation, but a mutiny in Pennsylvania in late June forces Congress to flee Philadelphia first for Princeton and later Annapolis.

The **Continental Army disbands** on June 13, but for a small core that remains with Washington until the British **evacuate New York** on November 25. A triumphant Washington appears before Congress on December 23 to resign his commission and retire into private life.

1784 The Revolutionary War officially **ends** on January 14, when Congress ratifies the Treaty of Paris. John Jay returns from Europe to become Secretary for Foreign Affairs, while Thomas Jefferson teams up with John Adams and Benjamin Franklin in Paris to negotiate commercial treaties. Meeting at Trenton in December, Congress votes for a federal capital to be laid out beside the Delaware, and to move to New York until it is ready.

The Spanish refuse to accept the 31st parallel as the boundary between Spanish Florida and the US. Claiming an additional hundred miles northward to the Yazoo, they close the lower Mississippi to American shipping.

By picking up a valuable cargo of tea and silks in Canton in August, an American vessel, the *Empress of China* from New York, opens a lucrative new trade with China.

The Russians establish their first permanent settlement on Alaska's Kodiak Island.

1785 The weakness of central government, and specifically the ability of individual states to reject national treaties, hampers efforts to form trade agreements with foreign nations. Thomas Jefferson becomes US ambassador to France, and John Adams to Britain. Adams cannot satisfy British demands over compensation of Loyalists and debts owed to British merchants, so the British continue to occupy western outposts and to deny American traders access to the West Indies.

On March 28, at the **Mount Vernon Conference**, commissioners from Virginia and Maryland consider maritime traffic in the Chesapeake Bay and along the Potomac. Their desire to standardize commercial regulations and charges, and establish a uniform currency, prompts an invitation for all states to discuss commercial problems at Annapolis in September 1786.

In May, the **Land Ordinance** provides for new land in the northwestern territories to be divided into rectangular townships of six square miles. Each township will be further divided into 36 lots of 640 acres each, and each lot sold for $640. One lot is set aside to pay for public education, but the proposal that another should support the majority religion is rejected.

1786 Virginia adopts Jefferson's **Statute of Religious Freedom**, which guarantees that no man can be forced to attend church or suffer other religious discrimination, and will be the model for the First Amendment.

Slavery and the Constitution

For the speed and eloquence with which it transcended apparently irreconcilable sectional differences, the Constitutional Convention is often hailed as 'the miracle at Philadelphia'. Behind closed doors, however, some very hard-nosed negotiations went on, and the Constitution's equivocation on slavery led Maryland delegate Luther Martin to call it rather 'an odious bargain with sin'.

According to James Madison, 'the States were divided into different interests not by their difference of size, but principally from their having or not having slaves'. In the most explicit trade-off, the New England states agreed to forbid Congress to abolish the slave trade for twenty years, while southern delegates consented to make federal regulation of commerce subject to a simple majority. However, it was surely no coincidence that the Great Compromise, which by counting a slave as three-fifths of a person gave slave-owners increased representation in Congress, was signed just one day before the Northwest Ordinance banned slavery from new territories north of the Ohio – though the latter could be read either as prohibiting slavery's westward expansion, or as endorsing its spread *south* of the river.

The contradiction between the Declaration of Independence's avowal that 'all men are created equal' and the Constitutional requirement for states to facilitate the return of runaway slaves remains self-evident. The true 'great compromise' – the one that allowed slavery to persist – can be ascribed to several factors. Six northern states had already outlawed slavery, and many northerners believed it would simply wither away in the light of the revolutionary dawn. Others saw slavery as the price of southern co-operation, without which the United States could not survive. And yes, it has to be acknowledged that the men who gathered at Philadelphia were predominantly members of the landed elite, and they themselves, Washington and Jefferson included, owned and profited from slaves.

When representatives from only five states – New York, New Jersey, Delaware, Pennsylvania and Virginia – turn up for September's **Annapolis Convention**, delegates decide not to discuss commercial issues. Instead they endorse Alexander Hamilton's proposal that all the states send commissioners to a new convention at Philadelphia in 1787, to consider all matters necessary to 'render the constitution of the Federal Government adequate to the exigencies of the Union'.

Congress tackles the instability of paper currency issued by individual states by introducing a national coinage system that includes $10 gold pieces and $1 silver coins.

1787 In an armed uprising triggered by the failure of Massachusetts' legislature to provide relief for debt-ridden and heavily taxed farmers, 1200 men under **Daniel Shays** attempt to capture the federal arsenal at Springfield on January 24. The insurrection is easily defeated, but a more sympathetic legislature reduces taxes and court fees, and makes the debt process more humane. However, fears of anarchy bolster the conservative resolve towards stronger central government.

The **Constitutional Convention** opens in **Philadelphia** on May 25, when a seven-state quorum finally gathers; twelve are represented in due course, only Rhode Island ignoring the proceedings altogether. George Washington is installed as its president, and it's agreed to give each state one vote in the convention itself. When Edmund Randolph introduces the **Virginia Plan** – largely the work of James Madison – on May 29, it becomes clear that the convention will go beyond its stated brief to revise the Articles of Confederation, and consider new forms of national government. The plan proposes that a bicameral legislature will make laws, choose an executive to carry them out, and appoint a judiciary including supreme and inferior courts to enforce them. A three-member 'council of revision', elected by both houses, will have a veto.

Opposition from smaller states focuses on the provisions for states to be represented unequally in both the proposed legislative houses, in proportion to their populations and/or tax. Many delegates also argue against direct popular elections, suggesting that state legislatures should choose their representatives in Congress. The alternative **New Jersey Plan**, advanced by William Paterson on June 15, suggests that the Confederation should be retained, with Congress given increased powers to tax and regulate commerce, and to appoint a supreme court and a plural – but veto-less – executive.

The deadlock is broken on July 16, when the **Great Compromise** is narrowly agreed. The lower house will be on a proportional basis, with each state having a representative for each thirty thousand of its population – a slave being counted as three-fifths of a person – while the upper house will have equal numbers from each state. A Committee of Detail is then given eleven days to draft a Constitution, before the **Great Debate**, from August 6 onwards, settles such issues as term lengths of two years for representatives, six years for senators, and four for the president.

The Constitution is finally **signed** on September 17, by 39 of the 42 delegates. To take effect, however, it must first be ratified by nine of the thirteen states, in special constitutional conventions rather than in the existing state legislatures. In the ensuing **ratification debate** between the Constitution's **Federalist** supporters and its **Anti-Federalist** opponents, 85 newspaper articles written by Hamilton, Madison and Jay, published collectively in 1788 as *The Federalist*, play a crucial role in forming public opinion. The first states to ratify, in December, are Delaware, Pennsylvania and New Jersey.

Meanwhile, in July, Congress issues the **Northwest Ordinance**, drafted in 1784, which sets out rules for the government of areas north of the Ohio River. This

The Federalist Papers

During the **ratification debate** of 1787–88, each state had to decide whether to ratify the newly drafted Constitution. The clearest articulation of the pro-Constitution case came in 85 articles credited to 'Publius', written for New York newspapers, additionally distributed in Virginia, and collected as *The Federalist*. Their actual authors were **Alexander Hamilton** – a New York delegate at the convention, left unable to vote after his two colleagues departed – who wrote around fifty, **James Madison**, responsible for thirty more, and **John Jay**, who contributed five.

Quite how many minds were changed by the '**Federalist Papers**' remains unquantifiable – the support of two titans, George Washington and Benjamin Franklin, probably did more to convince waverers – but they provide a definitive insight into the reasoning that went into the framing of the Constitution. In essence, they articulate the need for a strong national government while countering charges that such a government, especially one able to impose taxation and holding a monopoly on the printing of currency, would simply mimic the worst excesses of British rule. As well as carefully explaining the intricate checks and balances contained within the Constitution, they argued – as in the best-known essay, no. 10 – that the sheer size and diversity of the new nation would prevent the government from ever being dominated by a single narrow faction.

Anti-Federalists argued that the Constitution amounted to an illegal rejection of both the Declaration of Independence and the Articles of Confederation, and that the Federalists were not really federalists at all. True federalism would consist in keeping the individual states powerful, not forcing them to submit to a far-off national government. It's simplistic to suppose that the Federalists completely defeated their opponents; the Constitution was duly ratified, but only after Anti-Federalist demands for a **Bill of Rights** had been acknowledged.

establishes the principle that newly settled lands will start out as '**territories**', but that once they have sixty thousand free inhabitants they will be admitted to the United States 'on an equal footing with the original States in all respects whatever'. While freedom of worship, trial by jury, and funds for public education are guaranteed, slavery is prohibited except as criminal punishment.

The first **steamboats** are demonstrated on the Delaware and Potomac rivers.

1788 Between January and May, Georgia, Connecticut, Massachusetts, Maryland and South Carolina ratify the Constitution. Following intense campaigning, **New Hampshire** becomes the vital ninth state to ratify on June 21. By the time the president of Congress declares the Constitution to be in force, on July 2, Virginia has followed suit, and New York does so soon after. Both, however, recommend the addition of a **Bill of Rights**, while North Carolina waits until November 1789, after the bill has been put forward. Rhode Island holds out until 1790.

Having affirmed New York as the temporary seat of government, Congress meets for the last time under the Articles of Confederation in October.

In August, the town of Losantiville is founded on the Ohio; it will be renamed **Cincinnati** in 1790.

In December, Maryland cedes the ten square miles that will become the **District of Columbia** to Congress, for the federal capital.

1789 In January, all the 'ratifying states' except New York choose the first presidential electors, who cast their ballots on February 4. Once enough members have reached New York to make both the House of Representatives and the Senate quorate, in early April, the votes are counted to

The Constitution

As signed in 1787 and ratified in 1788, the **Constitution** stipulated the following form of government:

All **legislative** powers were granted to the **Congress of the United States**. The lower of its two distinct houses, the **House of Representatives**, was to be elected every two years, with its members in proportion to the number of each state's 'free Persons' plus 'three fifths of all other persons' (meaning slaves). The upper house, the **Senate**, would hold two Senators from each state, chosen by state legislatures rather than by direct elections. Each Senator was to serve for six years, with a third of them to be elected every two years.

Executive power was vested in the **President**, who was also Commander in Chief of the Army and Navy. He would be chosen every four years, by as many '**Electors**' from each individual state as it had Senators and Representatives. Each state could decide how to appoint those Electors; almost all chose to have direct popular elections. Nonetheless, the distinction has remained ever since between the number of 'popular votes', across the whole country, received by a presidential candidate, and the number of state-by-state 'electoral votes', which determines the actual result. Originally, whoever came second in the voting automatically became **Vice President**.

reveal that **George Washington** is unanimously elected as the first **President of the United States**, with John Adams as his Vice President. On April 30, Washington is inaugurated; that evening, he writes: 'I greatly fear my countrymen will expect too much from me.'

In July, Congress creates the Department of Foreign Affairs, renamed the **Department of State** in September. **Thomas Jefferson**, its first head, is still in Paris – where

The President could veto acts of Congress, but that veto could be overruled by a two-thirds vote in both houses. The House of Representatives could impeach the President for treason, bribery, or 'other high crimes and misdemeanors', in which instance the Senate could remove him from office with a two-thirds majority.

Judicial power was invested in a Supreme Court, and as many 'inferior Courts' as Congress should decide.

The Constitution has so far been altered by 27 Amendments. Those that have introduced significant governmental changes include 12, which instigated separate elections for President and Vice President, in 1804; 14 and 15, which extended the vote to black males in 1868 and 1870; 17, which made Senators subject to election by direct popular vote, in 1913; 18, introducing women's suffrage, in 1920; 22, restricting the President to two terms, in 1951; 24, which stopped states using poll taxes to disenfranchise black voters; and 26, which reduced the minimum voting age to 18, in 1971.

on July 14 he witnesses the fall of the Bastille, heralding the start of the **French Revolution** – so John Jay fills the post for the first few months.

The **Treasury Department** is created in September, with **Alexander Hamilton** as its first secretary.

Also in September, Congress proposes twelve **amendments to the Constitution**; the first ten will become the **Bill of Rights** in 1791.

The Bill of Rights

Proposed by Congress in 1789, and adopted in 1791 after being ratified in amended form by the separate states, the first ten Amendments to the Constitution are known as the **Bill of Rights**.

1 Congress shall make no law respecting an establishment of religion, or prohibiting the free exercise thereof; or abridging the freedom of speech, or of the press; or the right of the people peaceably to assemble, and to petition the Government for a redress of grievances.

2 A well regulated Militia, being necessary to the security of a free State, the right of the people to keep and bear Arms, shall not be infringed.

3 No Soldier shall, in time of peace be quartered in any house, without the consent of the Owner, nor in time of war, but in a manner to be prescribed by law.

4 The right of the people to be secure in their persons, houses, papers, and effects, against unreasonable searches and seizures, shall not be violated, and no Warrants shall issue, but upon probable cause, supported by Oath or affirmation, and particularly describing the place to be searched, and the persons or things to be seized.

5 No person shall be held to answer for a capital, or otherwise infamous crime, unless on a presentment or indictment of a Grand Jury, except in cases arising in the land or naval forces, or in the Militia, when in actual service in time of War or public danger; nor shall any person be subject for the same offence to

be twice put in jeopardy of life or limb; nor shall be compelled in any criminal case to be a witness against himself, nor be deprived of life, liberty, or property, without due process of law; nor shall private property be taken for public use, without just compensation.

6 In all criminal prosecutions, the accused shall enjoy the right to a speedy and public trial, by an impartial jury of the State and district wherein the crime shall have been committed, which district shall have been previously ascertained by law, and to be informed of the nature and cause of the accusation; to be confronted with the witnesses against him; to have compulsory process for obtaining witnesses in his favor, and to have the Assistance of Counsel for his defence.

7 In suits at common law, where the value in controversy shall exceed twenty dollars, the right of trial by jury shall be preserved, and no fact tried by a jury, shall be otherwise reexamined in any Court of the United States, than according to the rules of the common law.

8 Excessive bail shall not be required, nor excessive fines imposed, nor cruel and unusual punishments inflicted.

9 The enumeration in the Constitution, of certain rights, shall not be construed to deny or disparage others retained by the people.

10 The powers not delegated to the United States by the Constitution, nor prohibited by it to the States, are reserved to the States respectively, or to the people.

4
The young Republic
1790–1849

I n the sixty-year span between George Washington's inauguration as president and the first intimations of the coming Civil War, the infant Republic found its feet, learned
to stand up for itself, and ate pretty much whatever it
could get its hands on. It grew fast, in terms of both area and
population.

In 1790, the United States held four million people, of
whom at least ninety percent lived within fifty miles of the
Atlantic. There were only four thousand non-Indians in the
entire region bounded by the Ohio and Mississippi rivers. In
each of the next six decades, the population increased by
over thirty percent, until by 1850 the nation was 23 million
strong. That increase was due not only to a high birthrate,
but also to extensive **immigration** from Europe. Over a
third of new arrivals consistently came from **Ireland** alone,
even before the potato famine of the 1840s spurred the
influx to even greater levels, while as political disruption on
the continent increased **Germans** eventually overtook even
the Irish.

What's more, by 1850 the United States extended across
the entire North American continent. At independence, it
had covered 890 million square miles. The **Louisiana
Purchase** of 1803 added 828 million more, and in 1848 the
defeat of **Mexico** another 919 million. Lesser morsels ingest-
ed included **Florida** in 1819, and **Texas** and **Oregon** in the
1840s.

The first of the period's two major wars, the **War of 1812**, was essentially a rite of passage in which the US showed it would not be bullied by Britain. Although neither side gained territory from the other, the Americans seized the chance to push back the Indians of the Northeast, and received a huge boost of confidence from the last-minute victory of **Andrew Jackson** in New Orleans. Jackson himself, hailed as the embodiment of the robust, confident frontiersman, was the main beneficiary. His rapid propulsion to the presidency finally broke the mould whereby, for all except four of the Republic's first 36 years, the president was drawn from Virginia's planter aristocracy.

These were confident times: Americans took advantage of the twenty-year conflict between Britain and France to boost their trade around the world, and the same driving entrepreneurial spirit fuelled expansion at home. Roads, canals and subsequently railroads began to knit the nation together, prompting new towns and cities to spring up along the way. It was only a small step from realizing that the United States might be capable of spreading across the whole continent to supposing that it had a quasi-religious duty to do so. Popularized by journalistic 'boosters', the idea became current that to displace both Native Americans and Hispanic colonists was simply the nation's '**Manifest Destiny**', and lay beyond any moral or ethical questioning.

However, there was more to expansion than landless settlers being drawn westwards by the availability of fresh land. What was formerly prime agricultural land in the East was becoming depleted by wasteful farming practices, and with federal land-sale policies favouring large-scale purchasers, wealthy plantation owners sold up and moved west. Wherever climate permitted, a reality of cotton-growing slave plantations replaced Jefferson's hallowed vision of a republic of independent yeoman farmers.

Meanwhile, as the new form of **government** took root, the strengths and weaknesses of the Constitution became apparent. The first flaw to emerge was that, although the 'Founding Fathers' had not anticipated the development of **political parties**, they were themselves riven by such fundamental differences within the first decade that they divided into **Federalists** and (Democratic-) **Republicans**. At first, the vice presidency automatically went to the runner-up in the presidential race; it took the emergence of party tickets with designated presidential and vice-presidential candidates to circumvent the problems of what to do when the president and vice president belonged to different parties (as in 1796), and what to do in the event of a dead heat (as in 1800). Next came the issue of whether the federal government could or should finance public works, whether benefiting one particular state or several; the answer was broadly decided to be 'no', so the Erie Canal, for example, was largely financed and constructed by the state of New York, and the railroads by private speculators.

The greatest issue needing to be resolved, however, was what to do if states disagreed with federal policy. Was it possible, *in extremis*, to **secede** from the Union? Portions of New England and the Northeast appeared to be conspiring to do so in both 1804 and 1815, while South Carolina overtly threatened secession during the **Nullification Crisis** of 1832.

With **slavery** as the biggest source of contention, it steadily became clear that the system only worked so long as there were equal numbers of 'Free' and slave-owning states. The only practicable way to keep the balance was to ensure that each time a new state was admitted to the Union, a matching state taking the opposite stance on slavery was also admitted. Thus the admission of every new state became subject to endless intrigue. The 1820

Missouri Compromise, under which Missouri joined as a slave-owning state and Maine as a Free one, was straightforward in comparison to the prevaricating and chest-beating that surrounded the admission of **Texas**, while the **Mexican War** was regarded in many quarters as a naked land grab for new slave states. As it transpired, the discovery of **gold** in California in 1848, on virtually the same day that the war ended, provoked a massive westward surge of free white settlers, and ensured that the economy of the West developed in unanticipated directions. Meanwhile, however, the invasion of Mexico had provided most of the future commanders of the Civil War with their first battlefield experience. For the moment, they were fighting on the same side.

1790 Secretary of the Treasury Alexander Hamilton proposes that the federal government should assume the debts of individual states, and buy back wartime securities at face value, making no distinction between payments to their original holders – many of them soldiers who accepted them in lieu of pay – and speculators who have bought them cheap. James Madison and Thomas Jefferson see this as pandering to merchant capitalists, but eventually back the measures, in return for Hamilton's support for locating the new capital on the Potomac.

In his final public act before his death on April 17, Benjamin Franklin supports an unsuccessful Quaker petition to Congress to ban slavery.

Rhode Island joins the Union as the thirteenth state.

1791 Hamilton pushes through the creation of the **Bank of the United States** – which opens in Philadelphia, and is quickly successful – despite Madison's insistence that it is not sanctioned by the Constitution.

With Virginia's ratification in December, the **Bill of Rights** – which Madison calls 'the most dramatic single gesture of reconciliation that could be offered the remaining opponents of the government' – comes into effect. These first ten **amendments** to the Constitution guarantee freedom of speech and religion, the right to keep and bear firearms, and protection against cruel and unusual punishment, and also clarify that individual states and citizens retain any powers not specifically granted to the government.

Samuel Slater, who has illegally left England with the Arkwright process committed to memory, draws on his expertise to set up a cotton mill at Pawtucket, Rhode Island. Using power-driven machinery to spin thread, it provides a major stimulus to the factory system.

Vermont becomes the fourteenth state.

1792 Amid growing factional divisions, there's a tacit general consensus that for the sake of national unity **George Washington** should continue as president. He is unanimously re-elected.

In the Pacific Northwest, Captain Robert Gray, of Boston, explores the **Columbia River**.

Kentucky becomes the fifteenth state.

1793 Days after Louis XVI is guillotined, France declares war on Britain. Alarmed by what he sees as the anarchic violence of the French Revolution, and convinced that trade with Britain is the key to American prosperity, Hamilton argues for US neutrality; Thomas Jefferson insists the US is tied to moral and treaty obligations to France. After Washington proclaims US neutrality in April, Jefferson resigns as Secretary of State. All this factionalism results in a development not anticipated in the Constitution – the emergence of **political parties**. Jefferson, who with

Cotton and tobacco

Between the Revolution and the Civil War, a major turnaround took place in American agriculture. During the 1770s, North American tobacco exports were worth five hundred times as much as those of cotton. Cotton, however, overtook tobacco in 1820, and was by the 1850s worth nine times more.

Tobacco's relative decline was due partly to its deleterious impact on the soil. By the early nineteenth century, some Chesapeake plantations were so depleted after two hundred years of growing tobacco that they had to change to wheat. Tobacco production began to move inland instead, first to the piedmont of Virginia and North Carolina and then into Kentucky and Tennessee.

It was technology that triggered the rise of 'King Cotton', an almost negligible crop until 1793. Only a long staple variety, which was easier to process, was then commercially grown, along the Georgia and South Carolina coasts; short staple cotton thrived on the upland slopes, but separating its green seeds from the fibre by hand was prohibitively painstaking work. That year, however, the young Eli Whitney, visiting Mulberry Hill plantation in Georgia, was challenged to devise a machine to do the job. In ten days, he produced the cotton gin (short for 'engine'), a device simple enough to be copied throughout the South via word of mouth before he had time to patent it.

Whitney's invention prompted not only the wildfire spread of cotton, which swiftly crossed the mountains to reach Alabama, Mississippi, Louisiana and Arkansas, but also that of the plantation system, and with it slavery. Northern dreams that slavery might wither away were dashed by the emergence of new slave-dependent Southern states, while the institution itself became crueller than ever, as slaves were forced to trek west to clear new plantations, or sold away from their families to satisfy the booming demand for cheap labour.

supporters like Madison charges Hamilton with favouring financial and commercial interests above the agricultural community, becomes identified as the leader of the **Republicans** (often also referred to as the **Democratic-Republicans**), while Hamilton and vice president John Adams retain the label of **Federalists**.

Eli Whitney invents the **cotton gin**.

1794 In the **Battle of Fallen Timbers**, south of Detroit, General Wayne defeats a Shawnee, Ottawa, Chippewa and Potawatomi alliance. As a result, the vanquished Indians sell the US much of modern Ohio and Indiana, as well as the sites of Detroit, Chicago and Vincennes, in 1795's **Treaty of Greenville**.

General Henry Lee and Alexander Hamilton lead an army into western Pennsylvania to put down the **Whiskey Rebellion**, a vigilante uprising prompted by resentment of a tax on distilled liquor imposed by Hamilton in 1791. By the time they arrive, however, the trouble has died down.

With the British Navy harassing American shipping, especially in the Caribbean, John Jay is sent to London to negotiate a settlement. Under **Jay's Treaty**, Britain agrees to honour its commitments to evacuate frontier posts in the Northwest, and to allow a trading relationship of 'reciprocal and perfect liberty'. As Jefferson and Madison have long argued for discriminating against British commerce, and the British fail to acknowledge American neutrality, the treaty is not well received in the US. It's narrowly accepted by the Senate in 1795; all the Republicans vote against it.

In March, Congress forbids the trading of slaves with foreign nations.

1795 Abandoning hopes of expanding between the Alleghenies and the Mississippi, the Spanish sign **Pinckney's Treaty**, conceding American rights to navigate the full length of the Mississippi, and acknowledging the 31st parallel as the frontier.

Hamilton retires from government.

Prompted by the Federalist belief that new immigrants tend to support the Republicans, the **Naturalization Act** requires five years' residence before an immigrant can become a citizen.

1796 By deciding to retire from politics, Washington establishes the principle of a maximum two terms as president, which is not enshrined in the Constitution until 1951. In his (written rather than spoken) **Farewell Address**, published on September 18, he proclaims a cornerstone of future US foreign policy: 'Tis our true policy to steer clear of permanent Alliances, with any portion of the foreign world.'

The **Land Act** doubles the price of public lands in the Northwest Territory to $2 per acre, still to be sold in minimum 640-acre lots, making speculators even more likely to benefit.

Tennessee joins the Union as the sixteenth state, while Connecticut settlers found **Cleveland**, Ohio.

Congress imposes a **stamp tax** on legal documents.

Both the presidential and Congressional elections are fought on party lines for the first time. The first contested presidential campaign is complicated by the dislike felt towards the Federalist candidate **John Adams** by the influential Federalist Alexander Hamilton. Adams nonetheless narrowly defeats Thomas Jefferson, but a weakness of the Constitution is exposed when Jefferson, as the second-placed candidate, becomes vice president despite being the leader of the opposition.

1797 Considering Jay's Treaty to reveal the US as pro-British, the French start to harass American shipping. US commissioners travel to Paris to negotiate, but give up in the face of French demands for bribes. This becomes known as the **XYZ Affair**, after Adams only identifies the Frenchmen involved by the letters X, Y and Z.

1798 Although President Adams declines to declare war, a '**quasi-war**' is fought at sea with the French, especially in the Caribbean. Congress creates the Department of the Navy, appoints George Washington as commander-in-chief of the army, and prohibits trade, and suspends treaties, with France.

Provoked by domestic opposition, the Adams administration introduces repressive legislation. The **Alien** and **Alien Enemies** acts permit the president to deport any foreigners, without stating reasons, while another **Naturalization Act** extends the residential qualification for citizenship to fourteen years. Under the **Sedition Act**, which sanctions fines or imprisonment for 'false, scandalous and malicious writing' against the government, Vermont Congressman Matthew Lyon is fined and jailed for referring to Adams' 'ridiculous pomp . . . and selfish avarice'.

In response, the **Kentucky** and **Virginia** legislatures adopt Resolutions, drafted by Jefferson and Madison respectively, that assert a state may nullify an Act of Congress within its borders that it regards as contrary to the Constitution.

1799 George Washington dies at Mount Vernon on December 14.

1800 President Adams is defeated in the presidential election, but both Republican candidates**, Thomas Jefferson** and **Aaron Burr**, receive equal votes. Burr is universally understood to be the vice-presidential candidate, but declines to stand down. The tie has to be decided by the (old, and thus still Federalist-dominated) House of Representatives early in 1801, where Federalists refuse to break the deadlock through 35 ballots, and threaten to nominate their own candidate, before finally electing Jefferson.

In June, Congress and president move from Philadelphia to the new, planned capital of **Washington**.

Starting around now, and sweeping through rural areas throughout the country – especially along the frontier – for the next few decades, religious revivals known as the second **Great Awakening** increase membership of **Methodist** and **Baptist** congregations among both blacks and whites.

September's **Convention of Mortefontaine** ends the **quasi-war** and renews commercial relations, but leaves the US and France not bound by any treaty. In the secret **Treaty of San Ildefonso**, not revealed in the US until 1801, Spain cedes **Louisiana**, west of the Mississippi, to Napoleon's France.

1801 Immediately before ceding power to the new Jefferson administration, the Federalists appoint **John Marshall** as Chief Justice of the Supreme Court, and pass a **Judiciary Act** which the Republicans repeal and replace in 1802. By 1805, clashes between the Supreme Court and the Republican-dominated judiciary establish both the Supreme Court's support for, and yet independence from, the federal government.

The Pasha of Tripoli, one of the Mediterranean '**Barbary Pirates**', declares war over the failure of US vessels to pay tribute. The fledgling US navy will blockade Tripoli until a treaty is signed in 1805.

1802 Congress abolishes all excise duties, including the Whiskey Tax, and restores the 1795 Naturalization Act stipulating five years' residence for citizenship.

In line with the desire to professionalize America's armed forces, **West Point Military Academy** in upstate New York opens on July 4 as a school for sappers and gunners.

1803 Alarmed that Napoleon may be planning a colonial empire in America, and that a re-closure of the Mississippi would deny sixty percent of American produce access to the ocean, Jefferson sends envoys to France with a budget of $10 million, hoping to buy New Orleans and the Floridas. Instead, Napoleon, embroiled in war with Britain and with the slave revolt in Santo Domingo, agrees to sell all Louisiana west of the Mississippi for $15 million. Jefferson and the Republicans jump at this **Louisiana Purchase**, albeit with qualms about its constitutionality. Federalists are fearful that the Republic will be overwhelmed by the addition of vast new lawless territories and, potentially, further slave states; some even plot a breakaway by New England and the Northeast.

Ohio is admitted as the seventeenth state, and the first drawn from the old Northwest Territory. The 1802 Enabling Act which facilitates this also provides for an **East–West Road**, which later becomes the National or Cumberland Road.

1804 The **Twelfth Amendment**, a response to the 1800 electoral tie, introduces separate ballots for president and vice president. Jefferson is **re-elected**, with George Clinton as vice president, defeating Federalist Charles C. Pinckney.

Lewis and Clark depart on their Voyage of Discovery.

Aaron Burr kills Alexander Hamilton in a **duel** on July 11.

1805 After a British court, in the case of the *Essex*, rules that American vessels trading between France and the Caribbean cannot circumvent British restrictions by calling at American ports, the British start to seize American ships.

Lieutenant **Zebulon Pike** sets off from St Louis in an abortive attempt to find the source of the Mississippi.

1806 Following Nelson's victory against a Franco-Spanish fleet at **Trafalgar**, the British instigate a naval blockade of continental Europe. Napoleon retaliates with a similar blockade of Britain. Both measures are strengthened in 1807, damaging American commercial interests.

The Lewis and Clark expedition

Long before he or anyone else knew very much about it, Thomas Jefferson was fascinated by the mysteries of the unexplored American West. He was determined not to let the British claim the regions explored by Captain Cook, who touched on the Pacific Northwest coast in 1778, or Alexander Mackenzie, who twice crossed Canada overland. Alarmed by the prospect of French expansion after France regained Louisiana in 1800, he set two secret plans in motion. Both came to fruition in July 1803 – July 3 saw confirmation of the **Louisiana Purchase**, while on July 5 the **Lewis and Clark expedition** (officially, the Voyage of Discovery) left Washington.

Reasoning that a large-scale military expedition might antagonize the Indians en route, Jefferson commissioned two young men – **Meriwether Lewis**, his own private secretary, and **William Clark**, a Virginian associate – 'to explore the Missouri River' and find 'the most direct and practicable water communication across this continent for the purposes of trade'. They only set off up the Missouri itself once it was officially American, in May 1804. Over the next two years they encountered such tribes as the Sioux, Mandan, Blackfoot and Nez Percé, and unfamiliar creatures ranging from the 'verry large and turrible' grizzly bear to the salmon, which Lewis hailed as 'the finest fish I ever tasted'. Aided by a young Shoshoni woman, **Sacagawea**, who had been kidnapped five years earlier, they struggled across the Rockies and spent the winter of 1805–06 at the mouth of the Columbia River. They then explored alternative routes home – Clark followed the Yellowstone, Lewis the Marias – before returning to Washington.

On the face of it, their report was negative – they found no straightforward water route across North America – but by mapping the full width of the continent they effectively set the agenda for the new century, in which the United States was to extend 'from sea to shining sea'.

The Burr-Hamilton duel

What Henry Adams called 'the most dramatic moment in the early politics of the Union' occurred at dawn on July 11, 1804, at Weehawken, New Jersey, across the Hudson from New York City. In a duel between two of the nation's most powerful men, **Aaron Burr**, its Republican vice president, killed **Alexander Hamilton**, the leading light of the Federalist party.

Such 'affairs of honor', were far from rare; though most were settled without bloodshed, Hamilton's son had died in a duel near the same spot three years earlier. Ostensibly they were always fought over personal, not political, issues. Burr challenged Hamilton after hearing reports that he was spreading 'despicable' libels; Hamilton acknowledged making many negative comments over the years, but insisted they were always in the political arena. It was Hamilton who persuaded the Federalists to support Jefferson over Burr in the tied election. More recently, Burr, dropped from the ticket for the forthcoming presidential election, had run unsuccessfully against the Republican candidate for the governorship of New York. He had obtained the support of many Federalists, though not Hamilton himself, by agreeing to a conspiracy in which New England and New York would secede to form a **Northern Confederacy**, with Burr as president.

Precisely what happened that morning is unknown; Hamilton probably fired in the air, whereupon Burr, perhaps aiming to wound, shot him dead. Popularly depicted as a cold-blooded murderer, Burr fled south, though he returned briefly to preside over the Senate as vice president. By 1807, he was on trial for **treason**, charged with a quixotic scheme to hive off Louisiana and the Southwest as a separate nation, again with himself as president. To Jefferson's fury, he was found not guilty, as no 'overt acts' could be proved; he eventually returned to practise law in New York, where he died in 1836.

In a separate expedition to explore the southern reaches of the Louisiana Purchase, **Lieutenant Pike** crosses the Great Plains, which he describes as inhospitable desert, and then as a Spanish prisoner sees Santa Fe and northern Mexico.

1807 British aggression against American shipping includes the forcible **impressment** into the Royal Navy of alleged deserters – often simply anyone of British ancestry – found on American vessels. After the British frigate *Leopold* fires on and boards the *Chesapeake* off Norfolk, Virginia, on June 22, Jefferson orders British warships to leave American waters.

In December, Congress passes the **Embargo Act**, to be supplemented in 1808, which bans all overseas trade from American ports. While the intention is to punish the French and British, the impact on American shipping, and on the economy of New England, is disastrous.

Aaron Burr is acquitted of treason, over a scheme to establish an independent state in the Southwest.

Robert Fulton's **steamboat** *Clermont* makes a return voyage up the Hudson between New York City and Albany.

1808 On January 1, the earliest moment permitted by the Constitution, Congress bans the **importation of slaves** into the US. Opposition from the South is muted, partly because new arrivals from Africa are seen as likely to bear diseases that might harm existing slaves, and also because Southern entrepreneurs are trading slaves raised in the US – effectively, as a cash crop. Nonetheless, by 1861 a further 300,000 slaves will have been illegally imported.

Thomas Jefferson retires, and his favoured Republican successor, **James Madison**, is elected president. Once again, Charles C. Pinckney is the defeated Federalist candidate.

In his *Report on Roads and Canals*, **Albert Gallatin**, Secretary of the Treasury, outlines a transportation network to connect the eastern rivers with the Mississippi Valley.

$100 REWARD!

RANAWAY

From the undersigned, living on Current River, about twelve miles above Doniphan, in Ripley County, Mo., on 2nd of March, 1860, A NE-GRO MAN, about 30 years old, weighs about 160 pounds; high forehead, with a scar on it; had on brown pants and coat very much worn, and an old black wool hat; shoes size No. 11.

The above reward will be given to any person who may apprehend this said negro out of the State: and fifty dollars if apprehended in this State outside of Ripley county, or $25 if taken in Ripley county.

APOS TUCKER.

The reward offered for the capture of runaway slaves often exceeded the price of the slave

John Jacob Astor incorporates the American Fur Company in New York City; through this and his Pacific Fur Company, founded in 1810, he will monopolize the lucrative fur trade within twenty years.

1809 As his final act, Jefferson replaces the Embargo Act with the **Non-Intercourse Act**, which reopens all trade except with France and Britain. Madison then briefly reinstates trade with Britain, before closing it again as the British continue their harassment.

1810 In May, **Macon's Bill No. 2** removes all restrictions on trade, but stipulates that if either France or Britain commits itself to respecting US neutrality, the president will renew non-intercourse with the other. Assured by Napoleon that he will do so, Madison reimposes non-intercourse on Britain, but in fact the French continue to seize American ships.

American settlers in the westernmost portion of **West Florida**, immediately east of the Mississippi, rise against their Spanish rulers; Madison responds by annexing the region to the Territory of Orleans.

1811 After his brother is defeated at the **Battle of Tippecanoe**, Shawnee leader **Tecumseh** flees to Canada (see p.119).

After intense debate, in which some Republicans argue that it's an unconstituional, Federalist institution, Congress does not renew the charter of the **Bank of the United States**, which is dissolved – creating problems with financing the imminent war.

The *New Orleans* becomes the first steamboat to travel down the Ohio and Mississippi rivers from Pittsburgh to New Orleans.

1812 Several young, vociferous Republican **War Hawks**, drawn especially from the South and West and including **Henry Clay** and **John C. Calhoun**, have been newly elected to Congress. They argue that to continue to submit to British naval bullying amounts to 'absolute recolonization', while British support from Canada is encouraging Indian opposition in the Northwest.

Despite unanimous Federalist opposition, and from New England in general, President Madison declares **war** on Britain on June 18, demanding that it rescind the various Orders in Council imposing the blockades, and abolish impressment. It later turns out that the British have already done the former, if not the latter, two days earlier, but the **War of 1812** – known at the time as the Second War for Independence – goes ahead anyway.

The initial American strategy, a three-pronged **invasion of Canada**, is at first thwarted by the inadequate size of the army, the refusal of New England states to allow their state militias to take part, and the refusal of the New York militia to cross the border. Instead, **Detroit** falls to a British counter-attack on August 16.

In the Atlantic, however, the Americans fare better. In October alone, the *Wasp* defeats the British *Frolic* off Virginia, and the *United States* captures the *Macedonian* off Madeira.

Louisiana – previously known as the Territory of Orleans – joins the Union as its eighteenth state.

Madison is **re-elected** as president, defeating a Federalist anti-war candidate, DeWitt Clinton.

1813 American forces are more successful in Canada. A combined naval and military expedition crosses Lake Ontario to capture and burn **York** (modern Toronto) in April, while Commodore Perry wins the naval **Battle of Lake Erie** in September, forcing the British to abandon Detroit. Victory in the **Battle of the Thames**, east of Detroit, in October, during which Tecumseh is killed, puts an end to the British–Indian alliance, though further campaigns fail to reach Montreal in the winter.

The British navy, however, blockade the Atlantic coast as far north as New England, where many merchants continue trading with them.

1814 British soldiers land in Maryland in August. Following an easy victory at Bladensburg on August 24, they enter **Washington, DC** unopposed, and burn the White House and Capitol. They advance on **Baltimore**, but are repelled on September 13; the watching Francis Scott Key writes *The Star-Spangled Banner*. Meanwhile, a British invasion from Canada is halted by an American naval victory on **Lake Champlain** on September 11.

Tecumseh (1768–1813)

The most determined Native American opposition to the westward expansion of the young Republic was co-ordinated by twin **Shawnee** brothers. From 1805 onwards, the warrior chief **Tecumseh** set about establishing a confederation of all the tribes of the Ohio and Mississippi valleys, arguing that no single tribe could sign away lands held by all in common. Meanwhile the half-blind Tenskwatawa – **The Prophet** – added a spiritual basis by insisting on temperance and a rejection of all contact with whites. Obstacles in Tecumseh's path included the fact that many tribes were as reluctant to yield sovereignty to such a confederation as they were to the Americans, and that only perhaps four thousand Indian warriors were still present in that entire vast area.

In 1808, Tecumseh established his headquarters at **Prophetstown** in modern Indiana, where the Tippecanoe Creek meets the Wabash River. Even Tecumseh's most implacable opponent, **William Henry Harrison**, the governor of Indiana Territory, called him 'one of those uncommon geniuses', adding 'the implicit obedience and respect which [his] followers pay to him, is really astonishing'. Harrison therefore waited until 1811, when Tecumseh was absent recruiting among the Creek in Alabama, before leading his militia up the Wabash. Against Tecumseh's express instructions, Tenskwatawa allowed his warriors to be drawn into attacking the Americans. Though Harrison at first believed himself defeated in the resultant **Battle of Tippecanoe**, the carnage caused the Shawnee to lose faith in the Prophet and abandon Prophetstown.

Tecumseh fled to Canada, where he was killed fighting alongside the British in 1813, in the **Battle of the Thames**, east of Detroit. Colonel **Richard Johnson**, who claimed to have delivered the fatal blow, was elected vice president in 1836 – campaigning on the slogan 'Rumpsey dumpsey, rumpsey dumpsey, Colonel Johnson killed Tecumseh' – while Harrison's triumph led him to the presidency in 1840.

The death of the Shawnee leader Tecumseh, at the Battle of the Thames in Ontario on October 5, 1813

A Creek uprising in the South is crushed at **Horseshoe Bend** on March 27, by **Andrew Jackson**'s Tennessee militia. Jackson continues down the Alabama River to strengthen US defences at Mobile and New Orleans.

Peace negotiations in Europe fluctuate with each latest piece of news, but as both sides come to see the war as an expensive stalemate they sign the **Treaty of Ghent** on December 24. This ignores the war's original causes, simply restoring all captured territories, and setting up commissions to settle ongoing boundary disputes.

However, a British expeditionary force from Jamaica lands downstream of New Orleans on December 14. Jackson repels an attack on the city on December 23, and on January 8 1815, with neither army aware that the war has ended, wins an overwhelming victory at the **Battle of**

New Orleans. That boosts American confidence, and causes the war as a whole to be seen as a triumph despite the lack of any concrete gains.

With similarly poor timing, Federalists gather to discuss the problems of New England at the **Hartford Convention** in December. Moderates ensure that there's no majority call for secession, but they suggest amendments to the Constitution such as ending extra representation for Southern states, limiting presidents to a single term, and prohibiting successive presidents from the same state. Delegates arrive to present these proposals in Washington in January 1815 to find the war is over, leaving the Federalists even more sidelined than before.

Francis Cabot Lowell opens the first **factory**, manufacturing textiles, at Waltham, Massachusetts.

1815 Congress proclaims a policy of worldwide trading reciprocity, while a commercial convention re-establishes relations with Britain.

In the Mediterranean, Captain Decatur ends the threat of the **Barbary Pirates** by forcibly securing treaties with Algiers, Tunis and Tripoli.

1816 Calhoun and Clay persuade Congress to charter a second **Bank of the United States**, for twenty years, and to pass the **Tariff Act** to protect American industry.

In December, Republican **James Monroe** is elected president, overwhelmingly defeating Federalist Rufus King, and **Indiana** joins the Union as a Free state.

1817 In his last official act, President Madison insists that a Constitutional amendment would be necessary in order for the federal government to finance public works, establishing a presidential reticence that remains powerful for the next hundred years.

As partisan politics decline, a goodwill tour of New England by President Monroe is hailed by a local newspaper as heralding an '**Era of Good Feelings**'; the label will stick.

The **First Seminole War** starts when Calhoun, as Secretary of War, assigns Andrew Jackson to lead a punitive expedition against the Seminole Indians of (still Spanish) Florida, following border skirmishes.

Mississippi becomes the twentieth state.

1818 Britain and the US sign the **Convention of 1818**, which fixes the 49th parallel as the border between the US and Canada – but only as far west as the Rockies. Beyond that, Oregon is to be open to settlers from both countries for the next ten years, an agreement extended in 1827.

In **Florida**, Jackson seizes St Marks in March and Pensacola, ending the fighting, in May.

Illinois joins the Union as the 21st state.

1819 After Secretary of State **John Quincy Adams** demands that Spain either maintain order in Florida or cede it, Spain signs the **Adams–Onís Treaty**. This cedes East Florida to the US, and renounces Spanish claims to West Florida, in return for writing off $5 million of debt, but defines the western boundary of the Louisiana Purchase as excluding Texas. Henry Clay fails to persuade Congress to censure Andrew Jackson for his alleged despotic tendencies during the campaign, which included the summary execution of prisoners.

The postwar economic boom is interrupted by the **Panic of 1819**, as restrictions on credit hit speculators. Many western banks fail.

Stephen Long of the US Topographical Engineers sets off to survey the Great Plains, which he describes as 'almost wholly unfit for cultivation'. Misleadingly but enduringly, he dubs the region the **Great American Desert**.

Alabama becomes the 22nd state.

> If the dissolution of the Union should result from the slave question, it is as obvious as anything that can be seen of futurity, that it must shortly afterwards be followed by a universal emancipation of the slaves . . . . If the Union must be dissolved, slavery is precisely the question upon which it ought to break. For the present, however, this contest is laid asleep.

John Quincy Adams, then Secretary of State, February 1820, describing his reluctant support for the Missouri Compromise

1820 In March, the **Missouri Compromise** addresses the fact that to grant statehood to Missouri would for the first time give slave-owning states a majority over 'Free' states, by admitting **Maine** immediately, with Missouri to follow in 1821. It also prohibits slavery north of latitude 36° 30' in the rest of the Louisiana Purchase,.

In the presidential election, **James Monroe** is all but unanimously **re-elected**; the Federalists fail to put up a candidate.

1821 Missouri duly becomes the 24th state. Andrew Jackson is appointed governor of what soon becomes the Territory of Florida.

With the Spanish monarchy weakened by domestic uprisings, **Mexico** achieves independence. Merchant William Becknell pioneers the **Santa Fe Trail** from Independence, Missouri, to New Mexico, while Moses Austin is granted land beside the Brazos River in **Texas**. The condition that he settle three hundred families there is soon satisfied by his son **Stephen Austin**.

Russian traders having been advancing down the Pacific Northwest coast, Russia claims the northern half of Oregon.

1822 The American Colonization Society founds a colony for freed slaves at Monrovia, **Liberia**.

In Charleston, black carpenter **Denmark Vesey** – who bought his freedom from slavery after winning a $1500 lottery – is charged with plotting a slave rebellion; 35 blacks are hanged, four white co-conspirators fined and jailed.

America is now effectively a one-party state. All the main rivals for the presidency are **Republicans**, and state legislatures start to nominate their own candidates: in the most prominent instances, Tennessee chooses **Andrew Jackson**, and Kentucky **Henry Clay**.

1823 In his message to Congress on December 2, President Monroe asserts the **Monroe Doctrine**, which though not initially seen as significant is to become a cornerstone of US foreign policy. Written by **John Quincy Adams**, it states that 'the American continents . . . are henceforth not to be considered as subjects for future colonization by any European powers', adding that any future European attempt 'to extend their system to any portion of this hemisphere' will not be viewed 'in any other light than as the manifestation of an unfriendly disposition toward the United States'. By the same token, the US will not intervene 'in the wars of the European powers.'

1824 Although **Andrew Jackson** receives the most popular and electoral votes in the presidential election, he has no majority in either. Thanks to the backing of the lowly placed Henry Clay, the House of Representatives declares **John Quincy Adams**, the preferred candidate of New England, to be the sixth president in February 1825.

Trapper **Jedediah Smith** identifies Wyoming's **South Pass** as the best route through the Rockies. With his partner William Sublette he returns in 1826, reporting to the Secretary of War that 'this is the first time that wagons have been taken to the Rocky Mountains; and the ease and safety with which it was done prove the facility of communicating over land with the Pacific ocean'.

Russia and America fix **latitude 54° 40'** as the boundary between their claims in the Pacific Northwest.

1825 Allegations that Adams has secured the presidency thanks to a 'corrupt bargain' with Henry Clay – though no wrongdoing is ever demonstrated – cause the Republican party to split, casting Clay and Adams loyalists as the **National-Republicans**, and supporters of Andrew Jackson as the **Democratic-Republicans**, which they eventually shorten to **Democrats**.

The completion of the **Erie Canal**, under construction since 1817, links **Albany** on the Hudson River with **Buffalo** on Lake Erie. It thus allows onward connections to Cleveland and Toledo, both of which will be linked by 1840 by further canals to the Ohio River and the Mississippi. Much the most commercially successful of the canals, it's immediately lined with towns and cities such as **Rochester**, establishing a model of development later followed by the railroads.

 I regret that I am now to die in the belief, that the useless sacrifice of themselves by the generation of 1776, to acquire self-government and happiness to their country, is to be thrown away by the unwise and unworthy passions of their sons, and that my only conclusion is to be, that I live not to weep over it.

The elderly Thomas Jefferson

1826 Both **Thomas Jefferson** and **John Adams** – the current president's father – die on July 4, the fiftieth anniversary of the Declaration of Independence.

1827 New York State abolishes slavery and frees 10,000 slaves.

1828 In a Machiavellian scheme, Jackson supporters including Vice President **Calhoun** devise the so-called '**Tariff of Abominations**', an exceptionally high tariff on raw materials. They expect its eventual defeat to discredit President Adams, while they themselves can at one and the same time attract support in the Northeast for advocating it, and elsewhere for opposing it. To their amazement, however, Congress passes it and Adams signs it into law. Previously an advocate of protectionism, Calhoun now finds himself writing the South Carolina Exposition, which defines the **Nullification** doctrine that states are entitled to nullify, or refuse to enforce, federal legislation they consider unconstitutional.

One by one the states have been dropping property or tax-paying requirements for voters, so **suffrage** is all but universal among white males, while all states except South Carolina and Delaware now choose presidential electors through direct ballot. **Andrew Jackson** wins the presidential election, with 178 electoral votes, all drawn from the South and West, to Adams's 83, all from the Northeast. Calhoun remains vice president.

In Maryland, the earth is turned on July 4 for both the **Chesapeake and Ohio Canal** and the **Baltimore and Ohio Railroad**; the latter will initially run horse-drawn trains.

Noah Webster publishes the *American Dictionary of the English Language*, and **John James Audubon** the first volume of *Birds of America*.

A daguerrotype of Andrew Jackson, made shortly before his death in 1845

The **Workingmen's Party** is founded in Philadelphia. It will spread throughout the northern seaboard states in the next few years, with a programme that includes social reforms, free public schools and the abolition of imprisonment for debt.

1829 Andrew Jackson – known as **Old Hickory** for his toughness – brings a new style to the presidency, replacing the mould of the aristocratic Virginia planter with that of the plain-speaking frontiersman. Governing with the aid of an informal 'kitchen cabinet', he's also responsible for introducing the 'spoils system' by which presidents fill federal posts with their own supporters – albeit on a low-key scale compared to later excesses.

1830 Proposals that the government should restrict land sales in the West lead to a **Great Debate** on states' rights in the Senate. **Daniel Webster** of Massachusetts insists that states cannot nullify federal laws or secede from the Union. The issue comes to a head at a dinner marking Jefferson's birthday on April 13, when President Jackson proposes the toast 'Our Union – it must be preserved!', and Vice President Calhoun responds 'The Union, next to our liberty most dear!'

In May, the **Indian Removal Act** entitles the government to exchange Indian lands in the East for unsettled regions west of the Mississippi.

Joseph Smith founds the **Mormon** Church in upstate New York, while **Chicago** is laid out on the site of Fort Dearborn.

The first US public **railroad**, the Baltimore and Ohio, carries its first steam-driven passengers, though the line won't reach the Ohio until the 1850s.

1831 Nat Turner leads a slave revolt in Virginia.

In the first **party conventions**, both held in Baltimore, the Anti-Masonic Party nominates William Wirt for president, while the National-Republicans nominate Henry Clay.

Elected to the House of Representatives, former president **John Quincy Adams** advocates the abolition of slavery.

Nat Turner's revolt

The largest **slave revolt** in the antebellum South broke out on August 22, 1831, in Southampton County, southeast Virginia. Its leader, **Nat Turner**, was an educated 30-year-old slave renowned as a Baptist preacher. Turner was motivated not by personal grievance – he characterized his owner Joseph Travis, the first victim of the uprising, as a 'kind master' – but by his sense, since early childhood, that 'I was ordained for some great purpose in the hands of the Almighty'. When the 'great day of judgment' came, his small band of followers, convinced that he was a prophet, killed around sixty white men, women and children. Swelling to around seventy strong, they marched on the county seat, Jerusalem, but were confronted by state and local militia. Dozens of randomly chosen blacks were slaughtered, including forty by a cavalry company that impaled their severed heads on poles. Almost fifty were tried, and nineteen executed, though Turner himself escaped capture for another eight weeks. Interviews he gave before he too was hanged on November 11 were published as *The Confessions of Nat Turner*; asked 'Do you not find yourself mistaken now?', he replied 'Was not Christ crucified?'

Despite the harsh reprisals, and general panic, the **Virginia assembly** conducted a unique debate just three months later. Spurred by Governor Floyd's aversion to slavery, it seriously considered abolishing slavery to prevent future revolts; once free, all blacks would be deported, to Africa or elsewhere. The proposal's narrow defeat was initially seen as a sign that abolition was imminent. However, delegates who had spoken against slavery were defeated in the state's 1832 elections, and instead there followed an upsurge in theoretical justifications of slavery by Southern academics and politicians, with Calhoun going far beyond the traditional defence that it was a 'necessary evil' to proclaim it a 'positive good'.

> The Anglo-American race fells the forests and drains the marshes; lakes as large as seas and huge rivers resist its triumphant march in vain. The wilds become villages, and the villages towns. The American, daily witness of such wonders, does not see anything astonishing in all this. This incredible destruction, this even more surprising growth, seems to him the usual progress of things in this world. He gets accustomed to it as to the unalterable order of nature.
>
> Alexis de Tocqueville, reporting on his travels in America during the 1830s

1832 Jackson vetoes a bill to re-charter the **Bank of the United States**, charging that it serves only to make 'the rich richer and the potent more powerful'.

Although a new **Tariff Act** modifies the Tariff of Abominations and reduces certain duties, a convention in South Carolina – guided by Calhoun, who is by now completely estranged from Jackson, and has been deselected as vice-presidential candidate – declares both tariffs unconstitutional, and therefore void within the state. Jackson responds to threats of secession with the **Nullification Proclamation** of December 10, calling such nullification an 'impractical absurdity' that's 'incompatible with the existence of the Union'.

Nominated by the first **Democratic** convention, in Baltimore in May, **Andrew Jackson** beats **Henry Clay** in the presidential election by 219 electoral votes to 49.

In the **Black Hawk War**, Sauk Indians led by Black Hawk attempt to retake their lands in Illinois and Wisconsin; the militia that defeats them includes both Abraham Lincoln and Jefferson Davis.

The **New England Anti-Slavery Society** is founded by supporters of **William Lloyd Garrison**, editor of *The Liberator*, to be followed by the American Anti-Slavery Society in 1833.

A **cholera** epidemic prompts New York City to improve its provision of clean water.

1833 In January, Jackson asks Congress to reassert his authority to use the army if South Carolina declines to obey federal law. Henry Clay brokers a deal in which the tariff will be progressively reduced over the next ten years; both this **Compromise Tariff**, and the president's **Force Bill**, are passed on March 1, thereby ending the Nullification crisis.

Boosted by his re-election, Jackson transfers all federal funds from the Bank of the United States to designated state banks, known as 'pet banks'.

As the **ice trade** from New England expands, 'Ice King' Frederic Tudor sends a 180-ton shipment from Boston to Calcutta.

Slavery is abolished throughout the British Empire.

1834 A disparate anti-Jackson coalition, including Southern believers in nullification, Northern industrialists, and supporters of the national bank, melds to form a new party, the **Whigs**, with **Henry Clay** and **Daniel Webster** prominent among its leaders.

A **National Trades Union** is set up in New York. Until its progress is halted when the Panic of 1837 makes it impossible for many members to pay their dues, Unionism appears likely to supersede working men's parties.

John Jacob Astor leaves the fur trade, as demand for beaver-skin hats dwindles with rising imports of Chinese silk.

Methodist missionaries, invited by a Flathead and Nez Percé delegation to St Louis, are among the first settlers to reach Oregon's **Willamette Valley**.

1835 When the Seminole resist transportation west, the **Second Seminole War** breaks out in Florida. Though guerrilla fighting will continue for seven years, Seminole resistance is effectively ended when their leader Osceola is taken prisoner, while under a flag of truce, at St Augustine in 1837.

Oberlin College in Ohio votes to admit **blacks**, making it the first racially integrated college; in 1837 it will similarly pioneer the admission of **women**.

Artists **Thomas Cole**, who first visited the Catskills around 1825, and **Asher Durand** lead the **Hudson River School**, renowned for their romanticized celebrations of the American wilderness.

1836 **Texas** declares itself independent on March 2. Mexican general Santa Anna's massacre of the defenders at the **Alamo** four days later is avenged by General Sam Houston's victory at **San Jacinto** on April 21. Houston becomes President of the **Republic of Texas**, which from now on makes repeated requests for annexation by the US.

The Senate decides that any abolitionist petition will automatically be rejected – 'laid on the table' – without discussion; so-called '**gag rules**' are readopted annually until 1844.

Samuel Colt patents his revolving pistol, the so-called 'equalizer' of the West.

Arkansas becomes the 25th state.

In the presidential election, Jackson's chosen Democrat successor, Vice President **Martin van Buren**, wins comfortably, with the Whig vote split three ways.

The Alamo

After Mexico achieved independence from Spain in 1821, it encouraged immigration into **Texas**, believing that American settlers would guard its frontiers not only against Indians, but even, strangely, against annexation by the United States. With land available on generous terms, Americans flooded in; despite a panicky border closure, there were by 1835 thirty thousand Americans in Texas, as opposed to three thousand Mexicans.

The emergence of a dictatorial, centralized government under General Antonio López de **Santa Anna** prompted Americans who had been hoping for greater regional autonomy to talk openly of secession from Mexico. Early in 1836, Santa Anna – the self-styled 'Napoleon of the West' – marched north with an army of six thousand.

The first serious opposition he encountered was at **San Antonio**, where a garrison of under two hundred volunteers, holed up in a former Spanish mission known as the **Alamo**, refused to surrender. Only a few were Hispanic – their commander, William Travis, wrote that 'the citizens of this municipality are all our enemies'. The rest were immigrants from the US, England, Scotland, Ireland and even Denmark, and included adventurers like **Davy Crockett**, a three-term Congressman from Tennessee once seen as a potential candidate for the presidency, and **Jim Bowie**, inventor of the famous knife.

Defeat at such odds was inevitable, and duly came on March 6 after a thirteen-day siege in which 1500 Mexicans died. All except one of the defenders were killed, in a massacre dismissed by Santa Anna as 'but a small affair'. Meanwhile, however, Texas had declared its **independence** on March 2, and General Sam Houston had scrambled together the army that on April 21, with the cry of 'Remember the Alamo', defeated Santa Anna in the **Battle of San Jacinto**. That victory secured Texan independence, and its eventual incorporation into the US in 1845.

1837 Jackson recognizes independent Texas on his last day in office.

The new President van Buren is immediately confronted by a major financial crisis, the **Panic of 1837**. Cotton prices drop, food prices and unemployment soar. Banks throughout the country refuse to hand over cash for paper money; more than six hundred fail altogether, including many of Jackson's 'pet banks'. Van Buren attempts to establish an independent Treasury to control federal funds, but due to Whig opposition no such measure is passed until 1840.

Mary Lyon opens **Mount Holyoke Seminary**, the first women's college, in South Hadley, Massachusetts.

Michigan is admitted as the 26th state.

1838 General Winfield Scott rounds up the **Cherokee** into prison camps, then forces them to walk west towards Oklahoma along the **Trail of Tears**. One in four dies en route.

Frederick Douglass escapes from slavery in Baltimore; he will later achieve fame as writer, orator and statesman. By now the informal network known as the **Underground Railroad** is assisting runaway slaves from the upper South to escape north, and potentially as far as Canada.

1839 Repeated incidents along the northeastern border with **Canada** never quite erupt into war.

The Spanish slave ship *Amistad* arrives in Connecticut, having been seized in a slave uprising off Cuba; in 1841 the Supreme Court will rule against handing the slaves back to Spain.

1840 Still defined solely by their opposition to the Democrats, the Whigs nominate former Indian fighter **William Henry Harrison** as their presidential candidate, adding Virginia's **John Tyler** to the ticket to attract supporters of states' rights. Harrison defeats Van Buren narrowly in the popular vote, but resoundingly in the electoral college.

1841 Harrison is expected to govern as a front man for Henry Clay and Daniel Webster, but catches pneumonia on inauguration day, and **dies** a month later. His successor, Vice President **John Tyler**, is in no way beholden to Clay; he sanctions repeal of the new Independent Treasury, and a raising of the tariff, but vetoes Clay's bill for a new national bank. The entire cabinet except Webster then resigns, leaving Tyler as a president without a party.

George Catlin, who has been painting and documenting Native Americans for twenty years, publishes his *Letter and Notes on the Manners, Customs, and Condition of the North American Indians*.

Ralph Waldo Emerson publishes his first volume of *Essays*.

1842 The **Webster–Ashburton Treaty** with Britain finally settles the Canadian border in Maine and Wisconsin.

Rhode Island has been continuing to use its 1663 charter as a constitution, without extending the franchise. In **Dorr's Rebellion**, Thomas Dorr is 'elected' governor under a rival constitution. With Tyler's active support, and the 1844 endorsement of the Supreme Court, Dorr is tried and convicted of treason. The old legislature remains in power, but agrees to a new constitution granting universal male suffrage in 1843.

Spurred by reports of fine agricultural land in the Pacific Northwest, '**Oregon fever**' sweeps the frontier. An annual ritual is established in which Conestoga wagons, known as 'prairie schooners', gather at Independence, Missouri, for the six-month trek along the **Oregon Trail**; nine hundred make the journey in 1843's **Great Migration**.

In successive government-sponsored expeditions, **John Frémont**, the **Pathfinder**, scouts for military sites along the Oregon and other trails, and by identifying the **Great Basin** in 1844 finally proves that there is no east–west waterway through the Rockies to the Pacific.

Phineas T. Barnum, destined to become nineteenth-century America's greatest showman, exhibits the diminutive **General Tom Thumb** – still a young boy, but only ever destined to grow 2ft 5in tall – in New York City.

1843 American settlers reach California's San Joaquin Valley.

1844 In April, Calhoun negotiates a secret treaty for the annexation of **Texas**, but the Senate rejects it in June, as Texas's admission as a slave state might provoke civil war.

Tyler stands down as president. Rejecting Van Buren as their nominee for his opposition to annexation, the Democrats choose the little-known Governor of Tennessee, **James K. Polk**, on a platform of 'the reoccupation of Oregon and the reannexation of Texas'. His Whig opponent, **Henry Clay**, wavers on his previous anti-annexation stance, but Polk triumphs when the anti-slavery Liberty Party denies Clay victory in New York.

Samuel Morse marks the completion of the first **telegraph** line, from Baltimore to Washington, by sending the message 'What hath God wrought!'

Charles Goodyear patents the vulcanization of **rubber**.

1845 Taking Polk's election as his cue, the departing President Tyler invites Congress to support the annexation of Texas by a joint resolution. It does so in March, and **Texas** formally joins the Union in December, as does **Florida** in March.

On March 6, two days after Polk takes office, **Mexico**

breaks off diplomatic relations. Polk sends John Slidell to Mexico City in an abortive attempt to buy **California**.

In the New York *Morning News*, John O'Sullivan writes that the US has a '**Manifest Destiny**' to spread across the entire continent.

1846 On January 13, Polk orders **General Zachary Taylor** to cross the Nueces River. On April 26, Mexican troops kill eleven American soldiers in the territory north of the Rio Grande to which America has a spurious claim, and the **Mexican War** begins on May 13. Taylor advances into northern Mexico, capturing Matamoros and Monterrey. Though welcomed in the West, the war is unpopular in the Northeast, where it's widely seen as intended to strengthen the 'slave power'.

On June 14, settlers in Sacramento Valley stage the **Bear Flag Revolt**, entering Sonoma and proclaiming **California** a republic, but the Pacific Fleet lands at Monterey on July 7 and claims California for the US. On August 18, Colonel Stephen Kearny occupies **Santa Fe**, having paid off the defenders, and claims **New Mexico**. Continuing west, he occupies **San Diego** on December 12, and is named as governor of California.

In August, after Polk asks Congress for $2 million to use in negotiations with Mexico, the House of Representatives passes the **Wilmot Proviso**, stipulating that 'neither slavery nor involuntary servitude' shall ever exist in any territory acquired from Mexico. The measure stalls in the Senate, but alarms the South.

The **Oregon Treaty** with Great Britain settles the 49th parallel as the Canadian border between the Rockies and the Pacific.

The **Independent Treasury Act**, repealed by the Whigs in 1841, is re-enacted.

Iowa is admitted as the 29th state.

John Banvard exhibits his vast *Panorama of the Mississippi*, a scrolling canvas supposedly three miles long.

Mormon leader Brigham Young, photographed by Matthew Brady

The Mormons

The Church of Jesus Christ of Latter-Day Saints, better known as the **Mormons**, was founded in 1830 by **Joseph Smith**, a 24-year-old farmhand in Palmyra, New York. Prompted perhaps by tales of Mound Builders (see p.10), Smith claimed he'd unearthed golden plates that held the *Book of Mormon*, telling of two Israelite families – the Lamanites, the ancestors of the Native Americans, and the Nephites – who had fled to America in 600 BC.

Of greater significance to Smith's poverty-stricken peers was his vision of a Utopian, communalist society. However, his advocacy of **polygamy**, and perceived opposition to slavery, attracted great hostility from unconverted 'Gentiles'. Smith moved successively to Ohio, Missouri, and Illinois, where he was killed by a mob in 1844.

Now led by **Brigham Young**, the Saints decided to leave the US, and trekked across the Rockies to found **Salt Lake City** in 1847. Within a year, however, the wilderness they called **Deseret** was annexed by the US. Suspicious of Deseret's religious underpinnings as a threat to the Union, the federal government rejected the subsequent petition for statehood. In 1856, the Republican party railed against slavery and polygamy in equal measure, as 'twin relics of barbarism'. When Congress sent a new non-Mormon governor west with 2500 soldiers – one-sixth of the US army – Salt Lake City was temporarily abandoned, but thanks largely to the Civil War, the much anticipated Mormon War never quite happened.

The Mormons survived by recognizing that individual farmers could make little impact on the uncompromising terrain of the West, and embarking instead on a massive communal effort to irrigate the desert. By 1860, they numbered over fifty thousand, including fifteen thousand from England; three thousand pushed their belongings across America in handcarts. After pressure from Washington forced the renunciation of polygamy in 1890, **Utah** became a state in 1896.

1847 General Taylor wins the battle of **Buena Vista** in February. Alarmed by his growing popularity, Polk sends a naval expedition under **General Winfield Scott** to land at Vera Cruz, which is captured on March 27. After victories at **Churubusco** and **Chapultepec**, Scott enters **Mexico City** on September 13.

The Mormons found **Salt Lake City**.

Liberia declares its independence.

1848 In February, the **Treaty of Guadalupe Hidalgo** ends the Mexican War. In return for $18.25 million, Mexico cedes **California** and **New Mexico** – which includes most of the modern states of New Mexico and Arizona, plus much of Utah and Nevada – to the US, and recognizes the Rio Grande as the border with Texas.

President Polk declines to stand for re-election. The Whig candidate, the apolitical (but slave-holding) war hero **Zachary Taylor**, defeats Democrat Lewis Cass, after the anti-slavery **Free Soil Party** once again splits the Democratic vote in New York.

The world's first **Woman's Rights Convention** gathers at Seneca Falls, New York, on July 19, with **Elizabeth Cady Stanton** and **Lucretia Mott** as its guiding lights. Proclaiming that 'woman is man's equal', participants call for an end to 'the monopoly of the pulpit' and restrictive inheritance laws, and for women to have the right to **vote**.

Wisconsin becomes the 30th state.

1849 In February, the first fortune seekers of the **Gold Rush** arrive in San Francisco.

Henry Thoreau publishes *Civil Disobedience*, inspired by his one-night imprisonment for refusing to pay Massachusetts's poll tax in protest against the Mexican War.

The Gold Rush

On January 19, 1848, James W. Marshall spotted **gold** in the millrace he was constructing for John Sutter on the American River, on the western flank of California's Sierra Nevada. Sutter, a Swiss immigrant who nine years earlier had founded Sacramento, attempted to keep the find secret. When the word got out, he was abandoned by his employees, lost his land, and wound up bankrupt.

The news reached **San Francisco** in March; as prospectors flocked to the hills, the port's population plummeted from a thousand to less than a hundred. New York heard in August, and in December President Polk told Congress of gold deposits that 'would scarcely command belief were they not corroborated by authentic reports'.

The **Gold Rush** was on. Twelve thousand wagons crossed the Missouri in 1849, and eighty thousand fortune seekers made their way to California by land and sea. By 1852, California's American population had risen from 14,000 to over 250,000, with San Francisco twenty thousand strong. Most previous western migrants had been family groups, expecting to remain forever; ninety percent of the **Forty-Niners**, however, were single males, hoping to return home soon as rich men.

At first, 'mining' in California amounted to little more than sieving mud and sand from streambeds to extract golden nuggets. Within three years, however, the easy 'placer' deposits were exhausted, and the work of crushing ore or sluicing away entire hillsides could only be done by heavy machinery. Some miners took steady jobs in the new large-scale mines, others headed east to prospect in Nevada and Colorado, or west to San Francisco, now crying out for skilled labourers and craftsmen. The Gold Rush had given California an economic clout that it never lost; San Francisco's banks were to finance and profit from mines and industrial development throughout the West.

5
The Civil War

1850–65

T he 1850s mark the moment when the South finally lost its grip on American national politics. For two-thirds of the period between the founding of the Republic and the coming of the Civil War, the President of the United States was a Southern slaveholder. By the time that era drew to an end, however, Southern efforts to ensure that one out of every two new states entering the Union embraced slavery were becoming ever more desperate. Southerners were convinced that were the North to gain the upper hand in Congress, the **abolition of slavery** would inevitably follow. To prevent that from happening, the slave-owning states had therefore to continue to match the 'Free' states in the Senate, which held two Senators per state; they had long since been outnumbered in the House, where the members were apportioned according to the population in each state. The effect of the South's frantic attempts to maintain parity was to alienate Northern sympathies and ultimately cause a break in the Union – with the South on the outside.

Although certain enterprising Southerners (known as 'filibusters') schemed to incorporate Cuba, Nicaragua and points south as slave states, attention focused primarily on the new territories in the West. Once options below the Missouri Compromise line of 36° 30' ran out in 1850, Southern pressure managed to get the Compromise repealed by the **Kansas–Nebraska Act** of 1854. That, however, opened a new can of worms – **popular sovereignty**, under which settlers in new territories could vote whether to allow slavery. For the act to achieve its purpose, Kansas had to vote for slavery, to match free Nebraska. However, not only was Kansas unsuitable for plantation agriculture, but slavery now faced national opposition from two different directions: not only from abolitionists, but also from **nativists** who wanted to live in whites-only states. Savage confrontations between pro-slavery and **free-soil** militia turned Kansas into **Bleeding Kansas**, and the conflict soon extended to Washington. Equally savage political infighting ruptured the existing party system – even the Methodist and Baptist churches split into separate, hostile Northern and Southern wings – and created the **Republican** party, explicitly opposed to slavery and rooted exclusively in the North. As the will to compromise disappeared, bluster about **secession** if Southern 'rights' were not respected was increasingly ignored. In 1860, **Abraham Lincoln** proved that it was possible to be elected president with no Southern support whatsoever, and the South felt that it had no choice but to leave the Union.

Whether or not slavery truly faced imminent abolition once the slave states were in the minority is impossible to judge. Abolitionism was not all that strong in the North in 1850, though it grew in the course of the decade in response to such conspicuous injustices as the Fugitive Slave Act, the **Dred Scott** decision, and the South's increasingly strident defence of its 'peculiar institution' with such slogans as 'Freedom is not possible without slavery'. Even when Lincoln was inaugurated in March 1861, he felt that his personal principles should remain distinct from his duty as president, and avowed that 'I have no purpose, directly or indirectly, to interfere with the institution of slavery in the States where it exists. I believe I have no lawful right to do so, and I have no inclination to do so.'

The two sides that squared up to fight the **Civil War** were clearly demarcated by slavery. Slaves constituted on average 46 percent of the population in the seven Deep South states that originally formed the Confederacy – South Carolina, Mississippi, Florida, Alabama, Georgia, Louisiana and Texas – and 28.5 percent of the four upper-South states that joined once war began – Virginia, Arkansas, North Carolina and Tennessee. Overall, more than a third of the Southern population were slaves; the corresponding figure for the North was just one percent.

The final Union victory is often attributed to sheer weight of numbers, and the economic might that went with it. In total, the war pitted the **Union** of 23 Northern states, holding over 22 million people, against the **Confederacy** of eleven Southern states, with nine million people. As for potential combatants, the North initially drew on 3.5 million white males aged between 18 and 45 – and later recruited blacks as well – whereas the South had more like one million. In the end, around 2.1 million men fought for the Union, and 900,000 for the Confederacy. 620,000 soldiers died during the conflict, around one third of them in battle and the rest from disease; 360,000 of those were from the North, but the 258,000 who came from the South represented four percent of its total population, and one quarter of its white men of military age.

Purely as an economic system, slavery was not in decline in 1860. Plantation agriculture had never been more profitable. The South produced three-quarters of the world's cotton, provided sixty percent of US exports, and held every one of the top 116 counties in terms of per capita wealth. Southern confidence was perhaps best expressed in James Hammond's **King Cotton** speech to the Senate in 1858, when he credited the South with rescuing the Union from the Depression of 1857: 'The difference between us is, that our slaves are hired for life and well compensated . . . yours are hired by the day, not cared for, and scantily compensated.'

When war came, the North swiftly imposed a devastating **naval blockade** on the South, which all but prevented the Confederacy from selling its cotton or other produce abroad. Whereas the North was able to continue trading with the rest of the world, and also succeeded in maintaining its industrial and agricultural output, the Southern war effort was primarily financed by printing $1.5 billion of paper currency, which with neither reserves nor income to support it was so eroded by inflation that it became worthless.

Even so, the Confederacy came much closer to victory than is usually appreciated. The repeated outmanoeuvring of federal forces by General **Robert E. Lee**, and his incursions into Union territory, meant that in each of three successive years, from 1862 to 1864, there was a genuine possibility that Northern morale would collapse, allowing opponents of the war to be elected to power and agree to peace. After all, the Revolutionary War had shown how such a war could be won: for the Union to triumph, it had to invade and occupy the South, and destroy its armies, but for the South to win it only had to survive until the North wearied of the struggle. By that token, Lincoln's eventual success in finding generals Grant, Sherman and Sheridan to replace failures like McClellan, Pope, Burnside and Hooker, was only part of the story. Arguably as instrumental in the Southern defeat was the fact that the dashing tactics of Confederate generals Lee and Jackson, forever counterattacking and carrying the fight to the enemy, may have been in the finest romantic traditions of the Old South, but they were no match for the grim, relentless total-war determination with which Grant and Sherman eventually ground them down.

There's a particular irony in the fact that had the Confederacy sued for peace before Lee gave it fresh hope, a negotiated settlement might not have included the abolition of slavery. In the event, as the war went on, with Southern slaves flocking to the Union flag and black soldiers fighting on the front line, emancipation did indeed become inevitable. Lincoln took the political decision to match his moral conviction by issuing his **Emancipation Proclamation** in 1862, though the **Thirteenth Amendment** outlawing slavery only took effect in 1865. By then, the final tragedy of Lincoln's **assassination**, on Good Friday less than a week after Lee's surrender, had sanctified the cause beyond all further debate.

1850 The admission of **California** and **Texas** to the Union is engulfed in controversy. Southern states feel that unless they permit slavery – something Congress can ordain for territories, whereas states are entitled to choose for themselves – there will from now on be a permanent majority of 'Free' states. Henry Clay's efforts to devise a compromise are opposed by the dying John Calhoun, and President **Zachary Taylor** threatens to veto any deal. However, Taylor dies on July 9 and is replaced by **Millard Fillmore**. A South-leaning Northerner, Illinois Senator **Stephen Douglas**, then manages to push through the **Compromise of 1850**, a series of separate and hotly contested acts that cumulatively satisfy both sides. California enters the Union as a 'Free' state; New Mexico and Utah become territories, so their ultimate status remains undecided; the borders of Texas and New Mexico are finalized, and Texas is paid $10 million for the loss of its claims; the slave trade, but not slavery itself, is abolished in Washington, DC; and a Fugitive Slave Act is passed, requiring federal law officers to help slave-owners regain their property, and stipulating heavy punishment for those who aid runaway slaves.

Nathaniel Hawthorne publishes his greatest novel, *The Scarlet Letter*, exploring the moral consequences of an adulterous liaison in Puritan New England.

1851 On May 19, the first rail connection to the Great Lakes – the 483-mile **Erie Railroad** between New York City and Dunkirk on Lake Erie – is completed. In October, the **Hudson Railroad** links New York City with Albany.

South Carolina threatens to secede in response to the Compromise of 1850, but attracts no support from other Southern states.

The **Fugitive Slave Act** attracts huge opposition in the North. In Boston, after one such slave, Shadrach, is freed in February from a courtroom by an angry crowd, and smuggled to Canada, in April more than five hundred US troops frogmarch another, Thomas Sims, to a waiting ship, which carries him back South. A Pennsylvania

> **❝** That man over there says that women have to be helped into carriages, and lifted over ditches, and to have the best place everywhere. Nobody helps *me* any best place! *And ain't I a woman?* Look at me! Look at my arm! I have ploughed and I have gathered into barns. And no man could head me. *And ain't I a woman?* I could work as much, and eat as much as a man – when I could get it – *And ain't I a woman?* . . . If the first woman God ever made was strong enough to turn the world upside down all alone, these women together ought to be able to turn it back and get it right-side up again. And now that they are asking to do it the men better let them. **❞**
>
> Former slave **Sojourner Truth**, addressing the women's rights convention in Akron in May, 1851

The calling card of former slave turned travelling preacher Sojourner Truth

newspaper reports another confrontation in September, in which a slave-owner is killed, with the headline 'Civil War – The First Blow Struck'. In all, 332 escapees are returned to slavery during the 1850s.

At a women's rights convention in Akron in May, former slave **Sojourner Truth** delivers her most famous speech, **"Ain't I A Woman?"**

In the **Treaty of Traverse des Sioux**, the Sioux give up Iowa and most of Minnesota.

Herman Melville publishes *Moby-Dick*.

1852 **Harriet Beecher Stowe** publishes ***Uncle Tom's Cabin***, whose graphic depiction of the horrors of slavery strikes a huge chord around the globe. In 1862, when it has sold two million copies in the US, Abraham Lincoln will greet her with the words 'So you're the little woman who wrote the book that made this great war.'

The Democratic convention commits the party to the Compromise of 1850, and opts on its 48th ballot to nominate the little-known **Franklin Pierce**. He wins the presidency by a landslide after Northern and Southern Whigs fail to agree a common platform.

1853 On July 8, a squadron commanded by Commodore **Matthew Perry** sails into Tokyo Bay, and presents a letter from President Fillmore to the Emperor. The two-century self-imposed 'closure' of **Japan** to foreigners is formally ended by a commercial treaty in February 1854.

Railroads now connect New York with **Chicago**. As the nation's trade increasingly becomes oriented east–west rather than north–south, Southerners are determined that the transcontinental railroad should follow a southerly route. When surveys reveal that the best available course runs through northern Mexico, the **Gadsden Purchase** is negotiated. Ratified by the Senate in 1854, it pays $10 million

Walt Whitman (1819–92) and Herman Melville (1819–91)

Two great American writers, both raised in New York City, produced their masterpieces during the 1850s. Poet **Walt Whitman** aimed 'mainly . . . to put a Person, a human being (myself, in the latter half of the Nineteenth Century, in America,) freely, fully and truly on record'. In 1855, in the first edition of his much revised *Leaves of Grass* – hailed by Ralph Waldo Emerson as 'the most extraordinary piece of wit and wisdom that America has yet produced' – he set about that task with breathtaking exuberance. Everything was there: 'Do I contradict myself? Very well then, I contradict myself. I am large, I contain multitudes.' Though Whitman's homosexuality lay obscured, contemporaries were shocked by his earthiness, and his attitude to traditional religion – 'the old cautious hucksters, the most they offer for mankind and eternity less than a spirt of my own seminal wet'. Sidney Lanier, who both admired Whitman's daring and was appalled by his morality, memorably paraphrased him as 'because a prairie is wide, therefore debauchery is admirable, and because the Mississippi is long, therefore every American is God'.

Herman Melville, who earlier tasted success with the South Seas romps *Typee* and *Omoo*, produced his epic novel *Moby-Dick* in 1851. Critic Edmund Wilson found echoes in Captain Ahab's relentless, obsessive pursuit of the White Whale in Grant's later pursuit of Lee, while Ahab's insistence that 'some certain significance lurks in all things, else all things are little worth, and the round world itself but an empty cipher' has parallels with Whitman.

Neither man fought in the Civil War, though Whitman became a frequent hospital visitor after his brother was wounded. He later eulogized Lincoln in 'Oh Captain! My Captain!', and lectured on his assassination: 'the actual murder, transpired with the quiet and simplicity of any commonest occurrence – the bursting of a bud or pod in the growth of vegetation, for instance'.

Poet Walt Whitman, photographed during the 1860s by Matthew Brady

for a strip of Mexican land south of the Gila River to the modern-day borders of Arizona and New Mexico.

1854 To secure Southern support for a more northerly transcontinental railroad route, Stephen Douglas introduces the **Kansas–Nebraska Act**, under which Kansas and Nebraska will become territories, with a free vote of residents – **popular sovereignty** – to decide whether to allow slavery. This explicit repeal of the Missouri Compromise is pushed through Congress and becomes law on May 30. However, with every Northern Whig voting against it, the old party alignments are shattered.

Newly formed parties reflect two major strands of Northern opinion. **Nativists**, opposed to further immigration (especially by Irish Catholics) and keen to bar slavery in order to maintain all-white settlements, join the **American** party. They are widely known as the **Know-Nothings** because they respond 'I know nothing' to queries about their secret platform. Abolitionists who oppose slavery on principle, and see the federal government as having a duty to halt its spread, coalesce to form the **Republican Party**. Democrats quickly charge that all Republicans support Negro equality, and thus call them '**Black Republicans**'.

Both advocates and opponents of slavery encourage their supporters to migrate into Kansas itself, which swiftly becomes known as **Bleeding Kansas**. The headquarters of '**free-soil**' settlement is **Lawrence**, while most pro-slavery agitation comes from across the border in **Missouri**.

President Pierce hopes to acquire **Cuba**, to add one or more slave states to the Union, but the Spanish reject an offer of $130 million. On October 18, the American ministers to Britain, France and Spain declare in the **Ostend Manifesto** that if Spain refuses to sell Cuba, then 'by every law, human and divine, we shall be justified in wresting it from Spain if we possess the power'. This incurs such hostile denunciation in the US that Pierce abandons the scheme.

Henry Thoreau publishes *Walden,* an account of his solitary two-year sojourn by Walden Pond in rural Massachusetts.

1855 By allowing the cheap shipment of iron ore, the new **Sault Sainte Marie Canal** between lakes Superior and Huron facilitates the development of the steel industry, while a railroad across the **Isthmus of Panama** in Central America speeds up transportation to California.

Filibuster leader **William Walker** sails from San Francisco to **Nicaragua**, where he takes over the army, installs himself as president, and reintroduces slavery. He's deposed in 1857 before he can turn Nicaragua into an American slave state.

Walt Whitman publishes *Leaves of Grass,* which he promotes himself by writing bogus reviews, and which he will revise for the rest of his life; see p.150.

1856 **Bleeding Kansas** is in turmoil. In May, denouncing 'The Crime Against Kansas' in the Senate, Massachusetts' **Charles Sumner** accuses the South of having lapsed into 'shameful imbecility from Slavery', and is beaten bloody in the chamber by Congressman Preston Brooks of South Carolina. Inflamed both by that, and by an attack on Lawrence by Missouri militiamen, **John Brown** leads the Pottawatomie Massacre of five pro-slavery male settlers.

The Know-Nothings divide into factions, with Southern nativists securing the nomination of **Millard Fillmore** as the American party's presidential candidate. The **Republicans** thus become the main opposition in the North, and nominate **John C. Frémont**, who campaigns on an explicit anti-slavery platform under the slogan of 'Free soil, free speech, and Frémont'. The Governor of Virginia threatens that if Frémont wins, the slave states will 'proceed at once to immediate, absolute and eternal separation'. Frémont does win eleven out of sixteen Northern states, but Democrat **James Buchanan** – known as "Old Public Functionary" for his years of unspectacular public service – wins all the future Confederate states, and gains a narrow overall victory.

1857 Buchanan becomes president on March 4. Two days later, the **Supreme Court** decides that **Dred Scott** – a slave suing for freedom because his master has taken him both to Illinois, and to unorganized territory where the Missouri Compromise forbade slavery – cannot as a Negro become a citizen, and that he cannot be freed by going north because Congress cannot deprive citizens of their property. Supported by all five Southern judges, and two Northern ones to whom Buchanan has applied covert pressure, this ruling amounts to a radical declaration that slavery is now theoretically legal anywhere.

Buchanan also introduces an exceptionally low tariff on imports, which is blamed in the North for the short-lived **Depression of 1857**, in which Northern businesses suffer heavily.

1858 By now, Kansas has two rival state legislatures: an official one, dominated by pro-slavery activists, at Lecompton, and an unofficial one at Topeka that's more representative of actual residents. After both draw up constitutions, President Buchanan chooses to submit the **Lecompton Constitution** to Congress, recommending the admission of Kansas as a slave state. In ferocious debates that split the Democratic party into Southern and Northern factions, Douglas denounces this as a violation of popular sovereignty. It passes the Senate but is defeated in the House, and defeated again by a referendum in Kansas.

The Lincoln-Douglas debates of 1858

In the 1858 Senate race in Illinois, the incumbent Democrat **Stephen A. Douglas** faced Republican lawyer and former Whig Congressman **Abraham Lincoln**. The campaign received such national attention, and so clearly articulated the issues confronting the country, that the same two candidates were to contest the 1860 presidential election.

Accepting nomination on June 16, Lincoln declared '**A house divided against itself cannot stand**. I believe this government cannot endure, permanently, half *slave* and half *free*.' To Douglas, such sentiments made Lincoln a 'Black Republican', out to destroy the Union. He declared: 'this government of ours is founded on the white basis. It was made by the white man, for the benefit of the white man to be administered by white men . . . I am opposed to taking any step that recognizes the Negro man or the Indian as the equal of the white man.' Lincoln responded: 'I should like to know if taking this old Declaration of Independence, which declares that all men are equal upon principle, and making exceptions to it – where will it stop? If one man says it does not mean a Negro, why does not another it does not mean some other man?'

The election culminated with seven head-to-head debates. Lincoln believed that slavery while wrong remained legal, and, like many Southerners, that if prevented from spreading it would inevitably die out. At Freeport on August 27, he demanded whether new territories could legally exclude slavery. Although Douglas supported the Dred Scott decision, he argued that territories could pass 'unfriendly legislation' precluding slavery. That view, favoured neither by the current president nor in the South, did much to damage his prospects in 1860. However, Douglas was re-elected as Senator for Illinois, after the election was decided in a state legislature dominated by sitting Democrats.

Contesting election to the Senate in Illinois, **Stephen Douglas** and **Abraham Lincoln** stage regular debates throughout the summer.

Minnesota becomes the 32nd state.

In what Buchanan calls 'a triumph for civilization and the Union', **John Butterfield** – a founder of the American Express Company – sends the first Overland Mail **stagecoach** from St Louis to San Francisco in 24 days.

1859 Sectional passions are further aroused by John Brown's raid on **Harpers Ferry** in October, and his subsequent execution.

The discovery of the Comstock Lode of **silver** in Nevada, and deposits of **gold** near Pike's Peak in Kansas (in what soon becomes Colorado), trigger another rush of westward migration.

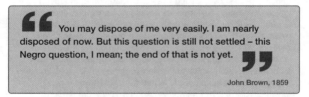

❝ You may dispose of me very easily. I am nearly disposed of now. But this question is still not settled – this Negro question, I mean; the end of that is not yet. ❞

John Brown, 1859

1860 In February, after heated opposition from Douglas in particular, Congress rejects resolutions from **Jefferson Davis** – who is regarded as President Buchanan's spokesman in the Senate – supporting a federal **slave code** and states' rights. That same debate splits subsequent Democratic conventions in both Charleston and Baltimore. In the end, Northern Democrats nominate **Stephen Douglas**, and Southerners **John C. Breckinridge**. The Republican convention in Chicago eventually nominates favourite son **Abraham Lincoln** rather than original front-runner William Seward. John Bell stands for the Union Party.

John Brown and the raid on Harpers Ferry

On October 16, 1859, a tiny militia of eighteen men – thirteen white, five black, and led by the 59-year-old, white, failed entrepreneur **John Brown** – seized the federal arsenal and armoury at **Harpers Ferry**, Virginia. Brown's hope that blacks would flock to Harpers Ferry, creating an army of former and runaway slaves that could advance to liberate the South, was swiftly dashed. Federal reinforcements arrived within 36 hours; ten of Brown's men, including two of his sons, were killed, and Brown was taken prisoner.

Brown's subsequent embrace of **martyrdom** reflected his awareness that the plan was never likely to succeed. Though he has often been dismissed as a crazed fanatic, according to Virginia's Governor Wise 'they are themselves mistaken who take him to be a madman'. His eloquence during his trial, and prior to his **execution** on December 2 – his last words were 'I am now quite certain that the crimes of this guilty land will never be purged away, but with Blood' – polarized the nation.

The South was appalled. Although Congress decided there was no overt conspiracy, Brown was clearly financed by a 'Secret Six' of abolitionist Northerners. While Lincoln repudiated his actions, Stephen Douglas called them 'a logical, inevitable result of the teachings of the Republican party'. Prominent Southerners who came into contact with Brown included Lieutenant Colonel Robert E. Lee and Lieutenant J. E. B. Stuart, who arrested him, and Stonewall Jackson and John Wilkes Booth, who saw him hang.

In the North, on the other hand, Emerson observed 'that new saint . . . will make the gallows as glorious as the cross', while William Lloyd Garrison commented: 'In firing his gun, John Brown has merely told what time of day it is. It is high noon, thank God.' Indeed it was. Within two years, Union soldiers were marching to war singing 'John Brown's Body'.

John Brown, the abolitionist leader of the attack on the federal arsenal at Harpers
Ferry, Virginia

The four-way presidential election boils down to two separate contests, between Douglas and Lincoln in the North, and between Breckinridge, Douglas and Bell in the South. **Lincoln**, who is not even on the ballot in the Deep South, gains just 39 percent of the popular vote, but wins all 18 'Free' states. He gains 180 votes in the electoral college; Breckinridge has 72, Bell 39 and Douglas 12.

Southern states see no future for themselves in a Union that has categorically voted against slavery despite their explicit threats of secession. On December 20, **South Carolina** becomes the first to **secede**, when a convention unanimously agrees to dissolve 'the union now subsisting between South Carolina and other States'.

In April, the **Pony Express** carries mail from St Joseph, Missouri, to San Francisco in ten days.

1861 Following advice from President-elect Lincoln, who argues that 'the tug has to come, and better now than any time hereafter', Republican opposition ensures the defeat in the Senate on January 16 of the **Crittenden Compromise** – a set of proposed constitutional amendments that would guarantee slavery in perpetuity. On February 28, however, both House and Senate agree an unamendable Thirteenth Amendment that forbids Congress ever to abolish slavery, which the Civil War will prevent from ever being ratified.

> **❝** You think slavery is *right* and ought to be extended; while we think it is *wrong* and ought to be restricted. That I suppose is the rub, It certainly is the only substantial difference between us. **❞**
>
> Abraham Lincoln, in a private letter to Alexander Stephens, soon to become Confederate vice president, December 22, 1860

Amid joyful celebrations, but with little expectation of war, six more Southern states **secede** in the three weeks following January 9: **Mississippi**, **Florida**, **Alabama**, **Georgia**, **Louisiana** and **Texas**.

On February 4, delegates from six seceding states (joined by the Texans in March) meet at **Montgomery**, Alabama, and form a provisional government as the **Confederate States of America**. Choosing **Jefferson Davis** as president and **Alexander Stephens** as vice president, they draw up a constitution closely modelled on that of the United States, with the same tensions between individual states and the federal authority. One cabinet member is drawn from each state, in what sympathetic observer Mary Chesnut calls 'a perfect magazine of discord and discontent'. Davis's call on March 6 for an army of 100,000 one-year volunteers is swiftly answered.

In his inaugural address on March 4, **President Abraham Lincoln** attempts to reassure the South that in exercising his new authority, whatever his own moral convictions, he neither plans nor desires to abolish slavery. While asserting that 'no state, upon its own mere motion, can lawfully get out of the Union', he insists that 'you can have no conflict without yourselves being the aggressors'.

As the Confederates seize federal funds and property through the South, Lincoln informs the governor of South Carolina that he intends to re-provision **Fort Sumter**, guarding the harbour at Charleston. Davis decides to reduce the fort before such help arrives; after Major Robert Anderson refuses to capitulate, General **Pierre Beauregard** commences an artillery bombardment on April 12 – the first shots of the **Civil War** – and the fort surrenders on April 13.

The two sides muster their armies. Lincoln follows up his appeal for 75,000 three-month volunteers on April 15 with a request for 42,000 three-year men in May, while Davis calls for 400,000 more three-year volunteers in May.

The start of war forces the border states of the 'upper South' to choose sides. **Virginia** votes to secede on April 17 – its militia immediately seizes the federal armoury at Harpers Ferry and the naval base at Gosport – and is followed in May by **Arkansas**, **North Carolina** and **Tennessee**. Although **Missouri** is riven by guerrilla violence, a strong Union show of force drives out its governor and much of its legislature, who join the Confederacy but remain in exile throughout the war. **Kentucky** at first declares itself neutral. After it's invaded by rival armies, the official legislature declares its allegiance to the Union in September, while a breakaway faction joins the Confederacy in December. Pro-secession rioters in Baltimore in late April briefly sever communications between Washington, DC, and the rest of the North, but **Maryland** eventually votes to stay in the Union, as does **Delaware**. The western portion of Virginia, where slavery is peripheral to the economy, starts the process of becoming the separate state of **West Virginia**.

On April 19, Lincoln orders a **naval blockade** of the South. Successful assaults on forts Clark and Hatteras on the North Carolina coast in August are followed by the capture of Port Royal, South Carolina, in November. By April 1862, only Charleston and Wilmington remain open to Confederate shipping. Although Confederate 'blockade-runners' continue to operate throughout the war, the blockade reduces Southern trade by at least two-thirds, and greatly contributes to Southern economic hardship.

The acceptance in May of Virginia's offer to make **Richmond** the Confederate capital means the two rival capitals are just one hundred miles apart. It will arguably hamper the Confederate war effort by making Virginia the main focus of the war, and creating an unnecessary preoccupation with the defence of Richmond.

Confederate States of America
The date of secession is given for each state.

State seceding before the outbreak of war on April 12, 1861

States seceding after the outbreak of war

INDIANA

ILLINOIS

Louisville

KANSAS

MISSOURI

KENTUCKY

New Madrid

Fort Donelson

Stones River ✗

Fort Henry

Nashville

OKLAHOMA

Memphis

Shiloh ✗

TENNESSEE
(May 7, 1861)

ARKANSAS
(May 6, 1861)

Corinth

Florence

MISSISSIPPI
(Jan 9, 1861)

ALABAMA
(Jan 11, 1861)

Shreveport

Vicksburg

Jackson

Montgomery

TEXAS
(Feb 1, 1861)

LOUISIANA
(Jan 26, 1861)

Mobile

Pensacola

Fort Hudson
Baton Rouge

New Orleans

Gulf of Mexico

0   100 miles

THE CIVIL WAR

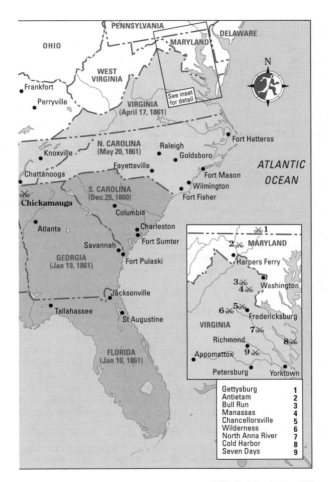

OHIO

PENNSYLVANIA

DELAWARE

MARYLAND

See inset for detail

WEST VIRGINIA

• Frankfort

• Perryville

VIRGINIA
(April 17, 1861)

N

N. CAROLINA
(May 20, 1861)

Raleigh •

• Goldsboro

Fort Hatteras

• Knoxville

Fayetteville •

• Chattanooga

Fort Mason

S. CAROLINA
(Dec 20, 1860)

Wilmington

Fort Fisher

✂ Chickamauga

Columbia •

ATLANTIC OCEAN

Charleston •

• Atlanta

Fort Sumter

Savannah •

Fort Pulaski

GEORGIA
(Jan 19, 1861)

Jacksonville •

• Tallahassee

St Augustine •

FLORIDA
(Jan 10, 1861)

✂ 1

2 ✂   MARYLAND

Harpers Ferry •

3 ✂

4 ✂   • Washington

6 ✂ 5 ✂

• Fredericksburg

VIRGINIA

7 ✂

Richmond •

8 ✂

Appomattox •

9 ✂

• Petersburg

Yorktown •

Gettysburg	1
Antietam	2
Bull Run	3
Manassas	4
Chancellorsville	5
Wilderness	6
North Anna River	7
Cold Harbor	8
Seven Days	9

The initial Union war strategy, devised by General **Winfield Scott**, is the **Anaconda Plan** to encircle the Confederacy with both the naval blockade and troops along the Mississippi. Public pressure in the North, however, inspired by the newspaper slogan 'On to Richmond', demands an assault on Virginia. On July 21, around 35,000 raw Union troops, under General **Irwin MacDowell**, attack 20,000 Confederates, led by General Beauregard, defending the junction of the railroads to the Deep South and the Shenandoah Valley at **Manassas**. In this **First Battle of Bull Run**, the Confederate Colonel Thomas Jackson earns his nickname **Stonewall** by repelling initial Union advances, before reinforcements under **Joseph Johnston** arrive, emit the chilling 'rebel yell' for the first time, and drive the Yankees from the field. As jubilation sweeps the South – contributing perhaps to a lasting Confederate overconfidence – there's panic in Washington. Within four days, Lincoln signs two bills to enlist a million three-year volunteers into what will become the **Army of the Potomac**, and replaces MacDowell with General **George McClellan**, who becomes general-in-chief on Scott's retirement in November.

By proclaiming its neutrality on May 13, the **British** government recognizes the Confederate states as belligerents. On November 8 the federal sloop *San Jacinto* stops the British steamer *Trent* at sea and arrests two Confederate commissioners being sent to Britain and France, James Mason and John Slidell. The furious British response is as close as Britain ever comes to siding with the Confederacy; after Lincoln climbs down and releases the two envoys, they achieve little impact in Europe. With slavery as the principal stumbling block in popular opinion, Britain will never recognize the Confederacy as an independent nation.

Kansas finally joins the Union as a 'Free' state in January.

In August, Congress enacts America's first **income tax**, levying three percent on all annual incomes over $800.

> **"** Our new government is founded on the opposite idea of the equality of the races . . . Its corner stone rests upon the great truth that the Negro is not equal to the white man. This . . . government is the first in the history of the world, based upon this great physical and moral truth. **"**
>
> Alexander Stephens, February 18, 1861, taking his oath of office as Vice President of the Confederacy

In September, the **Pacific telegraph** is completed, and drives the Pony Express out of business.

1862 Although McClellan turns the Army of the Potomac into a disciplined and efficient fighting force, he displays a strange reluctance to do anything with it, and consistently overestimates the strength of his opponents. Convinced that he's outnumbered by Joseph Johnston's army, entrenched at Manassas – in fact his own is three times the size – he refuses to attack. Instead he plans a **Peninsula Campaign**, embarking with 112,000 men and landing southeast of Richmond between the York and James rivers in April. Once there, he's so unwilling to advance that Johnston has time to move his entire army to confront him. Nonetheless, in May McClellan slowly approaches to within seven miles of Richmond.

The North is so confident of victory that all recruiting offices are closed, while the beleaguered Confederacy introduces the first **conscription** law in American history on April 16. Declaring all able-bodied white males between 18 and 35 (later extended to 17–50) liable for three years' service, it's deeply unpopular; the ease with which the wealthy can escape the draft leads to the charge that this is 'a rich man's war and a poor man's fight'.

The myth of the Old South

The vague sense of romantic despair that still surrounds the defeat of the Confederacy – and obscures the cause for which it fought – owes much to the lingering myth of the **Old South**. In fact, the *Gone with the Wind* world of courtly, chivalrous planters and belles was largely the invention of Southern novelists, erected on the shaky premise that whereas Northerners were Puritans, 'Southrons' were Cavaliers. Mark Twain knew who to blame for setting the South in love 'with the sillinesses and emptinesses, sham grandeurs, and sham chivalries of a brainless and worthless long-vanished society . . . **Sir Walter Scott** had so large a hand in making Southern character, as it existed before the war, that he is in a great measure responsible for the war'.

Insofar as the Old South ever existed, it was probably limited to a few hundred families in tidewater Virginia, and destroyed by soil depletion long before the war. That didn't stop Confederates such as **J. E. B. Stuart**, with his red-lined cape, yellow sash, and felt hat with ostrich-feather plume, or **George Pickett**, with his long ringletted hair, goatee beard and drooping moustache, from turning themselves into Cavaliers. Union General Sherman characterized such men as 'the young bloods of the South . . . men who never did work and never will. War suits them, and the rascals are brave, fine riders, bold to rashness . . . they care not a sou for niggers, land or anything.'

Arguably, the attachment to honour, as seen in Lee's faith in attack as the best form of defence, may have lost the South the war. If he had instead allowed the Union war effort to become bogged down with endless, fruitless pursuits into the Deep South, the Confederacy might have secured a negotiated peace.

The tide changes in early May, when '**Stonewall**' **Jackson**, who appears to be withdrawing to defend Richmond, suddenly launches 17,000 men on a northwards assault up the **Shenandoah Valley**. In a month of swift manoeuvring, he defeats Union forces in four separate battles and greatly disrupts Northern strategic planning, tying up troops that would otherwise be able to reinforce McClellan.

Rather than submit to a siege of Richmond, General Johnston launches an abortive counterattack against McClellan, but is wounded in the battle of **Seven Pines** (or Fair Oaks) on May 31, and replaced as commander of the Army of Northern Virginia by General **Robert E. Lee**. Lee swiftly goes on the offensive, calling Jackson back from Shenandoah and embarking on June 25 on the **Seven Days'** Battle, a succession of bloody encounters starting at **Mechanicsville** and ending at **Malvern Hill**. Although the Union armies repel virtually every attack, inflicting heavy Confederate losses, the intimidated McClellan consistently retreats, and loses the opportunity to capture Richmond.

During the Peninsula Campaign, both sides revolutionize naval warfare by launching **ironclad** ships. On March 8, the Confederate *Virginia*, more usually known as the *Merrimac*, sinks the federal *Cumberland* and *Congress* in Hampton Roads, but it's confronted and driven off the next day by the Union *Monitor*, which pioneers the revolving gun turret. The *Merrimac* is deliberately destroyed to prevent it falling into Union hands in May, while the *Monitor* sinks in December.

Out West, in a hugely successful campaign between February and May for which General **Henry Halleck** has overall responsibility, Union forces set out to control the major waterways of the South. Starting from Cairo, Illinois, Brigadier General **Ulysses S. Grant** forces the surrender of **Fort Henry** on the Tennessee River on February 6, and of **Fort Donelson** on the Cumberland River on February 16. This forces Confederate General **Albert Johnston** to evacuate **Nashville** on February 23, and fall back on **Corinth**, the major railroad intersection of the Mississippi Valley.

> **❝** I want to push on as rapidly as possible to save hard fighting. These terrible battles are very good things to read about for persons who lose no friends, but I am decidedly in favor of having as little of it as possible. The way to avoid it is to push forward. **❞**
>
> Ulysses S. Grant to his wife Julia, February 1862

Together with Beauregard, Johnston launches a surprise attack on Grant's advance guard at **Pittsburg Landing**, twenty miles north, on April 6. Though Johnston is killed confronting fierce resistance from General **William Tecumseh Sherman**, Beauregard reports he has won a 'complete victory' on the first day of the **Battle of Shiloh**. However, Grant is reinforced overnight and makes an equally unexpected counterattack the next morning, driving the Confederates back and securing a Union victory. The total losses of around 24,000 men exceed all American casualties in the Revolutionary War, the War of 1812, and the Mexican War put together.

In the ensuing weeks, Union forces capture Confederate forts on the Mississippi, and occupy **Memphis** and **Corinth**. Meanwhile, **New Orleans** has been left poorly defended; after bombardment by federal warships under David G. Farragut, General **Benjamin Butler** enters the city with 15,000 troops on May 1. Farragut's fleet continues upriver to take Baton Rouge and Natchez, but the Confederate fortress of **Vicksburg** will remain impregnable for another year.

The Peninsula Campaign ends with McClellan in open conflict with the exasperated Lincoln, who orders him to withdraw to the Potomac in early July, and appoints Halleck as commander-in-chief of all Union forces. Before McClellan can return to defend Washington, Lee and Jackson push northwards. Jackson defeats General Nathaniel Banks at **Cedar Mountain** on August 9, and the two together force General John Pope from the field at the **Second Battle of Bull Run** (or Second Manassas) on August 29 and 30.

Now the tables are turned, with the Confederates just twenty miles from Washington. Lee crosses the Potomac on September 4 to invade the North, but receives a less than enthusiastic welcome in Maryland. After he divides his already small army to secure his supply lines, a careless officer loses his written campaign plans, which when found by a Union private offer McClellan a great opportunity to destroy Lee's forces piecemeal. Instead McClellan's lethargy allows Lee to regroup, first to resist the Union onslaught at **Antietam** on September 17 – the war's bloodiest day, during which 22,000 men die – and then to withdraw safely across the Potomac.

Lincoln's fury with McClellan's failure either to win a decisive victory at **Antietam** or to pursue Lee into Virginia culminates with the memorable one-sentence letter 'If you don't want to use your army, I should like to borrow it for a while.' In November, he dismisses McClellan and replaces him with General **Ambrose Burnside** (whose whiskers give us the word 'sideburns'). Nonetheless, coupled with a Union victory at **Perryville** in Kentucky on October 8, Antietam is enough of a success to prevent the election of a Democratic House of Representatives in the autumn – which might have negotiated a peace settlement – and to convince European powers not to recognize the Confederacy.

By July, tens of thousands of so-called '**contrabands**' – runaway slaves from the South – have reached Union lines, creating a practical problem for the generals at the front and a political one in Washington. Abolitionist sentiment combines with the twin realization that not only does it make no sense to continue respecting Southern notions of 'property', but that freed slaves can make a significant contribution to the war effort. Lincoln informs his cabinet that Emancipation is now 'a military necessity, absolutely essential to the preservation of the Union', but decides to delay any announcement to coincide with success on the battlefield. Victory at Antietam furnishes the right moment, and on September 22 President Lincoln issues a preliminary **Emancipation Proclamation**, declaring that all slaves in states or areas of states still in rebellion on January 1, 1863, will be free, and that blacks will be 'received into the armed services of the United States'.

As the year closes, General Burnside attempts to satisfy public demands for action by invading Virginia. He, too, moves too slowly to attack separate components of the Confederate army, and instead makes a disastrous head-on assault against the united, entrenched Confederate position at **Fredericksburg** on December 13. The resultant carnage shatters Northern morale.

Meanwhile, Congress takes advantage of the absence of the Southern states to pass a raft of federal legislation that will shape the future course of the United States. The **Legal Tender Act**, obliging all individuals, banks and federal institutions to accept US currency notes, is complemented in July by the **Internal Revenue Act**, which introduces taxes on an extraordinary range of products and services, profits and inheritances, and creates the **Bureau of Internal Revenue**. May's **Homestead Act** grants 150 acres of public land to any settler who occupies (and improves) it for five years, while in July the **Morrill Act** gives land to each state to finance colleges devoted to 'agriculture and the mechanic arts', and the **Pacific Railroad Act** provides federal land and loans to build a railroad from Omaha to San Francisco.

> Abraham Lincoln may not wish it; he cannot prevent it; the nation may not will it, but the nation cannot prevent it. I do not care what men want or wish; the negro is the pebble in the cog-wheel, and the machine cannot go on until you get him out.
>
> Abolitionist Wendell Phillips, May 1862

By the end of the year, prices in the South have increased sevenfold since the start of the war, while in the North they've risen by just fourteen percent.

1863 On January 1, the **Emancipation Proclamation** comes into effect. Jefferson Davis calls it 'the most execrable measure recorded in the history of guilty man', while **Clement Vallandigham**, the most prominent **Peace Democrat** in the North and a candidate for the governorship of Ohio, denounces the war as being 'for the freedom of the blacks and the enslavement of the whites'. He is arrested and deported to the Confederacy.

On March 3, Congress passes the **Enrollment Act**, allowing the **conscription** of males aged between 20 and 45; its main intention is to encourage volunteering, for which a bounty of $300 is paid. The first draft drawing in **New York City** on July 11 triggers the worst **riot** in American history, in which 120 people die as a predominantly Irish mob rampages against the city's black population. The South also experiences civil unrest, as hungry women stage **bread riots** from Mobile to Richmond.

Lincoln replaces Burnside with General **Joseph Hooker** – whose name also enters the language on account of the prostitutes who frequent his headquarters – on January 25. After months of reorganization, he lures Lee into open battle at

Robert E. Lee (1807–70) and 'Stonewall' Jackson (1824–63)

The two most renowned Confederate generals were both Virginians, graduates of West Point, and veterans of the Mexican War. In other respects, however, they differed enormously. Where the charm, modesty and fairness of **Robert E. Lee** have been widely hymned, **Thomas 'Stonewall' Jackson** was a colder fish, a dour Presbyterian – more Roundhead than Cavalier – who observed 'I like strong drink, so I never touch it', and sucked incessantly on lemons.

Lee, the son of a Revolutionary general who became governor of Virginia, was offered command of the Union forces by Abraham Lincoln on April 18, 1861. That same day, however, he learned of Virginia's secession, and decided his duties lay with his native state. It is a common misconception: that he opposed slavery, he owned and traded slaves, and even in 1865 described it as 'the best [relation] that can exist between the white and black races while intermingled as at present in the country'. Jackson, an uninspiring professor at Virginia Military Institute until war broke out, was known as 'Old Tom Fool' until he held his troops firm 'like a stonewall' at Manassas in July 1861.

The two men teamed up in 1862. Lee took command of the Army of Northern Virginia that June, shortly after Jackson's most celebrated exploit – the daring **Shenandoah** campaign in which his 17,000 men tied down 45,000 Union troops. Over the ensuing year, Jackson served as the chief tactical instrument of Lee's offensive–defensive strategy, operating under the maxim of 'always mystify, mislead, and surprise the enemy'. Then he was shot by his own men, returning from a moonlight reconnaissance after a triumphant day at **Chancellorsville** on May 2, 1863. After his arm was amputated, Lee observed 'he has lost his left arm, but I have lost my right'; pneumonia set in, and Jackson died eight days later.

Chancellorsville, Virginia, only to lose his nerve and be comprehensively outmanoeuvred between May 1 and 4. Lee's greatest triumph comes at a heavy price, however, when **'Stonewall' Jackson** is accidentally shot by his own men as he returns from reconnoitring.

Lee now decides to carry the war out of Virginia, and invades the North again, via the Shenandoah Valley. As his advance guard reaches **Gettysburg** in southern Pennsylvania on July 1, they encounter outposts of the Army of the Potomac, now commanded by General **George Meade** in place of the demoted Hooker. Troops and generals alike converge on the region, where over the next three days they fight the largest, and perhaps the most crucial, battle of the war. Initial Confederate successes simply push the Union forces into stronger defensive positions, from which increasingly despairing Confederate assaults – culminating in the doomed **Pickett's Charge** on July 3 – fail to dislodge them. Gettysburg is celebrated as a huge Union victory.

Meanwhile, along the Mississippi, **Grant** wins perhaps the most tactically brilliant campaign of the war. In April, he runs navy ships past the guns of Vicksburg while marching his troops south through Louisiana, then ferries 23,000 men across the river into Mississippi. Living off the land, they seize and ravage **Jackson**, then besiege **Vicksburg**. Its commander, John Pemberton, acknowledges the town as 'the most important point in the Confederacy'. He eventually **surrenders** it on July 4 – the same day that news of Gettysburg reaches Washington – leaving the Confederacy cut in two, with the Union controlling the entire Mississippi river. Lincoln exults: 'The Father of Waters again goes unvexed to the sea', and declares 'Grant is my man, and I am his the rest of the war.'

> **I** have heard of your recently saying that both Army and Government needed a Dictator. Of course it was not for this, but in spite of it, that I have given you the command . . . What I ask of you now is military success, and I will risk the dictatorship. **"**

Abraham Lincoln, appointing General Joseph Hooker to command the Army of the Potomac, on January 25, 1863

Union successes in the West continue. General **William Rosecrans** pushes the Confederates out of central Tennessee, and occupies the rail junction of **Chattanooga** on September 9. Continuing into Georgia, he's badly defeated by General **Braxton Bragg** at **Chickamauga** on September 19 and 20 – the only major victory ever won by the Confederate Army of Tennessee, and one of the very few engagements where the Confederates outnumber the Union. Rosecrans falls back on Chattanooga, which briefly becomes the only Union-held city to fall under siege, but is soon joined by reinforcements from both Vicksburg, under Sherman, and from the Potomac under Hooker. Grant arrives in October, shortly after being given command of all operations in the West. In the two-day **Battle of Chattanooga**, on November 24 and 25, Union forces drive the Confederates from apparently impregnable positions on first Lookout Mountain and then the even more redoubtable Missionary Ridge. Bragg retreats all the way to Atlanta, where he resigns and is replaced by **Joseph Johnston**.

On July 18, the **Fifty-Fourth Massachusetts Volunteer Infantry** – consisting of black soldiers commanded by white officers – suffers almost fifty percent casualties in an unsuccessful attack on **Fort Wagner** outside Charleston, and thereby conclusively answers the much debated question 'Will the Negro fight?'

On August 21, Confederate 'bushwhackers' from Missouri, led by **William Clarke Quantrill** and avenging the arrest of their wives and sisters, launch their bloodiest raid on neighbouring **Lawrence**, Kansas. They kill 182 men and boys – almost the entire male population.

Abraham Lincoln dedicates the Union cemetery at **Gettysburg** on November 19.

West Virginia is formally admitted to the Union on June 20.

> **"** Fourscore and seven years ago our fathers brought forth on this continent a new nation, conceived in liberty, and dedicated to the proposition that all men are created equal. Now we are engaged in a great civil war, testing whether that nation, or any nation so conceived and so dedicated, can long endure . . . We here highly resolve that these dead shall not have died in vain – that this nation, under God, shall have a new birth of freedom – and that government of the people, by the people, for the people, shall not perish from the earth. **"**
>
> Abraham Lincoln, dedicating the Union cemetery at Gettysburg, in the
> **Gettysburg Address** of November 19, 1863

1864 On March 9, Grant is promoted to the rank of **Lieutenant General** – the first such since George Washington – and appointed general in chief of all Union armies. His immediate aim is to prevent the Confederate forces from linking up. The Army of the Potomac – still commanded by Meade, with **General Philip Sheridan** in charge of cavalry – is assigned to follow Lee, while Sherman takes over in the West with instructions to break up Johnston's army.

Grant crosses the Rapidan on May 3, and confronts Lee in the **Wilderness**, close to Chancellorsville. In the ensuing confused battle on May 5 and 6, Grant is no more successful in displacing the Confederates than Hooker a year earlier, but rather than retreating he keeps moving south, and engages Lee for five more days, from May 8 to 12, at **Spotsylvania**. Sheridan's cavalry branch off towards Richmond, and defeat their Confederate counterparts, killing 'Jeb' Stuart (see p.166), at Yellow Tavern on May 11.

'Collecting Remains of the Dead at Cold Harbor'; a gruesome Matthew Brady photograph from 1864

Announcing that 'I propose to fight it out along this line if it takes all summer', Grant continues south. Ten days of clashes around the **North Anna River**, from May 21 to 31, are followed by three more at **Cold Harbor**, from June 1 to 3. Grant's desire for a major battle is consistently thwarted by Lee, and he loses 44,000 men to Lee's 25,000. The carnage of the final day's attack on Confederate trenches at Cold Harbor convinces him to try a new approach. His weary forces move still further south, crossing the James River via a perilous 700-yard pontoon bridge, but fail to act decisively enough to take **Petersburg**, twenty miles below Richmond, before Lee's army can reach it, and instead settle for besieging the city. Lee attempts to create a diversion by sending **General Jubal Early** on a foray to within five miles of Washington, where he's turned back on July 11.

Meanwhile, on May 5, **Sherman** sets off from Chattanooga towards **Atlanta** with 100,000 men. General Johnston, with 65,000 men, draws Sherman forward, harassing him all the while but avoiding a major battle, but Jefferson Davis becomes frustrated by this progressive withdrawal and replaces him with the reckless **General John Hood**. Hood sustains heavy casualties attempting to halt Sherman's advance at Peachtree Creek on July 20, but digs in at Atlanta, and a siege commences.

As the sieges at Petersburg and Atlanta drag through the summer, Confederate strategy focuses on protracting the conflict long enough for war-weariness in the North to result in a Democratic victory in the presidential election. In late August, Lincoln tells a friend: '**I am going to be beaten**, and unless some great change takes place, badly beaten.' The next week, the Democratic convention in Chicago adopts a **peace** platform, supporting an 'immediate cessation of hostilities' that would leave 'the rights of the States unimpaired' – in other words, preserve slavery.

However, it muddies the waters by selecting the rejected General **George McClellan** as its candidate, who retains considerable popularity but still supports the war.

Lincoln's 'great change' arrives three days later. The Confederates **evacuate Atlanta** on September 1, when Hood realizes that Sherman has severed almost all his communications. Hood's army is still intact, so after occupying Atlanta Sherman feels obliged to pursue him. When Hood heads into Alabama and Tennessee, however, Sherman delegates that task to General George Thomas, who duly defeats Hood at **Franklin** on November 30 and **Nashville** on December 15 and 16.

Convinced by his earlier experiences in Tennessee that 'the entire South, man, woman and child, is against us, armed and determined', Sherman persuades Lincoln and Grant to endorse his plan to 'make Georgia howl'. On November 15, having burned what little remains of military use in Atlanta, he cuts loose and starts the **March to the Sea**, a pioneering example of 'total war' in which his 62,000 men systematically destroy the agricultural and industrial resources sustaining the Confederate war effort. They enter **Savannah** on December 22.

Shortly after the fall of Atlanta, **Sheridan**, whom Grant has ordered to follow Early 'to the death', inflicts heavy defeats on him in the **Shenandoah Valley**, at Winchester on September 19 and Fisher's Hill on September 21. After laying waste to the valley, he finally ends its role as a Confederate stronghold with a decisive victory at **Cedar Creek** on October 19.

In the wake of these successes, **Lincoln is re-elected** to the presidency on November 8, officially as the 'Union' rather than Republican candidate. He defeats McClellan by 2.2 million to 1.8 million in the popular vote; by 212 to 21 in the electoral college; and, perhaps most significantly, where it's possible to tell, by 78 percent to 22 percent among voting soldiers. **Andrew Johnson**, a 'War Democrat' from Tennessee who has been added to the Union ticket, is the new vice president.

During the spring, the first Union dead are buried in Robert E. Lee's front lawn, across the Potomac from Washington, which becomes the site of **Arlington National Cemetery**.

Nevada is admitted to the Union in October. At **Sand Creek**, Colorado, in November, Colonel John Chivington's troops massacre around 450 peaceful **Cheyenne** displaced by the mining boom. Further south, nine thousand **Navajo** of what's now northeastern Arizona are rounded up by General James Carleton and scout Kit Carson and forced to march to the barren Bosque Redondo camp in New Mexico.

1865 As the year starts, Lee's army is the last significant Confederate force left in the field, with the **Carolinas** as its main source of supplies. **Sherman** sets off north from Savannah in February and ravages the Carolinas just as he has Georgia, while the Union capture of Fort Fisher outside **Wilmington** on January 15, and **Charleston** on February 18, complete the naval blockade of the South. Sherman takes **Columbia** on February 17 and defeats Johnston's remaining forces at **Bentonville** on March 21.

So many 'contrabands' attach themselves to Sherman's army that in January he issues his '**Special Field Orders, No. 15**', designating the entire Southern coastline for thirty miles inland for settlement by former slaves; 40,000 freedmen claim their forty acres per family by June.

On February 1, Congress proposes the **Thirteenth Amendment** to the Constitution, prohibiting slavery within the United States. Also in February, Jefferson Davis concludes that 'we are reduced to choosing whether the

Abraham Lincoln (1809–65)

Abraham Lincoln was born in the proverbial **log cabin**, near Hodgenville, Kentucky, in 1809. Raised in Indiana, he spent less than a year in school before taking jobs that ranged from splitting fence rails on the family farm to rafting down the Mississippi as a flatboatman. As the postmaster in New Salem, **Illinois**, he entered the state legislature as a Whig in 1834, before becoming a lawyer and moving to state capital **Springfield** in 1837. A single term in Congress ended in 1849, when his opposition to the war with Mexico lost him his seat.

While Lincoln stated that 'if **slavery** is not wrong, nothing is wrong', he saw it as a 'minor question on its way to extinction', whose right to exist was unassailable under the Constitution. His mind was changed by the **Kansas–Nebraska Act** of 1854. Leaving the Whigs for the new Republican Party in 1856, he became a national figure when he opposed **Stephen Douglas** for a Senate seat in 1858, as detailed on p.155.

Propelled to the presidency in 1860, Lincoln subordinated not just when, but also whether, to free the slaves to what he saw as a greater end: the need to preserve the Union, 'the last, best hope of earth', at all costs. When he finally issued the Emancipation Proclamation in 1862, he acknowledged that 'I claim not to have controlled events, but confess plainly that events have controlled me'. Thus there's some truth to modern claims that the slaves 'freed themselves', by abandoning the plantations of the South and attaching themselves to the Northern war effort. However, it was Lincoln, by his immense skills both as a politician and as a military strategist – a role the early failures of his generals forced him to develop – and above all by his sheer single-mindedness, who kept the war effort going, shaped its eventual victory, and made that freedom possible. Whether, had he lived, he might also have achieved a successful Reconstruction, with 'malice toward none and charity for all' as he promised in his second inaugural address, is one of the great imponderables of US history.

President Abraham Lincoln, photographed in 1865

negroes shall fight for or against us', acknowledging that any slave soldiers will be entitled to their freedom. The Confederate House authorizes the conscription of slaves, but the Senate does not; only Virginia actually enlists any black soldiers, and they never see action. Davis uses the promise of emancipation in a fruitless last-ditch bid for British and French recognition.

With Petersburg all but encircled, Lee attempts to break out in strength at the end of March, but is badly defeated on March 25 and April 1, and forced into ignominious retreat. Both **Petersburg** and **Richmond** are evacuated on April 2, and entered by Union forces the next day. Visiting Richmond on April 4, Lincoln is mobbed by grateful former slaves.

His retreat blocked by Sheridan, **Lee surrenders to Grant** at Appomattox Courthouse on April 9; he accounts to his soldiers for their defeat with the words 'the Army of Northern Virginia has been compelled to yield to overwhelming numbers and resources'. Grant's terms, which extend to apply to the surrenders of Johnston's southern army to Sherman on April 26, and General Kirby Smith in Louisiana on May 26, guarantee Confederate soldiers freedom from prosecution for treason. **Jefferson Davis** is captured in Georgia on May 10, and imprisoned.

Speaking from a White House balcony on April 11, Lincoln advocates extending the franchise to literate or war-veteran blacks. Actor **John Wilkes Booth**, in the crowd below, comments 'That means nigger citizenship . . . that is the last speech he'll ever make.' On the evening of April 14 – Good Friday – Booth **shoots President Lincoln** as he watches *Our American Cousin* at Ford's Theatre, as part of a conspiracy in which Secretary of State William Seward is badly wounded. Vice President **Andrew Johnson**, however, is unhurt, and succeeds Lincoln as president upon his death the next day.

The process of postwar **Reconstruction** has already started. In March Congress creates the **Freedmen's Bureau**, to provide relief for those impoverished and displaced in the South. This applies most obviously to former slaves, and promises further distribution of forty-acre plots. On May 29, however, Johnson proclaims an **amnesty** for all rebels who swear an oath of allegiance to the US. All those owning property worth more than $20,000 have to apply for individual pardons, but these soon turn out to be readily forthcoming, and to include restitution of former property – which leaves the Freedmen's Bureau without land to distribute. Many who have claimed land under Sherman's Field Order 15 are forcibly expelled.

Already casting an eye towards his potential re-election, with Southern support, in 1868, Johnson declines to impose prolonged military government on the South, but instructs the seceded states to draw up revised constitutions so they can resume full participation in the Union. This they do, offering minimal contrition beyond a grudging ratification of the Thirteenth Amendment, and a repudiation of Confederate debts. When former Confederate generals and politicians, such as Alexander Stephens in Georgia, triumph in state and federal elections, Johnson observes that 'there seems . . . something like defiance, which is all out of place at this time'. One by one the Southern states enact **Black Codes**, typically obliging newly freed slaves to hire themselves out by the year, and imposing stiff penalties for 'vagrancy' or unemployment, thus preventing them from leaving plantations to find work in cities.

In Washington, Radical Republicans are appalled by the inadequate progress of Reconstruction, and in particular the absence of black suffrage. At least the **Thirteenth Amendment**, banning slavery, is ratified, and becomes law on December 18.

6
Reconstruction, expansion and industrialization
1866–1912

The end of the Civil War marked the moment when the nation finally came to see itself as something considerably more than the sum of its parts. That change was reflected in the language: Americans started to say 'the United States is . . .' instead of 'the United States are . . .'. Tellingly, while eleven of the twelve constitutional amendments passed before the war had limited the powers of the federal government, six of the next seven were to restrict those of the individual states instead. Which is not to say that the wounds of war were successfully healed. The attempted **Reconstruction** of the South – doomed perhaps when the assassinated Lincoln was replaced by **Andrew Johnson**, who swiftly fell out with the Radical Republicans in the North and came to see his own future as dependent on mollifying the South – was a fiasco. For a brief period, after black men were granted the vote, the Southern states elected black political representatives, but without a sustained effort to enable former slaves to acquire land, social relations in the South swiftly deteriorated, and Southern blacks were soon disenfranchised once more, by repressive state legislation. Anyone working to transform the South came under attack as either a **carpetbagger** (a Northern opportunist who headed south for personal profit) or a treacherous **scalawag** (a Southern collaborator).

With the completion of the **transcontinental railroad** in 1869, **Manifest Destiny** acquired an unstoppable impetus. Among the first to head west were federal troops, to do battle with the remaining Native Americans. Treaty after treaty was signed, only to be broken as it became expedient to do so – as a rule, upon the discovery of gold. When the whites overreached themselves, or when driven to desperation, the Indians fought back. The defeat of General Custer at **Little Bighorn** in 1876, by **Sitting Bull** and his Sioux and Cheyenne warriors, provoked the full wrath of the government. Within a few years, leaders such as **Crazy Horse** of the Oglala Sioux and **Geronimo** of the Apache had been forced to surrender, and their people confined to reservations. Federal authorities further attempted to eliminate the Indian way of life by doling out land to individuals rather than tribal units, hoping to force them to farm separately rather than hunt en masse.

The late nineteenth century was also an era of massive **immigration** from the rest of the world, with influxes from Europe to the East Coast paralleled by those from East Asia, and China in particular, to the West Coast. The fastest growth of all was in the greatest **cities**, especially New York, Chicago and Boston. Their industrial and commercial strength enabled them to attract and absorb migrants not only from throughout Europe but also from the old South – particularly ex-slaves, who could now at least vote with their feet.

The various presidents of this so-called **Gilded Age**, from the victorious General Grant (a man palpably out of his depth in the political arena) onwards, now seem anonymous figures compared to the industrialists and financiers who manipulated the national economy. These '**Robber Barons**' included such men as **John D. Rockefeller**, who controlled seventy percent of the world's oil almost before anyone else had realized it was worth controlling; **Andrew Carnegie**, who made his fortune introducing the Bessemer process of steel manufacture; and **J. P. Morgan**, who went for the most basic commodity of all – money. Their success was predicated on the willingness of the government to co-operate in resisting the development of a strong labour movement. A succession of widely publicized strikes – such as those on the railroads in 1877, in the mines of Tennessee in 1891 and in the steel mills of Pittsburgh in 1892 – were forcibly crushed.

Even though the federal union was now beyond challenge, the country remained far from united, with class and factional differences echoed by the geographical split between the industrial East and the agricultural West. Both the presidential elections of 1896 and 1900 pitted the Republican **William McKinley**, seen as the representative of the East, against the populist Democrat **William Jennings Bryan**, champion of the West, the farmers and free silver.

Many Americans saw the official 'closure' of the Western frontier in 1890, which ended the era of Manifest Destiny, as tantamount to depriving the country of its *raison d'être*, and were prompted to search for new frontiers further afield. Such **imperialist ventures** reached a crescendo in 1898, with the annexation of Hawaii, and the double seizure of Cuba and the Philippines in the **Spanish–American War**, which catapulted **Theodore Roosevelt** to the presidency. Though he took the African proverb 'speak softly and carry a big stick' as his motto – and was hardly, if truth be told, noted for being soft-spoken – Roosevelt in office did much to heal the divisions within the nation. While new legislation reined in the worst excesses of the Robber Barons, and of rampant capitalism in general, it also alleviated popular discontent without substantially threatening the business community, or empowering the labour movement. A decade into the twentieth century, the United States had advanced to the point that it knew, even if the rest of the world wasn't yet altogether sure, that it was the strongest, wealthiest country on earth. **Woodrow Wilson** was to get the chance to demonstrate that new status sooner than he or anyone else imagined.

1866 On February 19, in opposition to the **Radical Republicans** who are coming to dominate Congress, President Johnson vetoes a bill to extend the life of the Freedmen's Bureau, saying that the country has returned 'to a state of peace and industry'. **Johnson** then rails against the Republicans, calling their leader **Thaddeus Stevens** a traitor.

In March, the **Joint Committee on Reconstruction**, dominated by Stevens, refuses to allow Southern representatives to take their seats in Congress. In response to the Black Codes proliferating throughout the South, Congress then passes the **Civil Rights Act**, overriding another Johnson veto in early April. It specifies that all persons born in the US, without distinction of colour or former status – but 'excluding Indians not taxed' – are citizens and equal before the law.

The Joint Committee then proposes the **Fourteenth Amendment**, which passes Congress on June 16 and is ratified in July. Giving the Civil Rights Act constitutional force, this forbids states to 'deprive any person of life, liberty or property, without due process of law'. The intention is that Southern states must ratify the amendment in order to be readmitted to the Union; Tennessee does so immediately, but the rest do not. Congress also overrides another veto to renew the Freedmen's Bureau in July.

Meanwhile in the South, police and white mobs massacre blacks in race riots in **Memphis** in April, and **New Orleans** in July. The **Ku Klux Klan** makes its first appearance, in Pulaski, Tennessee.

Johnson attempts to rally support by organizing an abortive **National Union Convention**, but in November's Congressional elections, Radical Republicans make sufficient gains against Copperhead Democrats – Northern Democrats with Southern sympathies – to have two-thirds majorities in both houses.

On February 13, the James-Younger gang carry out the first armed **bank robbery** in Liberty, Missouri, while the Reno brothers commit the world's first **railroad robbery**, in Indiana on May 22.

Resentful of increased traffic along the **Bozeman Trail** to Montana, Sioux warriors including **Crazy Horse** kill Captain William **Fetterman** and eighty US soldiers in Wyoming on December 21.

In Baltimore in the summer, William Sylvis attempts to consolidate labour and craft associations in the **National Labor Union**.

1867 In early March, the outgoing Congress passes three major bills. The **Military Reconstruction Act** divides the South into five military districts – five former Union generals will be appointed as governors – and specifies that the former rebel states will only be restored to the Union once they frame and ratify new constitutions via universal male suffrage, and elect new legislatures that ratify the Fourteenth Amendment. The **Command of the Army Act** requires all the President's military orders to pass through the General of the Army – currently **Ulysses S. Grant** – and thus stops Johnson dealing directly with Southern military leaders. The **Tenure of Office Act** obliges the president to obtain Senate consent to dismiss or appoint office-holders.

Congress also agrees that the new Congress will convene after a gap of two days instead of the usual nine months.

Secretary of State William H. Seward negotiates the purchase of **Alaska** from Russia for $7.2 million, though Congress won't actually pay for 'Seward's Folly' until 1870, after a few judicious Russian bribes.

To combat isolation, encourage mutual co-operation, combine against high railroad rates, and generally resist exploitative middlemen, **farmers** form the Patrons of Husbandry, better known as **the Grange**.

Joseph McCoy sets up a rail depot at **Abilene**, Kansas, so Texan drovers can drive their cattle north without passing through hostile settled areas: 35,000 cattle come up the **Chisholm Trail** in the first year.

Nebraska is admitted to the Union.

1868 To test the constitutionality of the Tenure of Office Act, President Johnson dismisses the one overt Radical in his cabinet, Secretary of War **Edwin Stanton**. Led by Thaddeus Stevens, Congress instigates the first-ever **impeachment** proceedings, centring on Stanton's dismissal but also accusing Johnson of 'unlawfully devising and contriving' to violate the successive Reconstruction Acts. In May, 35 senators vote for impeachment, and 19 against; with seven Republicans voting against their own party, the prosecution thus falls one short of the 36 votes necessary to convict by a two-thirds majority. Although this defeat is a major blow to the Radicals, Johnson agrees not to continue blocking Reconstruction.

Both major parties woo the apolitical **General Grant** to be their presidential candidate. His mutual antipathy with Johnson, and mild Radical sympathies, lead him to opt for the Republicans. Campaigning on the slogan 'Let us have peace', he defeats Democrat **Horace Seymour** in the November election by 300,000 popular votes; 700,000 black voters participate, and probably determine the result.

C. Latham Scholes of Milwaukee, Wisconsin, patents his **Type-Writer**.

Formed out of parts of Utah, Dakota and Idaho, **Wyoming** becomes a territory.

Beside the Washita River in Indian Territory, General Sheridan and Colonel George Custer destroy a peaceful **Cheyenne** encampment, killing their leader Black Kettle, whom Sheridan dismisses as 'a worn-out and worthless old cypher'. Further north, Red Cloud signs the **Treaty of Fort Laramie**, which cedes the Black Hills to the **Sioux** in perpetuity.

1869 On February 26, Congress passes the **Fifteenth Amendment**, which provides that voting rights may not be denied 'on account of race, color, or previous condition of servitude'. It will be ratified on March 30, 1870.

On May 10, a 'golden spike' is driven into the ground at Promontory Point, Utah, linking the Union Pacific and Central Pacific railroads, and completing the **first transcontinental railroad**.

> **"** The more we can kill this year, the less will have to be killed next war, for the more I see of these Indians the more convinced I am that all have to be killed or maintained as a species of pauper. Their attempts at civilization are simply ridiculous. **"**
>
> General William Tecumseh Sherman, in a letter to his brother, mid-1860s

In the first of several scandals to tar Grant's presidency – though not Grant himself – rogue financiers **Jay Gould** and **Jim Fisk** exploit contacts within the administration in a scheme to hoard gold and push up prices. They sell out just before Grant cottons on and orders the sale of federal gold on **Black Friday**, September 24. Hundreds of investors suffer heavy losses.

The **American Equal Rights Association** meets in Washington, DC, in January; its president, **Susan B. Anthony**, demands that the Fourteenth Amendment should extend voting rights to women as well as black males. Both the **National Woman Suffrage Association**, led by Anthony and Elizabeth Cady Stanton, and the **American Woman Suffrage Party**, led by Lucy Stone and Julia Ward Howe, are organized. Wyoming Territory grants women the vote.

The National Temperance Convention, meeting in Chicago in September, forms the **Prohibition Party**, the latest in a long line of anti-alcohol organizations.

On December 9, nine Philadelphia tailors, led by Uriah S. Stephens, and hoping to unite all workers regardless of colour or gender, establish the **Knights of Labor**.

One-armed Union veteran **John Wesley Powell** leads the first expedition to float down the Colorado River through the **Grand Canyon**.

1870 Three **Enforcement Acts** make it a federal offence to interfere with anyone's right to vote; establish federal supervision of Congressional elections; and outlaw the **Ku Klux Klan**. Though prosecutions in the Carolinas and Mississippi secure few convictions, the Klan goes into decline. Racial intimidation, however, continues, and the Klan will reappear in the twentieth century.

On February 25, Senator **Hiram P. Revels** of Mississippi becomes the first black man to sit in Congress.

1871 The *New York Times* exposes the **Tweed Ring**, which by controlling patronage and rigging elections has dominated New York city and state since 1866, and embezzled vast sums. 'Boss' William Marcy Tweed is subsequently imprisoned, and **Tammany Hall**, the headquarters of the Democratic Party, becomes a byword for political corruption.

With the **Indian Appropriation Act**, Congress forbids any further Indian treaties, declaring that henceforth 'no Indian nation or tribe . . . within the United States shall be acknowledged as an independent nation, tribe or power'.

In October a fire destroys much of Chicago, killing 300 people and leaving 100,000 homeless.

1872 Britain resolves an ongoing dispute by agreeing to pay $15.5 million compensation for wartime damage caused by Confederate raiders built in British shipyards, including the *Alabama*.

Republicans dissatisfied with Grant's administration and the progress of Reconstruction hold a breakaway **Liberal Republican** convention, and nominate **Horace Greeley** for president. Even though Greeley has long opposed the Democrats, they choose to nominate him too, and he runs as a Democratic Liberal. Grant, however, easily wins

> **“** Railroads in Europe are built to connect centers of population; but in the West the railroad itself builds cities. Pushing boldly out into the wilderness, along its iron track villages, towns and cities spring into existence, and are strung together into a consistent whole by its lines of rails, as beads are upon a silken thread. **”**
>
> Horace Greeley, 1872

re-election, and the disappointed Greeley dies three weeks later.

During the campaign, it's revealed that **Credit Mobilier**, the company responsible for constructing the Union Pacific Railroad, has with the connivance of the railroad's directors skimmed off almost half the project's $50 million federal funding. Over the next few months, many Congressional leaders, including Vice President Schuyler Colfax, and future president James Garfield, are shown to have benefited from free or heavily discounted stock.

Yellowstone is established as the country's first **national park**.

1873 When a European financial crisis diminishes European interest in American stocks and bonds, railroad investment is hardest hit, forcing **Jay Cooke and Company** into bankruptcy in **September**. The resulting **Panic of 1873** causes the New York Stock Exchange to close for ten days, and launches a six-year depression that lowers agricultural prices, and worsens the economic problems of the South.

The first effective **barbed wire** is demonstrated to cattlemen in San Antonio, Texas, making it possible to enclose land in the West.

With new finds on Nevada's Comstock Lode greatly increasing the availability of silver, the Coinage Act – later known as the **Crime of 1873** – bans silver coinage.

Cable cars are introduced in San Francisco.

1874 Lieutenant Colonel **George Custer** leads a survey party into the Black Hills of Dakota; within two days, they discover gold, precipitating a headlong gold rush.

Led by Quanah Parker, an alliance of Comanche, Kiowa, Cheyenne and Arapahoe warriors open the **Red River War** by attacking buffalo hunters in Texas. They will be defeated by General Sheridan in 1875.

The extermination of the buffalo

Perhaps fifty million **buffalo** roamed the Great Plains in the mid-nineteenth century, the pivotal species in the prairie ecosystem and the largest mass of living creatures ever recorded. Buffalo hunting was the basis of life for the **Plains Indians**, who ate buffalo meat fresh, or pounded it with berries to preserve it as pemmican, and lived in bull-hide tepees. The buffalo-skin robes they wore, laboriously prepared by women, were a major source of both prestige and income, with 100,000 hides per year being sold to the American Fur Company.

In 1871, a Philadelphia tannery developed a cheap way to turn buffalo hides into **leather**, which the British hailed as ideal for military boots. Now that the **railroad** had made it possible to ship them east, buffalo skins were a saleable industrial commodity. White hunters swarmed onto the Plains. The transcontinental railroad having created separate northern and southern buffalo herds, the southern herd was wiped out between 1872 and 1874. The northern herd followed between 1880 and 1882, after the railroad reached North Dakota. In 1883, 5000 hunters found just 200 animals. A rancher told Theodore Roosevelt that in a thousand miles of travel he was 'never out of sight of a dead buffalo, and never in sight of a live one'. Millions of carcasses rotted where they lay, before being ground up for fertilizer.

While not literally a federal project, buffalo killing certainly gelled with the government's desire that Indians should farm rather than hunt. As General Sheridan put it, the hunters 'have done . . . more to settle the vexed Indian question than the entire regular army. They are destroying the Indians' commissary . . . for the sake of a lasting peace, let them kill, skin and sell until the buffaloes are exterminated. Then your prairies can be covered by the speckled cow and the festive cowboy.'

On September 14, in the so-called **Battle of Liberty Place**, a militia of former Confederates known as the White League that seeks to halt the 'Africanization' of New Orleans overthrows Louisiana's Republican governor. He's soon reinstated, but it's seen as a triumph for white supremacy.

The November elections give the Democrats control of the House of Representatives for the first time since the Civil War.

1875 The **Civil Rights Act** marks the final Congressional attempt to legislate Reconstruction. It guarantees blacks equal rights in theatres, restaurants and other public places, and forbids their exclusion from jury service; but its most significant proposal, compelling racial integration in schools, is stricken out. It includes no provisions for enforcement, and will in any case be declared unconstitutional by the Supreme Court in 1883.

1876 Ruling in the **Granger cases**, prompted by the Grange movement's attempts to bring railroad and grain-elevator pricing under state control, the Supreme Court establishes that state legislatures may regulate businesses where there is a public interest.

Secretary of War **William W. Belknap** resigns to avoid impeachment for selling trading posts in Indian Territory.

During a Sioux uprising triggered by white incursion into the Black Hills, George Custer and 266 men of the Seventh Cavalry die at **Little Bighorn** on June 25.

The presidential election focuses on the record of the retiring Grant. Democrat candidate **Samuel Tilden** of New York defeats Republican **Rutherford B. Hayes** of Ohio in the popular vote by 250,000 votes. However, in the electoral college Tilden has only 184 of the necessary 185 votes, with twenty votes in Oregon, Florida, South

John D. Rockefeller (1839–1937)

John D. Rockefeller – whose father, a snake-oil salesman, cheated his sons to 'make 'em smart' – was a Cleveland grain trader when associates sent him to Pennsylvania in 1862 to investigate recent **oil** discoveries. Despite reporting there was 'no future' in sinking more wells, he began to invest his own money in **refining**.

Just one of thirty Cleveland refineries in 1869, Rockefeller's **Standard Oil Company** secretly bought up its rivals and kept them operating as though still independent. Soon he secured secret bulk discounts from the **railroads**, and even 'fined' them for carrying oil for competitors. He then became the world's first **billionaire** by following a strategy of vertical integration; under the motto 'pay nobody a profit', he dominated every stage of the oil industry.

Though by 1879 Standard Oil controlled ninety percent of US oil production, Rockefeller's ambition led him in 1882 to establish the **Standard Oil Trust**. This first **trust** ingeniously twisted an ancient legal institution to enable companies to own property and operate in multiple states. The fact that few of Rockefeller's activities to ensure his monopoly were actually illegal was simply because no one had yet devised laws to prevent them. His ruthlessness and skulduggery, as revealed in court cases and legislative hearings, appalled public opinion. In 1886, a Senate committee reported that Standard Oil 'fitly represents the acme and perfection of corporate greed in its fullest development'. The company became known as 'the **Anaconda**', while Rockefeller was the definitive '**Robber Baron**'.

After Ohio's Supreme Court dissolved the Standard Oil Trust in 1892, Rockefeller's lawyers came up with the '**holding company**' instead, and business continued as before. Rockefeller himself retired in 1897, and spent forty years giving away $500 million. It did little to improve popular perception; as Theodore Roosevelt put it, 'No amount of charity in spending such fortunes in any way compensates for misconduct in making them.'

Carolina and Louisiana remaining in dispute. After rival boards send different returns for the three Southern states, Congress appoints an Electoral Commission.

Colorado becomes a state.

Nineteeen members of the **Molly Maguires** – an Irish secret society that has organized strikes in the coalfields of Pennsylvania – are hanged for the murder of a mine boss.

Alexander Graham Bell patents and demonstrates the **telephone**.

Eight **baseball** teams, including the very first, the Cincinnati Red Stockings, form the National League of Professional Baseball Leagues.

Mark Twain captures the vernacular of the frontier in his novel *The Adventures of Tom Sawyer* – the first book to be written on a typewriter.

1877 Deciding the **contested presidential election**, the Electoral Commission votes on party lines, and awards the presidency to the Democrat **Hayes** on March 2, 1877. In a behind-the-scenes deal, the Republicans agree to withdraw federal troops from Louisiana and South Carolina and allow their Republican governments to fall, and Hayes promises to restrict himself to one term. Neither Republicans nor Democrats emerge from the debacle with much credit, as both show themselves as open to bribery and corruption.

Wage cuts precipitate the nationwide **Great Railroad Strike**. After federal troops kill 25 protesters in Pittsburgh on July 19, a mob destroys a large swathe of the city, and alienates public opinion.

The **Bland–Allison Act**, supported by farmers and producers who favour **silver coinage**, passes over President Hayes' veto, authorizing the Treasury to purchase $2–4 million of silver per month.

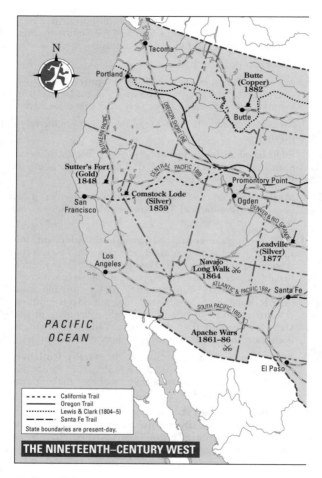

N

Tacoma

Portland

Butte
(Copper)
1882

Butte

OREGON SHORT LINE

SOUTHERN PACIFIC

CENTRAL PACIFIC 1869

Sutter's Fort
(Gold)
1848

Comstock Lode
(Silver)
1859

Promontory Point

Ogden

San
Francisco

DENVER & RIO GRANDE

Los Angeles

Navajo
Long Walk
1864

Leadville
(Silver)
1877

ATLANTIC & PACIFIC 1884

Santa Fe

SOUTH PACIFIC 1882

PACIFIC
OCEAN

Apache Wars
1861-86

El Paso

- - - - - California Trail
——— Oregon Trail
· · · · · · Lewis & Clark (1804–5)
— · — Santa Fe Trail

State boundaries are present-day.

THE NINETEENTH–CENTURY WEST

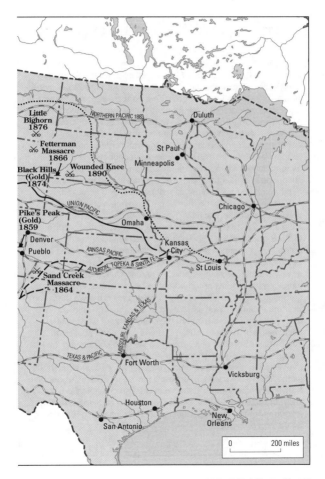

General Custer and the Battle of the Little Bighorn

Early in 1876, the visionary **Sitting Bull** inspired the **Sioux** and **Cheyenne** to resist the incursion of miners into the Sioux-owned **Black Hills**. Massive army detachments were sent to Montana in response, including the flamboyant Lieutenant Colonel **George Armstrong Custer** at the head of the crack **Seventh Cavalry**.

Few US soldiers have achieved the fame or opprobrium of the self-mythologizing Custer. During an erratic career, he graduated last at West Point in 1861; became the youngest-ever brigadier general, after a triumph at Brandy Station, Virginia, in 1863; was suspended for executing deserters from a forced march that he led through Kansas in order to visit his wife; and achieved notoriety for allowing the murder of Cheyenne women and children beside the Washita River in 1868.

On June 25, 1876, Custer's was the first unit to arrive in the **Little Bighorn Valley**. Disdaining to await reinforcements, he set out to raze a riverside tepee village, dividing his 600-strong command to form a three-pronged attack. Unaware that his advance flanks had been forced to retreat, Custer charged headlong towards what turned out to be the largest-ever gathering of Plains Indians, only to be encircled by two thousand warriors emerging from either side of a ravine. The soldiers dismounted and tried to shoot their way out, but were swiftly overwhelmed; simultaneously, Custer's command post on a nearby hill was wiped out. Archeologists have discounted the notion of **Custer's Last Stand** as a heroic defiance, with Custer the last cavalryman left standing; the battle lasted under an hour, as the 266 soldiers were effortlessly picked off. The most decisive Native American victory in the West was also their final great show of defiance. An incensed President Grant piled maximum resources into a campaign that crushed Plains Indian resistance by the end of the decade.

George Custer, photographed during the Civil War by Matthew Brady

After Chief Joseph is ordered to deliver his people onto an Idaho reservation within thirty days, the **Nez Percé** make a break for Canada, where they hope to rendezvous with Sitting Bull. A 1700-mile chase ends when they are forced to surrender at Snake Creek, Montana, in October, and dispatched to Oklahoma.

Thomas Alva Edison invents the phonograph.

1878 New Mexico's Lincoln County War brings **Billy the Kid** to prominence (see p.204).

1879 In January, for the first time since 1861, it becomes possible to exchange **greenbacks** – paper dollars – for **gold**. Almost no one does so, however, thanks in part to sales of the bumper 1878 wheat crop for gold in Europe.

Former slaves despairing of Reconstruction in the South are now migrating west in increasing numbers; more than six thousand such **Exodusters** reach Kansas in 1879 alone.

George B. Selden, of Rochester, New York, applies for a patent for a two-horsepower 'gasoline carriage'; he will deliberately delay being *granted* the patent until 1895, so his seventeen-year right to claim royalties on all such 'road engines' will not come into force until they are actually being produced. Meanwhile, after endless experiments, Edison invents a workable **electric light**, using carbonized bamboo as a filament.

F. W. Woolworth opens his first 'Five and Ten Cent Store' in Utica, New York.

1880 The Republicans split into two ill-defined groups – the **Half-Breeds**, who support the vaguely reformist Senator James Blaine of Maine, and the **Stalwarts**, who back Senator Roscoe Conkling of New York, and favour Radical policies in the South and maintaining the 'spoils system' under which the president has extensive rights to appoint federal office-holders. The Stalwarts almost succeed in

Billie the Kid, a copy from a very old tin-type.

William Bonney, aka Billy the Kid

The Western Civil War of Incorporation

The popular image of the West as being 'won' by rugged, self-reliant individualism dovetails with Frederick Jackson Turner's thesis of the frontier as shaped by individual enterprise, and in turn shaping the rest of the nation. Many historians, however, speak of a **Western Civil War of Incorporation**, in which large, Republican-affiliated mining and cattle-raising concerns, backed by eastern corporations and the federal government, wrested control of the land from Democratic ranchers, prospectors and cowboys – and from its previous Indian or Hispanic inhabitants. By this reckoning, the famed gunslingers were simply pawns.

Thus the Republican mine-owners of **Tombstone**, seeking to boost investment by ending Arizona's frontier anarchy, hired **Virgil Earp** as marshal, and his brothers **Wyatt** and **Morgan** as deputies. Their opponents in the 1881 **Gunfight at the OK Corral**, the Clanton gang, were freebooting cattle rustlers aligned with the Democrat county sheriff. Typically, both factions were family-based; it was hard for individuals to prosper alone in the West, but equally hard to find trustworthy partners. After three Clantons were killed, the *Tombstone Epitaph* reported: 'the feeling among our best citizens is that the Marshal was entirely justifiable'.

Similarly, New Mexico's 1878 **Lincoln County War** centred on a feud between a Republican-backed store managed by James Dolan, and Englishman John Tunstall's rival store. After Dolan's men murdered Tunstall, Tunstall's **Regulators** – including **Billy the Kid** – were deputized to find his killers. As well as the two culprits, they gunned down Sheriff Brady, a Dolan man. Several Regulators died in an ensuing siege by federal troops. New Mexico's Republican Governor **Lew Wallace** (the author of *Ben Hur*) promised amnesty to anyone testifying against Dolan, but kept Billy in jail when he surrendered. Billy escaped to become a full-time rustler, whereupon Republican cattlemen put up the money to hunt him down. An election in which Billy naturally lobbied for the Democrats installed a new Republican sheriff, **Pat Garrett**, who shot the Kid on July 14, 1881.

nominating Grant for the presidency again, but the Republican convention opts for a compromise candidate, **James A. Garfield**. He wins a narrow plurality, but a wider electoral margin, over Democrat **Winfield Scott Hancock**.

1881 On July 2, four months after taking office, **President Garfield is shot** in Baltimore by a disappointed office seeker, Charles Guiteau. He dies from blood poisoning in September, and is succeeded by his Stalwart vice president, **Chester A. Arthur**. However, Guiteau's boast that 'I am a Stalwart' obliges Arthur to distance himself from his erstwhile allies.

By requiring railroads to maintain separate first-class carriages for blacks and whites, Tennessee introduces the first of the **Jim Crow** laws – the name comes from an 1830s' minstrel song – that swiftly institutionalize **racial segregation** throughout the South.

Black leader **Booker T. Washington** founds the Tuskegee Institute for Negroes in Alabama.

In **Tombstone**, Arizona, on October 26, the Earp brothers and 'Doc' Holliday kill three men in the **Gunfight at the OK Corral** (see opposite).

1882 Chinese labourers have been attracting resentment from white settlers in California, partly because they have been used as strike breakers, and paid such minimal wages as to approximate a reintroduction of slavery. Now they are no longer needed for railroad construction, the **Chinese Exclusion Act** in May suspends Chinese immigration for ten years; it will be extended in 1892, and made permanent in 1902.

On September 4, the **Edison Illuminating Company** uses electricity to light up lower Manhattan. That same day, outlaw and former Confederate guerrilla **Jesse James** is shot in St Joseph, Missouri.

Having long searched to find a legal way to form a 'corporation of corporations', **John D. Rockefeller** secretly establishes the **Standard Oil Trust** (see p.196).

Huge deposits of **copper** are discovered in Butte, **Montana**, in what becomes the Anaconda Mine.

1883 Thanks to Garfield's assassination, and the support of President Arthur, **civil service reform** has become a national priority. January's **Pendleton Act** introduces competitive examinations for prospective federal employees and forbids the solicitation of campaign contributions from them.

The second transcontinental railroad, the **Northern Pacific**, is completed in September. Responding to the need to co-ordinate railroad timetables, the **General Time Convention** establishes four separate time zones in the US from November 18.

Hailed as an engineering marvel, the **Brooklyn Bridge** connects Brooklyn with Manhattan, while a **telephone** service links New York and Chicago. Construction starts on the first true **skyscraper**, Chicago's Home Insurance Building.

Joseph Pulitzer takes over New York's *World*; under his sensationalist direction, it swiftly becomes the nation's first mass-circulation daily **newspaper**.

Buffalo Bill Cody stages his first **Wild West** show; featured artists will include Sitting Bull and Annie Oakley.

1884 Dropping President Arthur, the Republican Party instead nominates **James Blaine**, but then splits when he is tainted by corruption charges. Republican reformists, known as **Mugwumps**, lend their support to the Democrat **Grover Cleveland**, a former mayor of Buffalo who calls himself 'ugly honest', and he's elected with 219 electoral votes to Blaine's 182.

Artist **Winslow Homer** makes his home in Prout's Neck, Maine, to devote himself to painting landscapes.

Mark Twain publishes his masterpiece, *The Adventures of Huckleberry Finn.*

1885 February's **Contract Labor** law prohibits employers to bring contract labourers – regularly used as strike breakers – as immigrants to the United States.

When Union Pacific attempts to replace white miners with lower-paid Chinese labourers, a mob burns the Chinese quarter of **Rock Springs**, Wyoming, killing between 25 and 50 Chinese.

1886 The **Knights of Labor** organize strikes against Jay Gould's Missouri–Pacific railroad system, which expand to include national strikes and demonstrations calling for an eight-hour day. On May 3, police fire into a crowd at the McCormick Harvester Works in Chicago, killing four strikers. The next day, the Black International **anarchist** group calls a protest meeting in Chicago's **Haymarket Square**. As a police riot squad attempts to break it up, a bomb kills six policemen; the police open fire and kill several demonstrators. Eight anarchists, only three of whom were present in Haymarket Square, are convicted of conspiracy to murder, and four hanged in 1887.

The Knights fall from mass favour, tarnished by their association with the 'Haymarket Affair', and also because their desire to unite skilled and unskilled workers is unpopular with specialist crafts workers. They're soon supplanted by a looser grouping of autonomous unions, the **American Federation of Labor**, which forms under the leadership of Samuel Gompers in December.

Geronimo, chief of the Chiricahua Apache, surrenders in Arizona (see overleaf).

Geronimo and the Apache War

The **Apache War** broke out in southeast Arizona in 1861, when **Cochise**, chief of the thousand-strong **Chiricahua** group, was falsely accused of kidnapping a child. After his brother and nephews were hanged, Cochise rampaged across Arizona, killing prospectors, stagecoach passengers and soldiers. When US forces were withdrawn to fight the Civil War, he imagined he had driven them out forever.

Within a year, the army was back. Adopting the new strategy of 'total war', **General George Crook** rounded the Apache onto a reservation in a ten-year campaign that claimed a hundred Apache, a thousand Americans, and cost $38 million. In 1877, however, five hundred warriors under **Victorio** fled reservation life, killing another thousand Anglos before they were wiped out in Mexico in 1880.

During the 1880s, **Geronimo**, a medicine man who grew to adulthood without ever seeing a white American, repeatedly burst out of the reservation and went on the warpath, his band of followers dwindling each time. In 1883, he captured Crook in Mexico's Sierra Madre, then surrendered to him instead. Geronimo fled again in 1885, and surrendered to Crook once more in 1886, only to get drunk and escape yet again. His ensuing five-month guerrilla campaign pitted 37 Apache, including just eighteen warriors, against 5000 soldiers, a quarter of the entire US Army. **General Nelson Miles** eventually managed to contact Geronimo in Mexico, and claimed that all remaining Chiricahua had been shipped to Florida. In despair, Geronimo surrendered for the fourth and final time in Skeleton Canyon, Arizona, on September 3, 1886.

The general's lie now became the truth. Geronimo and five hundred Chiricahua – along with the army's own Apache scouts – were indeed despatched to Florida. Geronimo never returned to the Southwest. Like many Indian leaders, however, once tamed he was lionized; among many public appearances, he rode at the head of Theodore Roosevelt's inaugural procession in 1905. He died in 1909.

Geronimo, war leader of the Chiricahua Apache, born in New Mexico c.1823 and originally named Goyahkla, 'One Who Yawns'

The **Statue of Liberty**, a centenary gift from the French Republic, is inaugurated in New York Harbor on October 28.

Atlanta pharmacist John Styth Permberton stirs up a new hangover tonic, **Coca Cola**; in 1887, he'll sell a two-thirds stake in his company for $283.29.

1887 In February, the **Interstate Commerce Act** regulates inter-company price-fixing on the railroads, though the commission set up to enforce it will be frustrated by the courts until 1903.

February's **Dawes Severalty Act** attempts to break up Indian tribes by turning them into individual farmers, stating that the president can end communal land ownership by giving the head of each family 160 acres. All such lands will be held in trust by the government for 25 years, after which the owner will receive full title and US citizenship. As speculators will ultimately buy up much of what is allocated, and lands not distributed are in any case sold to others, this will have a catastrophic effect on Indian landholdings.

A tremendous blizzard sweeps the western plains, from the Dakotas to Texas, in January, with temperatures dropping to -68°. Thousands of cattle die in this **Great Freeze**, which ends the era of the open range by convincing ranchers to erect fences. When the winter is followed by the harshest summer since the plains have been extensively farmed, many settlers despair that agriculture will ever take hold. Thousands of western farms are abandoned altogether, as their owners migrate beyond the Rockies.

1888 The presidential election focuses on tariff reform. President Cleveland, advocating tariff reduction and free trade, wins a popular majority against Republican **Benjamin Harrison**, but Harrison triumphs in the electoral college.

The result is largely decided by manoeuvring in New York, where thanks partly to Republican bribes, and also to an anti-Prohibition coalition, Tammany Hall Democrats defect to Harrison.

The first electric **street trolley** system is constructed and opened in Richmond, Virginia.

George Eastman of Rochester, who has in 1884 patented the first photographic 'film', registers the trademark **Kodak**, and starts selling his black-box 'detective camera'. Meanwhile, Thomas Edison patents his **Kinetoscope**; when Eastman introduces celluloid film in 1889, Edison will seize on it to pioneer motion pictures.

1889 In January, Congress forces the Creek and Seminole of the **Indian Territory** to renounce their land claims for $4.19 million, and on March 23 President Harrison announces that **Oklahoma** district – a subsection of the territory smaller than the modern state – will open for settlement in a month. On April 22, prospective settlers, known as **boomers**, wait on the border until a trumpeter blows the signal for them to rush in. To obtain land, they only have to stake a claim, pay a small fee, and cultivate it for five years. By the evening, **Guthrie** holds 15,000 inhabitants, and **Oklahoma City** over 10,000.

The **Johnstown Flood** kills 2200 people, after a dam bursts on Pennsylvania's Conemaugh River on May 31.

North and **South Dakota**, **Washington** and **Montana** are admitted as states; all are expected to vote Republican, and to support silver.

The Otis Elevator Company installs its first **electric elevator**, which will greatly facilitate the emergence of skyscrapers.

The Ghost Dance and Wounded Knee

The **Ghost Dance** of **1890** belonged to a long tradition of messianic Indian cults. The visionary responsible this time was **Wovoka**, a Nevada Paiute, who preached that if a tribe put aside warlike things and danced for five days, then come next spring – 1891 – both living and dead would be reunited on a regenerated and abundant earth. The whites would vanish, and the buffalo return. Although Wovoka never left his native valley, delegations from other tribes crossed the Rockies to visit him, and his message spread like wildfire across two-thirds of the United States. Many dancers experienced similar visions, and came to believe that the Ghost Dance shirts they wore could ward off bullets.

Frontier whites, however, imagined these fundamentally peaceful ceremonies to be war dances, and feared that a massive Indian uprising was about to take place. The order went out that the Ghost Dance must stop. Although the Hunkpapa Sioux chief, **Sitting Bull**, was not involved, the anxious agent at the Standing Rock reservation had him arrested, and he died in a scuffle on December 15. Many Sioux fled, to seek refuge on the Pine Ridge reservation. The agent there cabled that 'Indians are dancing in the snow and are wild and crazy . . . we need protection and we need it now'.

On December 29, the Seventh Cavalry surrounded the Sioux at **Wounded Knee**, and ordered them to surrender their weapons. A deaf Indian, not understanding what was going on, raised his gun above his head, and accidentally fired a shot. The soldiers panicked, and opened fire with four Hotchkiss machine guns. As a blizzard descended, three hundred Sioux men, women and children lay dead in the snow. Though Wovoka himself lived on until 1932, Wounded Knee is widely regarded as the final death knell for Indian resistance.

1890 Mississippi adopts a new constitution, imposing litera-cy tests that will reduce its black voters from 190,000 to 8000 within two years. In the face of federal inaction, other states will soon follow suit.

In February, the Supreme Court unexpectedly reverses its earlier Granger rulings by declaring that a state cannot set railroad fees at a level that would deny a 'reasonable profit', because a railroad corporation counts as a 'person' and is thus protected by the Fourteenth Amendment. In July, the **Sherman Anti-Trust Act** attacks monopoly by outlawing 'every contract, combination in the form of trust or other-wise, or conspiracy in restraint of trade or commerce among the several states or with foreign nations', but little attempt will be made to enforce it during the coming decade.

Two more Republican, silver-supporting states, **Wyoming** and **Idaho**, join the Union, and **Oklahoma** becomes a territory.

With the support of the new states, and in return for pass-ing the high **McKinley Tariff**, Congress promotes silver coinage with the **Sherman Silver Purchase Act**, requir-ing the Treasury to buy 4.5 million ounces of silver per month.

Three hundred Sioux, who by taking up the **Ghost Dance** have alarmed the federal authorities, are massacred at **Wounded Knee**, South Dakota, on December 29.

The poetry of **Emily Dickinson**, of Amherst, Massachu-setts, known only to a small circle of intimates until her death in 1886, is published for the first time.

New Orleans police superintendent **David Hennessy** is assassinated after declaring that the city is home to Sicilian criminal gangs. Eleven Italian suspects are lynched, and a grand jury confirms 'the existence of the secret organiza-tion styled **Mafia**'.

The Bureau of the Census announces that the **frontier** is officially closed. In 1893, historian **Frederick Jackson Turner**, in *The Significance of the Frontier in American History*, will argue that 'the existence of an area of free land, its continuous recession, and the advance of American settlement westward, explain American development'. His

The Reliance Building, erected during the early 1890s, was one of Chicago's first skyscrapers

> **"** Up to and including 1880 the country had a frontier of settlement, but at present the unsettled area has been so broken into by isolated bodies of settlement that there can hardly be said to be a frontier line. In the discussion of its extent, westward movement etc., it can not, therefore, any longer have a place in the census reports. **"**
>
> Bureau of the Census report, 1890

theory that the frontier fostered the individualism, practicality, earthiness and attachment to democracy that characterize the New World, and that 'never again can such an opportunity come to the sons of men', will be hotly debated a century later.

1891 Dr James Naismith invents **basketball** in the YMCA at Springfield, Massachusetts.

1892 In June, the Amalgamated Association of Iron, Steel and Tin Workers calls a **strike** over wage scales at the **Homestead Plant** of the Carnegie Steel Company, outside Pittsburgh. Company president H. C. Frick calls in three hundred detectives from the Pinkerton agency as strike breakers. After seven workers and three Pinkertons die in a pitched gun battle, state militia are used to protect more strike breakers. Frick is subsequently shot but not killed by an anarchist. This violence alienates public support; the strike collapses and the union dissolves.

The **Populist or People's Party** organizes in St Louis in February, amalgamating smaller farmers' alliances that have been forming for a decade. In July, it nominates **James B. Weaver** for the presidency, advocating the nationalization of railroads, telephones and telegraph; a graduated income tax; and the free coinage of silver. Weaver eventually wins four states, and 22 electoral votes. The major parties nominate the same candidates as in 1888, but the result is reversed. With opposition to Harrison's McKinley Tariff as the central issue, **Grover Cleveland** is elected president once again.

Ellis Island in New York Harbor opens as a federal immigration depot. In the 62 years before it closes in 1954, twelve million immigrants will pass through.

White mobs **lynch** 161 blacks in the South. After three black grocers are murdered over a business rivalry in Memphis, Tennessee, former slave **Ida B. Wells** denounces lynching in the *Free Speech* newspaper with such vehemence that she's forced to flee to New York.

The General Edison Electric Company merges with its greatest rival, Thomson-Houston, to form **General Electric**.

1893 Immediately before President Cleveland takes office, the Philadelphia and Reading Railroad fails. In the ensuing **Panic of 1893**, a quarter of the overextended railroad system follows suit, including the Northern Pacific, Union Pacific and Santa Fe. Wall Street panics, over 150 banks collapse in the South and West, and the country's largest **depression** yet throws millions out of work. Deciding that the essential remedy is to return to the **gold standard**, Cleveland pushes through the repeal of the Sherman Silver Purchase Act in October, despite strong Congressional opposition.

The World's Columbian Exposition in Chicago, better known as the **World Fair**, inspires interest in urban landscape and architecture, and stimulates the 'city beautiful' movement.

Czech emigré **Antonín Dvořák**, the director of the National Conservatory of Music, conducts the premiere of

The annexation of Hawaii

For a century after Captain Cook reached **Hawaii** in 1778, the islands struggled to remain independent. The British, French, Russians and Americans competed for influence and control, with the great prize being Honolulu, the finest deep-water harbour in the Pacific.

During the US Civil War, the North's need for a new source of **sugar** caused sugar plantations to spread across Hawaii. The eagerness of their American owners to secure favourable prices in the US thereafter moved the islands inexorably towards **annexation**. In 1887 an armed group of 'concerned businessmen' forced through the 'Bayonet Constitution', and **King Kalakaua** surrendered power to an assembly elected by property owners (of any nationality) rather than citizens. This swiftly granted exclusive rights to **Pearl Harbor** to the US.

In 1891, Kalakaua's successor **Queen Liliʻuokalani** proclaimed her desire for a new constitution. The same businessmen, now calling themselves the '**Annexation Club**', called in the US warship *Boston*, and declared a provisional government. President Cleveland was furious: 'As I look back upon . . . this miserable business . . . I am ashamed of the whole affair . . . Hawaii was taken possession of by the United States forces without the consent or wish of the government of the islands. . . . not merely wrong but a disgrace.' With phenomenal cheek, the provisional government rejected his demand for the restoration of the monarchy, saying the US should not 'interfere in the internal affairs of their sovereign nation', and declared themselves a **republic** on July 4, 1894.

In 1897 the new Republican President McKinley announced 'annexation is not a change. It is a consummation.' With the strategic value of Pearl Harbor emphasized by the war in the Philippines, Hawaii was formally **annexed** as a US territory on August 12, 1898.

his 9th symphony, *From the New World*, at Carnegie Hall on December 15.

1894 Railroad workers in the company town of **Pullman**, Illinois, strike in May after the Pullman Company cuts jobs and wages but not rents. As many belong to **Eugene V. Debs'** new **American Railway Union**, the strike spreads throughout the railroads of the Midwest. In July, the Attorney General wins an injunction to stop the union obstructing the mails or damaging railroad property, on the basis that the strike violates the Sherman Anti-Trust Act, and President Cleveland sends in troops. The strike collapses, and Debs is jailed for six months for ignoring the injunction, which turns him into a folk hero. However, court rulings on the Debs case in 1895 and 1897 will decide that the Sherman Anti-Trust Act applies to labour combinations – a considerable victory for capital.

Cleveland wants to lower tariffs, but the **Wilson–Gorman Tariff Act**, raising them, passes despite his veto. It includes a provision for a two percent **income tax** on incomes above $4000.

1895 In May, the Supreme Court rules that the income tax is unconstitutional, because as a direct tax it should be apportioned among the states according to population.

> ❝ Cast down your bucket where you are – cast it down in making friends . . . of the people of all races by whom we are surrounded . . . In all things that are purely social we can be as separate as the five fingers, yet one as the hand in all things essential to mutual progress. ❞
>
> Booker T. Washington, speaking in Atlanta on September 18, 1895

Speaking in Atlanta on September 18, **Booker T. Washington** puts forward what becomes known as the **Atlanta Compromise**, suggesting that blacks in the South should concentrate on economic co-operation rather than political conflict. Washington will remain America's most influential black leader until his death in 1915.

1896 Ruling in **Plessy v Ferguson**, brought by a New Orleans Creole barred from riding in an all-white streetcar, the Supreme Court asserts that 'if one race be inferior to the other socially, the Constitution cannot put them upon the same plane'. This doctrine of **'separate but equal'** provision for whites and blacks gives Southern states carte blanche to establish a system of **racial segregation** that will endure until 1954.

The presidential election focuses on the currency issue. **William Jennings Bryan** is nominated by the Democratic convention in Chicago after a rip-roaring speech in support of **silver** that culminates with 'You shall not press down upon the brow of labour a crown of thorns, you shall not crucify mankind upon a **cross of gold**.' Rather than split the silver vote, the Populists back him, effectively dooming their party to oblivion. Republican **William McKinley** favours the gold standard, and receives heavy financial backing from big business. Bryan sweeps the South and West, but McKinley carries major cities and the entire Northeast, winning the popular vote by 7.1 million to 6.5 million and the electoral college by 271 to 176.

Utah finally becomes a state – Congress has consistently refused to admit it to the Union until the Mormon Church renounced **polygamy** in 1890 (see p.139).

Gold deposits are discovered along the **Klondike River** in Alaska, triggering another **Gold Rush**.

Black composer **Scott Joplin** from Texas, a pioneer of polyrhythmic 'syncopation' on the piano, writes the *Maple*

Leaf Rag, which will make his reputation as the 'King of **Ragtime**'.

1897 With McKinley as president, the economy begins to recover, helped by increased world production of gold, and growing demand for American agricultural produce.

In a crucial moment for the emergence of **jazz**, New Orleans cornet player **Buddy Bolden** founds his own band.

1898 Pressure has been growing in **Cuba** for independence from Spain. Spanish repression has won Cuban guerrilla fighters support from the American 'yellow press' – notably from **William Randolph Hearst**'s *Journal* in New York – and President McKinley is an avowed supporter of independence. On February 15, the US battleship *Maine*, during what's ostensibly a courtesy visit, **explodes** in Havana harbour, killing 260 American sailors. Modern historians generally see this as an accident, but it's widely reported as a Spanish attack. McKinley attempts to avoid war, and the Spanish seem ready to capitulate, but US popular opinion is adamant, and the **Spanish–American War** is declared on April 25.

On May 1, the US Navy launches a surprise attack in the **Philippines**, and Admiral George Dewey defeats the Spanish fleet in **Manila Bay**. He now waits for land reinforcements to arrive, and the navy also blockades Cuba.

A 17,000-strong American army **invades Cuba** in June. **Theodore Roosevelt**, who calls the sinking of the *Maine* 'an act of dirty treachery', has resigned as Assistant Secretary of the Navy and is second in command of the First Volunteer Cavalry, known as the **Rough Riders**. Americans overwhelm the outnumbered Spaniards outside Santiago on July 1, when Roosevelt leads a bloody but successful charge up **San Juan Hill**. Two days later, the Spanish fleet is destroyed as it attempts to leave Manila, and Santiago surrenders on July 17.

The Spanish sue for peace, and terms are agreed on August 12, although US troops have now reached the Philippines, and capture Manila on August 13. Under December's **Treaty of Paris**, **Cuba** is promised its **independence**, though for the moment the US installs a military government, while in addition to handing over the **Philippines** to the US in return for $20 million, Spain cedes **Puerto Rico** and **Guam**, which have been occupied during the summer.

On the strength of his exploits, **Theodore Roosevelt** is elected Republican governor of New York in November.

1899 What to do with the **Philippines** tops the political agenda. Neither McKinley nor anyone else has previously advanced any US claim to the islands, but now the president – along with imperialists such as Senator Beveridge, who exults 'the Philippines are ours forever' – is reluctant to give them up again. The US is soon at war with independence-seeking **Filipino insurgents** under **Emilio Aguinaldo**, originally brought back to the islands by Admiral Dewey to goad the Spanish.

In September, Secretary of State John Hay announces what becomes known as the **Open Door Policy**. In notes to major world governments, he suggests that **China**, which following war with Japan has been divided into 'spheres of influence', should remain open to trade with all countries on an equal basis. Despite little response, Hay then announces the arrangement has been agreed.

1900 After **Boxer** rebels lay siege to foreign embassies in **Peking**, the US participates in an international force sent to relieve the city, and reasserts the Open Door Policy.

The same two candidates as in 1896 contest the presidential election, though to his free-silver platform Bryan now adds an outspoken opposition to the imperialist adventure in the Philippines. **McKinley** is comfortably **re-elected**, this time with **Theodore Roosevelt** as his vice president.

> **"** We have done our best. We have scratched our heads to find out how we could eliminate the last one of them. We stuffed ballot boxes. We shot them. We are not ashamed of it. **"**
>
> Senator Ben "Pitchfork" Tillman of South Carolina boasts to the Senate in 1900 of Southern success in disenfranchising blacks after the collapse of Reconstruction.

The national **census** records a total population of **76 million**. Just eighteen of those live in **Las Vegas**, Nevada.

1901 Despite widespread anticipation that the US will annex **Cuba**, the island achieves independence – on condition that it will make no treaties with foreign powers that affect its independence; the US can intervene to protect that independence; and the US can buy or lease land for naval stations. This will lead to the opening of the US naval base at **Guantanamo Bay**, still in use a century later.

The **Filipino Revolt** is effectively ended when Aguinaldo is captured and persuaded to swear loyalty to the US. Federal judge **William Howard Taft** becomes civilian governor of the Philippines.

The **Supreme Court** recognizes the new imperial reality by ruling that territories can be subject to jurisdiction without being incorporated into the US, and that the Constitution does not apply in its entirety to all lands over which sovereignty is exercised.

Andrew Carnegie, John D. Rockefeller and J. P. Morgan combine forces to end competition in the steel industry, by chartering the **United States Steel Corporation**, the first billion-dollar corporation, on April 1. A battle between Morgan and **Edward Harriman** for control of rival railroads then causes a stock market panic on May 9, 'Blue Thursday'.

On September 6, while visiting the Pan American Exhibition in Buffalo, President **McKinley is shot** by the anarchist Leon Czolgosz. His death on September 14 makes the 42-year-old **Theodore Roosevelt** the youngest-ever president.

Booker T. Washington dines at the White House on October 16, for the first and only time. Senator Benjamin Tillman of South Carolina declares: 'The action of President Roosevelt in entertaining that nigger will necessitate our killing a thousand niggers in the South before they will learn their place again.'

CORBIS

Theodore Roosevelt, photographed after he relinquished the presidency in 1908

Theodore Roosevelt (1858–1919)

Theodore Roosevelt became America's youngest-ever president at the start of the twentieth century. Bursting with vitality and enthusiasm, he was actually 42, though one friend observed 'you must always remember that the President is about six'. Born in New York, he blended North and South – his mother was a Georgia belle – East and West.

The young Roosevelt gloried in Manifest Destiny, exalting 'the rude, fierce settler who drives the savage from the land'. Devastated by a double tragedy in 1884, when his mother and his wife died separately within eleven hours, he briefly reinvented himself as a Dakota rancher. His embrace of American 'expansionism' followed hard on the realization that the frontier era at home had ended. The **Spanish–American War** brought him to prominence. As Assistant Secretary of the Navy, he engineered the conquest of the Philippines, before personally leading the charge up San Juan Hill that secured victory in Cuba. President McKinley's previous vice president having died, Roosevelt joined his ticket in 1900, only for McKinley's assassination to make him president.

As president, he cut a less bellicose figure, positing himself as the natural arbiter of both national and international disputes – he even won the Nobel Peace Prize for ending the Russo-Japanese war. Thus he summoned owners and labour leaders to the White House during the 1902 anthracite strike, and railed against both the 'law-defying wealth' of the Robber Barons and the 'vindictive and dreadful radicalism' of their 'socialistic' opponents. H. G. Wells' comment that Roosevelt possessed **'receptivity to the point of genius'** testifies to a very modern-sounding ability – shades of Bill Clinton – both to tune into, and to shape, public opinion. Even with his grasp on popular affection, however, he could not beat the Republican machine to secure re-election in 1912, after he'd fallen out with his chosen successor President Taft.

Under the **Hay–Pauncefote Treaty**, on November 18, the British agree to America's right to build, maintain and police a **canal** across Central America. Two days later, the Isthmian Canal Commission recommends it be constructed in Nicaragua, but allows the possibility that **Panama**, currently a region of Colombia, might offer a better route.

A 'gusher' of oil is struck at **Spindletop**, Texas; among those who prosper in the ensuing boom is the father of reclusive billionaire **Howard Hughes**.

1902 In May, in the greatest labour stoppage yet seen, 147,000 Pennsylvania **anthracite miners strike** for higher wages and recognition of the United Mine Workers. After Roosevelt threatens the owners that he will take over the mines and use troops to run them, they accept arbitration, and miners resume work in October. The eventual settlement in 1903 will improve wages by ten rather than twenty percent, while union recognition will not be achieved until 1916.

On June 17, the National Reclamation Act becomes law, creating the **Bureau of Reclamation**, whose schemes to irrigate the West will ultimately include the **Hoover Dam** and the **Glen Canyon Dam**.

While hunting in Mississippi in November, Roosevelt declines to shoot a captured bear. Although someone else kills it with a knife, this act of 'mercy' is widely publicized, and soon toy bears are being sold using the president's nickname – **Teddy bears**.

1903 In January, under the **Hay–Herrán** treaty, Colombia agrees to grant the US a 100-year lease to a ten-mile-wide strip of Panama for $10 million plus $250,000 per year. When the Colombian senate later holds out for more money, Roosevelt loses his patience. An uprising is engineered in Panama on November 3, with a US gunboat stationed offshore to prevent Colombian reinforcements from landing. **Panama declares its independence** on November 4, and the US recognizes it on November 6. On November 13, a Panamanian ambassador reaches Washington, DC, where he signs the **Panama Canal Treaty**, granting the US a canal zone in perpetuity, on the same terms as before.

Wisconsin is the first state to adopt **direct primary elections**; by 1948 all states will do so.

Waiting for a train at Tutwiler, Mississippi, orchestra leader W. C. Handy hears a ragged black man play 'the weirdest music I had ever heard' on a guitar – the first recorded mention of the **blues**.

On December 17, Wilbur and Orville Wright make the **first powered flight** at Kitty Hawk, North Carolina.

Jack London, whose rugged frontier tales and identification with ordinary working-class lives will soon make him the world's best-selling author, publishes *Call of the Wild*.

1904 After the Senate ratifies the Panama Canal Treaty, Roosevelt authorizes $40 million to buy out French rights in the scheme. With the largest-ever real-estate deal completed, the largest-ever construction project can begin.

In February, the **Japanese** launch a surprise counterattack against **Russian** expansionism, annihilating Russia's Oriental fleet at Port Arthur.

Roosevelt comfortably wins **re-election** in November, gaining 57 percent of the popular vote to Democrat Alton B. Parker's 38 percent. By now, thanks to repressive state legislation, literacy tests, and sheer intimidation in the South, not one black man in a thousand is eligible to vote.

On December 2, spurred by threatened European intervention over the public debt in the Dominican Republic,

Roosevelt sets out the **Roosevelt Corollary** to the Monroe Doctrine. This states that the US may 'exercise an international police power' to react to 'chronic wrongdoing' by governments in the Americas, and thus forestall European intervention. The US consequently takes over customs collection in the Dominican Republic.

1905 After the Japanese destroy Russia's Baltic fleet on May 27, both sides suggest that Roosevelt mediate between them. In September, the resulting **Treaty of Portsmouth** ends the war. Meanwhile, the US secretly agrees not to interfere with Japanese ambitions in Korea so long as the Japanese do not try to conquer the Philippines.

In June, the International Workers of the World – the **Wobblies** – organize in Chicago, led by William D. 'Big Bill' Haywood. They aim to create 'One Big Union' that will ultimately take over the functions of government.

Edith Wharton depicts the stifling pressures of New York society in her novel *The House of Mirth*.

1906 On April 18, an **earthquake** devastates **San Francisco**, killing 500 people and leaving 500,000 homeless.

Roosevelt's move towards '**Progressive**' policies culminates in June. He signs the **Hepburn Act** on June 29, entitling the Interstate Commerce Commission to set maximum railroad rates. The next day, in response to Upton Sinclair's novelized account of the meat-packing industry in *The Jungle*, and other such exposés of unsavoury practices among food producers, he signs two pioneering regulatory laws: the **Meat Inspection Act** and the **Pure Food and Drug Act**.

1907 A dramatic **crash** on the New York Stock Exchange on March 14, precipitated by worldwide borrowing, is slowed by the deposit of $12 million of federal gold in New York's banks. During the summer, the market slumps again after Standard Oil is fined $29 million in an anti-rebate case. A deeper **panic** hits in October, when the Knickerbocker Trust collapses. The federal government injects another $25 million, and financier J. P. Morgan puts together a consortium to import $100 million more from Europe, but a year-long **depression** still ensues.

On December 16, Roosevelt dispatches the entire US fleet of sixteen battleships – the **Great White Fleet** – on a two-year round-the-world cruise. The idea is partly to display US naval strength in the Pacific for the first time; some anticipate the Japanese will attack it, but in fact it will be welcomed in Japan.

One million immigrants pass through Ellis Island, in its busiest year.

Oklahoma becomes the 46th state.

MEPL

Henry Ford, pictured in his first 'quadricycle'

Henry Ford (1863–1947) and the Model T

Henry Ford was working for Thomas Edison in Detroit when he tested his first 'quadricycle' in 1896. His **Ford Motor Company** sold its first **automobile** in 1903, when there were 23,000 vehicles in the whole US, each individually crafted in some small workshop. Ford hoped to 'democratize the automobile', by producing a car everyone could afford. When a friend warned that all those automobiles would frighten the horses, he replied 'when I'm through . . . the horses will have disappeared from our highways, the automobile will be taken for granted, and there won't be any problem'. Having unveiled the **Model T** in 1908, Ford announced in 1909 that he would build no other model. He soon added the immortal sales pitch 'any customer can have a car painted any color he wants so long as it is black'.

To manufacture millions of identical 'tin lizzies', Ford copied the **assembly line** from the overhead trolley used by Chicago meatpackers, and used time-and-motion specialists to break down tasks into tiny components. His primary genius was for **flow**; aiming to ensure that raw materials never stopped moving from the mine to the highway, he bought up his own mines, forests and railroads. His showpiece factory Highland Park opened in 1909, and by 1913 had perfected **mass production**. In 1918, one of every two cars in the world was a Model T.

When the Model T was finally discontinued in 1927, over fifteen million had been made, and the price had fallen from $850 to $300. With secondhand sales booming, dealers were finding it hard to persuade customers to buy a new car identical not only to their old one, but to everyone else's as well. As the chief designer at rival **General Motors** observed, 'the great problem of the future is to have our cars different from each other and different from year to year'.

1908 On May 13, Roosevelt hosts a conference including 45 state governors and the entire cabinet and Supreme Court, to consider 'Conservation as a National Duty'. Seeking to ensure 'the wise use of our natural resources', he goes on to create a **National Conservation Commission**. Ironically, perhaps, **Henry Ford** introduces the **Model T** on October 1.

Roosevelt abides by his 1904 pledge not to stand for a second elected term, a decision he will come to regret. In November, his preferred successor, the Republican **William Howard Taft** – whom at this stage he calls 'just a dear' – easily defeats the persistent William Jennings Bryan.

1909 President Taft, who has campaigned against protectionism and in favour of a lower tariff, does little to resist the passage of the **Payne–Aldrich Tariff** on April 9. It's generally regarded as a high-tariff measure, so Taft's apparent support appals many progressive Republicans. He's also seen as practising '**dollar diplomacy**', when he intervenes with the Chinese government to allow New York bankers to join British, French and German interests in financing railroad construction.

Largely in response to a horrendous lynching in Springfield, Illinois, in 1908 – which arouses fears that Southern racial oppression may spread to the rest of the country – the **National Association for the Advancement of Colored People** is founded in New York City on May 31.

1910 In January, Taft further antagonizes progressive Republicans when he dismisses **Gifford Pinchot**, the Chief of Forestry, for protesting against Secretary of the Interior Ballinger's actions in withdrawing certain Western lands from the protection they were given by Roosevelt. Progressives go on to join Congressional Democrats in cutting the powers of the **Speaker** by enlarging the Rules Committee, making it elected by the House rather than appointed by the Speaker, and excluding him from membership. Progressive Republicans do well in the autumn elections, as do the Democrats, who now control Congress. By now Roosevelt is referring to his principles as the **New Nationalism**.

The **Mann–Elkins Act** extends the powers of the Interstate Commerce Commission to regulate railroads, and also gives it jurisdiction over telegraph and telephone companies.

1911 Senator Robert La Follette of Wisconsin is the driving force in the January foundation of the **National Progressive Republican League**, which promotes such increasingly popular democratic reforms as the initiative, the referendum, the recall, and direct primaries.

Interpreting anti-trust legislation in May, the Supreme Court invokes a new '**rule of reason**' doctrine, that government should only intervene against combinations that lead to the 'unreasonable' restraint of trade, to order the dismantling of the **Standard Oil Company**, and the reorganization of the **American Tobacco Company**.

A **fire** at the **Triangle Shirtwaist Company** in New York City on May 25 kills 146 people, mostly women, who are unable to escape. The public outcry following a failure to convict the owners of responsibility will lead to a raft of reforming legislation on labour laws, factory inspections and building codes.

Architect **Frank Lloyd Wright**, who has made his name with the **Larkin Building** in Buffalo in 1904 and the Unity Temple in Oak Park, Illinois, in 1906, sets up a studio and school at **Taliesin**, Wisonsin.

1912 After La Follette collapses during a speaking tour in February, **Theodore Roosevelt** announces that he would accept the Republican nomination for president. Now calling Taft a 'hopeless fathead', he defeats him in all but two of thirteen state primaries, but cannot overcome the party machine or the president's power of patronage. The Republican convention nominates Taft in June, whereupon Roosevelt calls a Progressive Party convention for August, in which few career Republicans participate. Roosevelt declares himself 'fit as a bull moose', and is nominated for what becomes known as the **Bull Moose Party**. Meanwhile the Democrats pick New Jersey Governor and former Princeton president **Woodrow Wilson** in June.

In March, Taft alienates Progressives by refusing to lend US support to a popular uprising against the ruthless **Mexican** dictator Porfirio Díaz. When Díaz does fall, Taft warns the revolutionary government of Francisco Madero to protect life and property (43 percent of the wealth in Mexico is American-owned). In October, by contrast, US marines invade **Nicaragua** after the government asks for help suppressing insurgency, and install an American collector of customs. The US will maintain a military presence until 1925.

On April 15, **RMS *Titanic*** sinks after striking an iceberg on her maiden transatlantic voyage, drowning 1513 passengers and crew.

In November, with the Republican vote split, Roosevelt wins 27 percent of the popular vote and 88 electoral votes, and Taft 23 percent and 8 respectively. That leaves **Wilson** the overall victor, with a 42 percent popular share and 435 electoral votes.

New Mexico and **Arizona** are admitted as the last of the contiguous 'lower 48' states.

7
The Great War and the Great Depression
1913–41

President **Woodrow Wilson** came to office in 1913 expecting to carry out an agenda of sweeping domestic reforms. As he told a friend, 'It would be an irony of fate if my administration had to deal with foreign problems, for all my preparation has been in domestic matters.' In the event, the **Great War** broke out the following year. Wilson managed to delay US involvement for three years, but when the time came in 1917, American intervention proved decisive. With the Russian Revolution evoking fears of anarchy, Wilson also took charge of supervising the peace. However, although he presided over the negotiations that resulted in the **Treaty of Versailles** in 1919, his stubborn refusal to compromise with isolationist sentiment at home – exacerbated by a near-fatal stroke – kept the US from joining his pet scheme to preserve future world peace, the **League of Nations**. Two major reforms did emerge from the Wilson years: the Eighteenth Amendment, which by banning alcohol ushered in the disastrous experiment of **Prohibition**, and the Nineteenth Amendment, giving **women** the vote.

The two Republican presidents who followed Wilson did little more than sit back and watch the Roaring Twenties unfold. At least until his premature death, **Warren Harding** enjoyed considerable public affection, but he's now remembered as probably the worst of all US presidents, thanks to the cronyism and corruption of his associates. It's hard to say quite whether **Calvin Coolidge** did anything at all; his laissez-faire attitude extended to working a typical four-hour day, and announcing shortly after his inauguration that 'four-fifths of our troubles would disappear if we would sit down and keep still'.

By the middle of the 1920s, the US was enough of an industrial powerhouse to be responsible for more than half the world's output of manufactured goods. After leading the way into a new era of prosperity, however, it suddenly found itself dragging the rest of the world down into economic collapse. It's hard to say exactly what triggered the **Great Depression**; the consequences seem out of proportion to any one specific cause. Possible factors include American over-investment in the floundering economy of postwar Europe, combined with high tariffs on imports that effectively precluded European recovery. Conservative commentators at the time chose to interpret the calamitous **Wall Street Crash** of October 1929 as a symptom of impending depression rather than a contributory cause, but the quasi-superstitious faith in the stock market that preceded it showed all the characteristics of such classic speculative booms as Britain's eighteenth-century South Sea Bubble. When the inevitable collapse came, many of the businesses that were destroyed were essentially sound.

National self-confidence, however shaky its foundations, has always played a crucial role in US history, but President **Herbert Hoover** was not the man to restore it. Matters only began to improve in 1932, when, pledging 'a new deal for America', the patrician **Franklin Delano Roosevelt** won a landslide victory in the presidential election. At the time of his inauguration, early in 1933, the banking system had all but closed down; it took the now proverbial

'**Hundred Days**' of vigorous legislation to turn around the mood of the country. Roosevelt cajoled America out of crisis, taking advantage of the new medium of radio to deliver reassuring 'fireside chats'.

The **New Deal** took many forms and worked through many newly created agencies, but was marked throughout by a massive growth in the power of the federal government. Among its accomplishments were the **National Recovery Administration**, which created two million jobs; the **Social Security Act**, introducing pensions to be paid for by payroll contributions; the **Public Works Administration**, which built dams and highways the length and breadth of the country; the **Tennessee Valley Authority**, which by generating electricity under public ownership for the common good marked probably the closest-ever approach in the US to institutionalized socialism; and measures to legitimize the role of the unions and revitalize the farmers of the **Dust Bowl** out on the plains.

Roosevelt originally saw himself as a populist who could draw support from every sector of society. By 1936, however, business leaders – and the **Supreme Court** – were making it clear that as far as they were concerned he had done more than enough already to kick-start the economy. From then on, as he secured an unprecedented four consecutive terms as president, he was firmly cast as the champion of the underdog.

Although the work-creation programmes of the New Deal put America back on its feet, it was the deadly pressure to achieve victory in **World War II** – increasingly visible on the horizon throughout the latter half of the 1930s – that finally spurred the economy back to full capacity. Once again, the US was able to stay out of the war at first, until it was finally forced in by the high-stakes gamble of the Japanese, who launched a pre-emptive strike on Hawaii's **Pearl Harbor** in December 1941.

1913 Woodrow Wilson becomes president in March, and spells out his reforming agenda to a joint session of Congress in April. Legislation in his first year includes a **lower tariff**, on the basis that 'we must abolish everything that bears even the semblance of privilege'. The graduated income tax that pays for this has been made possible by the adoption in February of the **Sixteenth Amendment**. In December, the **Federal Reserve Act** gives the banking system greater security and flexibility, by dividing the US into twelve districts, each with its own Federal Reserve Bank. All national banks must deposit at least half of their reserves.

The **Seventeenth Amendment**, passed in May, means that Senators will henceforth be elected by direct popular vote rather than by state legislatures.

1914 Wilson has refused to recognize General Victoriano Huerta's 'government of butchers' in **Mexico**, which has deposed the democratically elected Francisco Madero. Taking advantage of a largely imaginary show of disrespect from Huerta in April, Wilson orders US marines to seize the port of **Veracruz**. The country descends into civil war, and Huerta flees. Both his successor, General Venustiano Carranza, and the world at large, see Wilson's intervention as American imperialism.

On April 20, Colorado's governor uses the National Guard to break up a strike at John D. Rockefeller's coal mines in Ludlow, Colorado; 39 people, including two women and eleven children, die in the **Ludlow Massacre**.

When the **Great War** breaks out between the European powers in August, Wilson declares that 'the United States must be **neutral** in fact as well as in name'. Later that month, the **Panama Canal** opens, although it will not be fully operational until 1920.

Wilson pushes through two anti-trust measures, to curb the power of trade monopolies. In September, the **Federal**

Trade Commission is set up to oversee corporations conducting interstate business, while October's **Clayton Anti-Trust Act** outlaws price-fixing and exclusive trade contracts, and frees labour unions from the restrictions inadvertently imposed by the 1890 Sherman Act.

Former nurse **Margaret Sanger** publishes a new magazine, *The Woman Rebel*, advocating 'the prevention of conception'. She will go on to found the **American Birth Control League** in 1921.

1915 While the US has grudgingly accepted a British naval blockade of the North Sea, the German response in February, declaring a war zone around the British Isles, is denounced as an 'indefensible violation of neutral rights'. On May 7, a German U-boat sinks the Cunard liner *Lusitania*, killing 1198 passengers including 128 Americans. Wilson resists calls to war, from Theodore Roosevelt and others, saying 'there is such a thing as a man being too proud to fight'.

D. W. Griffiths releases the epic film *Birth of a Nation*, glorifying the role of the Ku Klux Klan in resisting Reconstruction. Wilson comments that 'it is all so terribly true', and it helps to trigger a resurgence of the Klan.

1916 Advocating military strength as the surest way to avoid involvement in the war, Wilson marches in one of many national '**preparedness parades**', and supports the passage of August's '**Big Navy Act**' to build up the navy. In May, an ultimatum from Wilson secures Germany's promise that it will no longer attack merchant vessels without warning.

In March, hoping to embroil the US in Mexico's civil war, guerrilla leader **Pancho Villa** launches a cross-border raid on Columbus, New Mexico. General John Pershing is dispatched into Mexico in ultimately fruitless pursuit. US marines land in the **Dominican Republic** in May, to take control of customs operations and thus guarantee debt repayments; they will remain until 1925. In August, the Jones Act gives the **Philippines** something close to territorial status, and promises to grant independence 'as soon as a stable government can be established'.

Campaigning on the slogan '**he kept us out of the war**', and on a generally progressive platform that closely mirrors Roosevelt's in 1912, Wilson is narrowly **re-elected** in November, defeating Republican challenger **Charles Hughes** by 277 electoral votes to 254. He then calls on each of the belligerent powers to state its war aims, but the German refusal to do so until a conference actually starts thwarts his attempt to broker a peace settlement.

Jeanette Rankin of Montana is the first woman to be elected to the House of Representatives.

1917 In January, in a last-ditch bid to achieve a breakthrough before the US can mobilize, Germany renews unrestricted submarine warfare. Wilson breaks off diplomatic relations on February 3. On March 1, the State Department releases the intercepted **Zimmermann Telegram**, in which Germany promises Texas, New Mexico and Arizona to **Mexico** in return for a military alliance. German U-boats then sink five US merchantmen. Having won Congressional approval by arguing that 'the world must be made safe for democracy', Wilson **declares war** on April 6.

May's Selective Service Act introduces **conscription**, requiring all men aged between 21 and 31 to register. Ultimately 2.8 million men will be drafted, and two million US soldiers will reach Europe. The first 14,500, under General Pershing, reach France on June 26, where the first of the 49,000 men to be killed in action die on November 3.

The **War Industries Board** is created in July to centralize economic planning, while August's Lever Act sets up a **Food Administration**, run by **Herbert Hoover**, to

Hollywood and the birth of the film industry

Thomas Edison opened his first Kinetoscope Parlor in New York in 1894, showing films that lasted less than a minute to a single viewer at a time, while the first purpose-built **movie theatre** opened in Philadelphia in 1905. By 1910, with 26 million Americans going to the movies each week, film-makers were gravitating from the East Coast to **southern California**, both for its varied terrain and climate suitable for year-round outdoor filming, and to distance themselves from Edison's Motion Picture Patents Company, whose stranglehold was eventually broken in 1915, on anti-trust grounds, by the Supreme Court.

By 1914, **Hollywood** – a former temperance colony that affiliated to Los Angeles in 1911 in return for regular water – was packed with movie-makers such as **Cecil B. DeMille**. The next year, D. W. Griffith's racist epic ***The Birth of a Nation***, which lasted an unprecedented twelve reels and cost $110,000, revealed the scale of potential profits by raking in an estimated $18 million (Griffith's next movie, **Intolerance**, cost $1.9 million and flopped). As business boomed, rival production companies sprang into being, and found themselves competing to sign the individual **stars** who offered the surest route to box-office success. The English-born **Charlie Chaplin** moved within a year from a weekly salary of $1250 at Essanay, to $10,000 per week at Mutual, and $1 million for eight pictures at First National.

Amid much publicity, the stars attempted to take control in 1919, when Chaplin, Griffith, Douglas Fairbanks and Mary Pickford formed **United Artists**. However, scandals such as comedian Roscoe 'Fatty' Arbuckle's trial for rape and murder in 1922 soon showed that stars could fall as well as rise, and in any case United merely distributed movies. True power was becoming concentrated in the **studio system**, under which the 'Big Five' – Warner Brothers, RKO, Twentieth Century Fox, Paramount and MGM – owned theatres and production studios as well as distribution. Between the late 1920s and 1948, when their operations were in turn dismantled by anti-trust legislation, they enjoyed a virtual monopoly over all movies shown in the US.

oversee the use and production of food and fuel. The war effort, combined with conscription and low immigration, will spur both a **Great Migration** of Southern blacks to work in the factories of the North, and increased job opportunities for **women**.

In December, Congress passes the **Eighteenth Amendment**, prohibiting the manufacture, sale and distribution of alcoholic liquors. It will be ratified in 1919.

1918 On January 8, President Wilson sets out US war aims to Congress. Designed to ensure that the victorious Allies will not annex large swathes of German territory, his **Fourteen Points** promote an idealized vision of a future world without armaments or trade barriers, and with freedom of the seas and a league of nations. French Premier Georges Clemenceau says 'President Wilson and his Fourteen Points bore me. Even God Almighty has only ten.' To Theodore Roosevelt they're 'a product of men who want everyone to float to heaven on a sloppy sea of universal mush'.

At home, opposition to the war is suppressed by measures including the **Sedition Act**; socialist leader **Eugene Debs** is among those imprisoned.

By October, with the Germans having lost control of the Atlantic, and the stalemate in Europe all but broken – over a million American soldiers take part in the Meuse–Argonne offensive – US intervention has played a decisive role in ending the war.

An **armistice** is signed on November 11, and President Wilson arrives in France on December 13 for the **peace conference**, the basis for which, the Germans have been promised, will be the Fourteen Points. Wilson's own position, however, has been weakened by his appeal to voters to treat the mid-term elections in the US as a referendum on his peace policies – only for them to reject him by electing Republican majorities in both houses.

Between September and June 1919, 675,000 Americans die in the worldwide **flu** epidemic.

1919 In the negotiations that produce the **Treaty Of Versailles**, eventually signed on June 28, Wilson concedes most of his Fourteen Points in order to secure a covenant establishing the **League of Nations**. Germany loses substantial territories, is obliged to disarm, and will have to pay punitive reparations, in a settlement that observers ranging from John Maynard Keynes to the young Adolf Hitler predict will inevitably result in another war.

Well before the treaty is signed, **Henry Cabot Lodge**, chairman of the Senate Foreign Relations Committee, signals that many Republicans oppose involvement in the League of Nations. When the Senate considers the treaty during the summer, Lodge leads a resistance to ratification that joins out-and-out isolationists with those who simply want guarantees that the US will not be obliged to go to war to avenge any slight violation. Wilson, however, refuses to make any compromise.

With the process stalled, Wilson embarks on a speaking tour to convince public opinion, only to suffer a major **stroke** in Pueblo, Colorado, on October 2. During the seven months that his wife and doctors keep him isolated, and conceal the gravity of his illness, the barely functioning Wilson becomes more intransigent than ever, and Congress finally **refuses to ratify** the treaty.

The ratification of the **Eighteenth Amendment** in January, and the passage of the **Volstead Act** to enforce it in October, herald the introduction of **Prohibition** on January 16, 1920. On June 4, Congress adopts the **Nineteenth Amendment**, giving women the vote, and submits it to the states for ratification.

In a shattering blow for the integrity of professional **baseball**, eight members of the Chicago White Sox, including 'Shoeless Joe' Jackson, are revealed to have taken bribes to throw the World Series. On a more encouraging note, **Babe Ruth** hits a record 29 home runs for the Boston Red Sox. Following changes to the ball, he will go on to hit 54 in 1920, 59 in 1921, and 60 in 1927.

1920 The **railroads**, placed under federal control during the war, are returned to their owners in March, subject to new regulations administered by the Railroad Labor Board.

> ❝ Boys, I told you before you went across the seas that this was a war against war, and I did my best to fulfil the promise. But I am obliged to come to you in mortification and shame and say I have not been able to fulfil the promise. You are betrayed. You fought for something you did not get. ❞
>
> Woodrow Wilson, trying to secure support for the League of Nations, shortly before his stroke in the autumn of 1919

In May, two Italian-born anarchists, Nicola **Sacco** and Bartolomeo **Vanzetti** are arrested for robbery and murder in Massachusetts. In a case that draws worldwide condemnation, they will be convicted despite flimsy evidence in 1921, sentenced to death by a judge who privately calls them 'those anarchist bastards', and executed in 1927.

Tennessee becomes the crucial 36th state to ratify the **Nineteenth Amendment** on August 18. **Women's suffrage** therefore finally arrives when it becomes law on August 26.

The death of Theodore Roosevelt in 1919 having left a political vacuum, the Republican Party chooses the affable, ineffectual **Warren G. Harding** of Ohio as its presidential candidate in a 'smoke-filled room' at its convention in June. According to Harry M. Daugherty, the party fixer responsible – later appointed as Attorney General – 'I found him sunning himself like a turtle on a log, and I pushed him into the water.'

Promising a return to what he calls 'normalcy', Harding comfortably defeats Democrat James M. Cox, whose running mate is **Franklin Delano Roosevelt**, by 404 electoral votes to 137 in November. On election night, Pittsburgh's KDKA station, recently granted the first commercial broadcasting licence, stages the first-ever national **radio broadcast**.

1921 In January, the Census Bureau announces that for the first time more than half of Americans now live in **towns**. In a year when 800,000 immigrants reach the US – adding to a total population of 106 million – Congress introduces its first serious restrictions on future immigration. May's **Immigration Act** limits the influx in any one year to 357,000, with no one country to supply more than three percent of the number of its people already resident in the US.

> **" "** I can't make a damn thing out of this tax problem. I listen to one side and they seem right, and then – God! – I talk to the other side and they seem just as right, and here I am where I started. I know somewhere there's a book that will give me the truth, but, hell, I couldn't read the book. I know somewhere there is an economist who knows the truth, but I don't know where to find him and haven't the sense to know him and trust him when I find him. God! What a job! **" "**
>
> President Warren Harding, to a friend

In June, the creation of the **Bureau of the Budget** enables the president for the first time to control all federal spending plans.

On July 2, President Harding signs a joint resolution of Congress that ends the war with Germany – something Wilson refused to do while the dispute over the treaty continued.

In the country's worst-ever **race riot**, 79 blacks die in Tulsa, Oklahoma.

On Britain's suggestion, the **Naval Disarmament Conference** opens in Washington in November. By February 1922, Britain, the US and Japan agree to restrict the tonnage of their battleships and aircraft carriers in the proportion 5:5:3, with a ten-year 'holiday' on building more ships. France and Italy are lesser partners. As the US Navy operates in two separate oceans, this will have the unintended effect of making the Japanese the most powerful Pacific fleet.

1922 Harding's administration favours big business, raising **tariffs** to their highest-ever level. This makes it even harder for European nations to raise the money they need to

The birth of jazz

What **Duke Ellington** called 'the only true American art' – **jazz** – developed in **New Orleans**. No other city was so ideally situated to synthesize the musical traditions of the Old World and the New. Not only did it pass from French to Spanish and then American hands, but it was the one American city that in the early 1800s allowed **slaves** to congregate freely, playing music on African instruments in public gatherings. Later in the century, local musicians began to merge African and Caribbean rhythms into both popular dance music, and the **brass band** music that, as pioneered by John Philip Sousa, had swept the nation after the Civil War. Among early jazz groups was one led by cornet player **Buddy Bolden**, while solo pianists playing syncopated, ragtime-influenced music in the city's brothels included **Jelly Roll Morton**, who later claimed 'I myself happened to be the creator of jazz in 1902'.

After 1917, when a clampdown closed New Orleans' Storyville red-light district, and a group of white New Orleanians, the Original Dixieland Jazz Band, made the first-ever jazz record in New York, there was a mass musical exodus. **Joe 'King' Oliver**'s Creole Jazz Band cut the first definitive jazz classics in Chicago in 1923, while his former trumpeter **Louis Armstrong** found glory with his Hot Fives in New York.

Seen as carefree and abandoned – or in sterner quarters as degenerate and obscene, with the **Ladies Home Journal** asking 'Does Jazz Put The Sin In Syncopation?' – jazz became the first product of black culture to win mass white acclaim, and contributed to a general flowering of black creativity known as the **Harlem Renaissance**. As racial barriers began to crack, white 'flappers' flocked to the **Cotton Club**, where Ellington led the house band, and white musicians such as Benny Goodman and Bix Beiderbecke found in jazz their own freedom of expression.

pay their wartime debts by trading with the US, and for Japan to stimulate its economy out of prolonged depression.

Attempting to assist struggling farmers, the **Capper-Volstead Act** enables them to buy and sell co-operatively without fear of anti-trust regulations.

1923 Harding **dies** suddenly on August 2, and is initially greatly mourned, before details of **corruption** emerge that permanently taint his reputation. Revelations range from his own adultery to the **Teapot Dome** scandal, in which Secretary of the Interior Albert Fall will eventually be jailed for leasing an oil reserve in Wyoming to cronies.

The new president is the taciturn **Calvin Coolidge**, a former governor of Massachusetts who has first come to prominence in 1919 for saying of a policemen's strike in Boston that 'There is no right to strike against the public safety by anybody, anywhere, any time.'

1924 On February 12, **George Gershwin**'s symphonic *Rhapsody in Blue* is performed for the first time.

In May a new **Immigration Bill** – signed into law by Coolidge with the words 'America must be kept American' – reduces the annual quota of immigrants from any country to two percent of the number of its nationals present in the US in 1890. This drastically curtails migration from Italy and Eastern Europe. No immigration at all is to be allowed from **Japan**, which declares a day of national mourning.

The **American Indian Citizenship Act** declares Native Americans to be US citizens, and gives them the right to vote.

Coolidge has sufficiently distanced himself from Harding to win comfortable **re-election** in November, gaining 15.7 million popular votes to 8.4 million for the Democrat John

W. Davis. Robert La Follette, standing with Socialist support for a newly reorganized **Progressive Party** that has little in common with Roosevelt's 1912 version, wins a creditable 4.8 million votes.

1925 Announcing that 'the chief business of the American people is business', Coolidge focuses his attention on freeing industry from government regulation. His ally Henry Cabot Lodge exults 'we have torn up Wilsonism by the roots'.

In Dayton, Tennessee, the **Scopes Monkey Trial** attracts international attention as it tests a new state law that forbids the teaching of Darwinian evolution in schools. Two renowned figures, populist politician and religious fundamentalist **William Jennings Bryan** and agnostic ACLU attorney **Clarence Darrow**, argue the case, which results in a conviction for teacher John Scopes. Bryan dies five days later.

The first **motel** opens in San Luis Obispo, California.

F. Scott Fitzgerald, who dubs this era the **Jazz Age**, publishes *The Great Gatsby*.

1926 On May 10, US marines land in **Nicaragua** to quell a revolt against 'el grotesco imperialismo Yanki' led by General Augusto **Sandino**. They will only leave the country in 1933, once Sandino has been executed by Colonel Anastacio **Somoza**.

A hurricane in southern Florida kills four hundred people on September 18, and in the process ends a speculative real-estate boom centred on **Miami**,

In October, the **Supreme Court**, which has become increasingly conservative with former President Taft as its Chief Justice, strikes down the 1867 Tenure of Office Act, and gives the president the right to appoint and dismiss cabinet members.

Prohibition: the 'noble experiment'

In December 1917, when Congress agreed the **Eighteenth Amendment**, banning the 'manufacture, sale, or transportation of intoxicating liquors', thirteen states were already totally 'dry', and only three had no restrictions on alcohol. The **temperance** movement had a long history. The **American Temperance Society** claimed a million members during the 1830s, while the **Anti-Saloon League**, founded in 1895, won considerable support for its charge that (all-male) saloons fostered political corruption, prostitution, ill-health and absenteeism.

That Prohibition was finally sanctioned during the **Great War** was no coincidence. Not only was its religious basis amplified by the high moral purpose of the war, but the brewing and distillery industry was dominated by German Americans, while grain was now arguably needed for food rather than drink. Once the amendment was ratified in January 1919, the 'noble experiment' of **Prohibition** began in January 1920.

However, as Daniel Boorstin put it, Prohibition 'created the greatest criminal bonanza in American history'. Liquor remained widely available, whether smuggled from Canada or Mexico, sold in ships moored outside territorial waters, or manufactured in dangerous backwoods stills. Illegal **'speakeasies'** mushroomed in every city – New York had 32,000, double its previous 16,000 saloons – and **bootleggers** raked in vast profits while the government lost perhaps $11 billion in tax revenue. The most famous of the **gangsters** who controlled the entire illegal trade was **Al Capone**, who took over Chicago in 1925, aged 26, and was soon earning an annual $60 million. Four years and 215 unsolved murders later, he retired to Florida, before being jailed for income tax evasion in 1931.

By and large, Republicans continued to advocate Prohibition, but crime and corruption gradually wore down public and political support. Democrat Al Smith opposed it in 1928, and Franklin Roosevelt signed the legislation to abolish it in 1933, saying 'I think this would be a good time for a beer'.

1927 On May 21, **Charles Lindbergh** becomes an international hero by landing his *Spirit of St Louis* in Paris, after flying non-stop across the Atlantic from New York in 33 hours 39 minutes.

After intense US pressure, **Mexico** agrees not to enforce the nationalization of foreign resources stipulated by its constitution, and return oil claims to American companies.

Television is publicly demonstrated for the first time in New York City in April, while October sees the release of the first commercially successful talking picture or '**talkie**', *The Jazz Singer* starring Al Jolson.

1928 Secretary of State **Frank Kellogg** responds to a proposal from French Prime Minister Aristide Briand that the US and France should sign a pact outlawing war by calling for a multilateral treaty. In Paris in August, therefore, all the main participants in World War II sign the **Kellogg–Briand Pact** to renounce war.

Walt Disney introduces **Mickey Mouse** in the cartoon *Steamboat Willie*.

President Coolidge having announced his intention not to run for re-election – though he probably hopes to be drafted anyway – the Republicans choose **Herbert Hoover** as their candidate. The fact that his Democratic opponent, New York governor **Alfred E. Smith**, is the first Catholic candidate of a major party alienates many white Southerners into voting Republican, and Hoover is elected by 444 electoral votes to 87.

1929 In the **St Valentine's Day Massacre** on February 14, five of Al Capone's gangsters murder seven of Bugs Moran's gang in a Chicago garage.

Automobiles replace cotton as the country's most valuable export.

A police 'mug shot' of gangster Al Capone

Two American authors publish seminal works: **William Faulkner** depicts his native Oxford, Mississippi, in *The Sound and the Fury*, while **Ernest Hemingway** looks back on his war experiences in *A Farewell To Arms*.

On September 4, exactly six months after Hoover states at his inauguration that 'I have no fears for the future of our country', the **stock market** begins to decline. As prices plummet, the **Wall Street Crash** deepens, with thirteen million shares being sold on Black Thursday, October 24, and sixteen million on Black Tuesday, October 29, which economist J. K. Galbraith will call 'the most devastating day in the history of markets'.

1930 In March, the State Department clarifies its position on the **Monroe Doctrine** by publishing the Clark Memorandum, drawn up two years earlier. This declares that the doctrine is concerned with 'the United States versus Europe, not . . . the United States versus Latin America', and thus does not justify US intervention in the Americas. Hoover's policy of recognizing even 'bad' governments is seen as a disavowal of the Roosevelt Corollary of 1904.

The Wall Street Crash

When the speculative financial boom of the Roaring Twenties – the **Great Bull Market** – peaked on September 3, 1929, the **New York Times** stock average stood at 452, having risen by 110 points in three months. Then it began to slide, gently enough at first for Yale Professor Irving Fisher to observe on October 15 that 'stock prices have reached what looks like a permanently high plateau'.

The rot set in the next week. When shares plummeted by ten percent on the morning of **Black Thursday**, October 24, the market went into blind **panic**. A consortium of big-name bankers stepped in at midday, making ostentatious purchases that turned initial losses of $9 billion into more like $3 billion. Attempting to reassure the nation, President Hoover ventured 'the fundamental business of the country . . . is on a sound and prosperous basis'. Newspapers reported the crisis was over.

Instead, on **Black Tuesday**, October 29, prices dropped by a third, wiping out $32 billion. Now, less conspicuously but with deadly effect, the bankers too started selling. The process began to feed on itself. As 'bad' stocks plummeted, investors could only cover their losses by selling 'good' stocks, which fell in turn, often triggering further preset selling instructions. To make matters worse, despite appalling individual days, this was not the proverbial instant crash. Prices just went on falling; speculators would rejoin the market, thinking the worst was over and hoping to pick up bargains, only for their new acquisitions to slump in turn.

Despite the occasional hopeful interlude, prices continued to fall until June 1932, by which time the general indices, as well as specific stocks like General Motors and US Steel, were a tenth of their 1929 high. By the next summer, industrial production and personal incomes had dropped by half in four years, while unemployment had increased from three million to fifteen million.

In summer, despite the opposition of many prominent economists, Congress passes, and Hoover signs, the **Hawley–Smoot Tariff Act**, greatly increasing duties. This devastates foreign trade and exacerbates the worldwide depression. By the end of 1931, 25 countries will have raised retaliatory barriers.

In the worst **bank failure** in American history – though just one of 1300 within the past year – New York's (private) Bank of the United States fails on December 11.

Grant Wood wins $300 and a bronze medal from the Art Institute of Chicago for his painting *American Gothic*.

1931 Nine black youths are arrested in Scottsboro, Alabama, on March 25, and eight are sentenced to death within twelve days on trumped-up charges of raping two white women on a train. The so-called **Scottsboro Boys** become a *cause célèbre* when the Communist-backed International Labor Defense carries their appeal to the Supreme Court, which will set aside the verdicts in 1932, and again after a retrial in 1935.

The **Empire State Building** is dedicated in New York on May 1.

Aiming to stem the growing international crisis, Hoover calls in June for a one-year **moratorium** on inter-governmental debts and reparations. All major world nations quickly accept, but soon confidence starts to slide once more.

Following the spurious **Mukden Incident** of September 18, Japanese troops occupy all of Manchuria, awakening American fears that Japan's expansionist ambitions may threaten the entire Pacific region.

On October 11, **Al Capone** is sentenced to eleven years' imprisonment for tax evasion.

Finally consenting to the notion of federal intervention to help corporations, if not individuals, Hoover asks Congress in December to create the **Reconstruction Finance Corporation**, to lend federal money to corporations in danger of failure.

1932 On March 1, the 19-month-old son of aviator Charles Lindbergh is **kidnapped**, only to be found dead in May. Bruno Hauptmann will be executed for the crime, still protesting his innocence, in 1936.

Twenty thousand impoverished war veterans stage the **Bonus March**, camping in Washington, DC, through May and June as they campaign for the early payment of a bonus promised for 1945. Hoover refuses to meet them, and Congress eventually rejects the necessary bill. On July 29, following clashes in which two policemen and two demonstrators die, Hoover sends in the army, under General **Douglas MacArthur**, who exceeds orders in the brutality with which he gases and burns them out.

On July 2, Governor **Franklin D. Roosevelt** of New York flies to Chicago to accept the Democratic nomination for president, with the words 'I pledge you, I pledge myself to a **new deal** for the American people'. In the ensuing campaign, he avoids being too specific about how he plans to tackle the economic situation, but exudes enough confidence to win an overwhelming **victory** in November by 23 million popular and 472 electoral votes to Hoover's 16 million and 59. This is the first Democratic popular majority since the Civil War.

1933 On January 30, **Adolf Hitler** becomes Chancellor in Germany.

The four-month interregnum between the election and Roosevelt's accession to power, during which Roosevelt declines Hoover's invitation to join him in a recovery plan of Hoover's devising, further depletes national confidence. In February, the **Twentieth Amendment** shortens future such hiatuses by changing the date for a new president to take office to January 20, and for a newly elected Congress to sit to January 3.

Roosevelt survives an **assassination attempt** in Florida on February 15, and is **inaugurated** as president on March 4. Announcing that 'the only thing we have to fear is fear itself', he promises to ask Congress for 'broad executive power to wage a war against the emergency'. Among his immediate appointees is **Frances Perkins**, who as Secretary of Labor becomes the first woman to join the cabinet.

With eighty percent of the nation's banks closed, Roosevelt declares a four-day '**bank holiday**', and summons a special session of Congress that opens on March 9. On the first of its **Hundred Days** of legislation, detailed on pp.256–257, it passes the necessary act to reopen the banks. On March 12, Roosevelt delivers the first of his popular radio '**fireside chats**', and listeners act on his exhortation to start depositing their money again.

On November 17, diplomatic relations with **Russia**, suspended since 1917, are resumed.

On December 5, the **Twenty-First Amendment** is ratified, repealing the Eighteenth and **ending Prohibition**.

Standard Oil acquires the first American **oil** concession in **Saudi Arabia**.

1934 New Deal legislation passed during the year includes January's **Gold Reserve Act**, which empowers the president to set the gold content of the dollar at between 50¢ and 60¢, and, in June, the **Communications Act**, regulating telecommunications, and the **Frazer-Lemke Farm Bankruptcy Act**, one of several measures to aid farmers

The Hundred Days

Summoned by the new President Roosevelt, the special session of Congress that opened on March 9, 1933, enacted in his first **Hundred Days** an astonishing programme of legislation. Not all was mutually consistent; the need to get the New Deal working meant that incompatible solutions were often tried and discarded. A day-to-day calendar reveals how quickly events moved:

March 9   The **Emergency Banking Relief Act** – debated, passed and signed in eight hours – reopens the banks and increases presidential regulatory powers.

March 20   The **Economy Act** cuts federal salaries by a minimum of 15 percent.

March 22   The **Beer and Wine Revenue Act** legalizes, and taxes, beer and wine.

March 31   The **Reforestation Relief Act** establishes the **Civilian Conservation Corps** for unemployed men.

April 19   The **gold standard** is abandoned, to stimulate foreign trade.

May 12   The **Federal Emergency Relief Act** provides $500 million – later increased tenfold – for local relief.

The **Agricultural Adjustment Act** tackles the agricultural glut, hoping to restore prices to prewar levels.

in difficulty. Additional acts set up agencies to mediate in labour disputes, and regulate the production of cotton, beet sugar and other agricultural products.

Prolonged drought is turning the Great Plains into the **Dust Bowl**. Thanks in part to poor farming techniques,

	The **Emergency Farm Mortgage Act** stops foreclosures and offers funds for refinancing.
May 18	The **Tennessee Valley Authority Act** provides hydroelectricity and economic empowerment to the Tennessee Valley.
May 27	The **Federal Securities Act** obliges issuers to provide full disclosure about, and the government to approve, all issues of stocks and bonds.
June 5	The **Gold Repeal Joint Resolution** removes any obligation to settle debts in gold.
June 13	The **Home Owners Refinancing Act** provides refinancing for home mortgages.
June 16	The **Farm Credit Act** encourages low-interest mortgages for farmers.
	The **Glass-Steagall Banking Act** restricts speculation by banks, and guarantees deposits up to $5000.
	The **National Industrial Recovery Act** creates the National Recovery Administration (**NRA**), to produce 'codes' for industry covering issues like maximum hours and minimum wages, and the Public Works Administration (**PWA**), to fund make-work projects.

over 300 million tons of topsoil are blown away, and refugees such as the **Okies**, immortalized in 1939 by John Steinbeck's *The Grapes of Wrath*, head for California.

The Tydings–McDuffie Act promises **independence** for the **Philippines** in ten years; it will eventually arrive in 1946.

On July 22, FBI agents shoot **John Dillinger** – Public Enemy No. 1 – outside Chicago's Biograph movie theatre. It's a personal triumph for **J. Edgar Hoover**, FBI Director since 1924, whose **G-men** (Government-men) are becoming national heroes.

1935 With employment still over twenty percent, April's **Emergency Relief Appropriation Act** provides another $4.8 billion of relief. Offshoots will include the Works Progress Administration (**WPA**), which funds make-work projects across the nation.

In May, stating that 'extraordinary conditions do not create or enlarge constitutional power', the **Supreme Court** undermines three key elements of the New Deal. It strikes down the Frazer-Lemke Farm Bankruptcy Act, declares the activities of the National Recovery Administration to be unconstitutional, and challenges the president's right to dismiss a member of the Federal Trade Commission who disagrees with his policies.

In response to a national grass-roots campaign for old-age **pensions**, originally inspired by Dr Frederick Townsend of California, August's **Social Security Act** requires workers and employers to contribute via payroll taxes to a fund that will pay not only pensions but death and other benefits.

> **❝** We put those payroll contributions there so as to give the contributors a legal, moral, and political right to collect their pensions and their unemployment benefits. With those taxes in there, no damn politician can ever scrap my Social Security program. **❞**
>
> President Franklin D. Roosevelt describes the thinking behind the Social Security Act of 1935

President Franklin Roosevelt delivers one of his 'fireside chats'

During the summer, Congress passes the **National Labor Relations Act**, guaranteeing the rights of unions; another **Banking Act**; and the **Revenue Act**, which moves against the 'unjust concentration of wealth and economic power' by raising income tax, adjusting corporation tax to hit large corporations harder, and imposing inheritance taxes.

On September 8, **Huey Long**, the 'Kingfish' (see overleaf), is assassinated in Baton Rouge, Louisiana.

George Gershwin's folk opera *Porgy and Bess* is premiered in New York and Boston.

1936 The Supreme Court continues to strike down New Deal legislation, only for new acts to be introduced that maintain the impetus.

Huey Long (1893–1935)

When a friend told Franklin Roosevelt that if his programmes failed, he would be remembered as the worst American president, Roosevelt replied 'if I fail, I shall be the last one'. In the event, the closest the American people ever came to acquiring a home-grown dictator was in their 1930s' flirtation with Huey Long.

A former travelling salesman from rural Louisiana, Long put himself through law school in just eight months. The self-proclaimed defender of the 'little people' – Catholic and Protestant, black and white – against corporations like Standard Oil, and the state's ruling elite in New Orleans, he was elected governor of Louisiana in 1928. Even after becoming a Senator in 1932, he retained autocratic powers in Louisiana. Boasting 'I can buy legislators like sacks of potatoes', he controlled every political appointment, legal proceeding, tax assessment and election. Benefits for Louisianans included extensive spending on road building, education and public amenities; among drawbacks were corruption, violence and intimidation.

Seen in Washington as a pudgy, cantankerous clown, Long established his reputation via radio. The first politician to buy time to broadcast directly to the nation, he called himself 'the Kingfish' after a character in the **Amos'n'Andy** show. Having initially supported Roosevelt, he charged the New Deal with doing too little to redistribute wealth, and launched the Share-Our-Wealth campaign in 1934. By confiscating any income over $1 million, or fortune over $3 million, this promised $2500 per year to every American family, plus old-age pensions and other benefits. Under the slogan 'Every Man A King', it soon claimed seven million members.

Roosevelt expected Long to run as a third-party candidate for president in 1936, and possibly split the vote to allow a Republican victory. However, he was shot on September 8, 1935, in Louisiana's state capitol at Baton Rouge, by the son-in-law of a judge whom he had manoeuvred out of office.

> **Better the occasional faults of a Government that lives in a spirit of charity than the constant omission of a Government frozen in the ice of its own indifference.**
>
> President Franklin Roosevelt, 1936

In November's **presidential election**, aided especially by women and blacks who shift their support to the Democrats, Roosevelt overwhelms Republican **Alfred Landon** by a popular margin of 27.7 million votes to 16.6 million, and an electoral one of 524 to 7.

1937 Roosevelt's second term begins amid industrial strife, including a major sit-down strike at General Motors' plant in Flint, Michigan. As the economy moves back into **recession**, unemployment increases by a further three million during the year.

On February 5, Roosevelt announces plans to ask Congress to appoint as many new judges to all federal courts as there are existing judges aged over 70. His intention is clearly to **'pack' the Supreme Court** with new judges who will support New Deal legislation. Portrayed as quasi-dictatorial, the proposal proves highly divisive. In the face of strong Democratic opposition in the Senate, it never comes to a vote, but despite its failure the Supreme Court will in any case over the ensuing months and years change its stance to rule in favour of New Deal programmes.

In May, the latest **Neutrality Act** in an ongoing series bans arms sales to foreign belligerents, and limits the sale and transportation of other materials.

On May 6, the German airship *Hindenburg* **explodes** at Lakehurst, New Jersey, killing 36 people and ending the era of commercial airship travel.

On June 22, boxer **Joe Louis** becomes the World Heavyweight Champion by knocking out James Braddock in Chicago.

In October, Roosevelt calls, in Chicago, for a '**quarantine**' against nations that are 'creating a state of international anarchy and instability', but advocates no specific programme and fails significantly to diminish the country's increasing **isolationism**.

1938 Roosevelt somewhat reluctantly agrees to a large increase in federal spending to combat continuing recession. In June, the **Emergency Relief Appropriation Act** authorizes $33 billion for public works. Although it's followed by a relative recovery, ultimately it will be the massive expenditures necessitated by the upcoming war – and revenues from arms sales – that turn the economy around.

Also in June, the **Fair Labor Standards Act** sets a minimum wage of 40¢ per hour, and a maximum working week of 44 hours, which will soon drop to 40 hours. Roosevelt calls this 'the most far-reaching, far-sighted program for the benefit of workers ever adopted in this or any other country'. Nonetheless, with conservative opposition growing, and now including some Southern Democrats, Republican gains in November's mid-term elections reduce the Democratic majorities in both houses.

On October 30, a radio broadcast of H. G. Wells' *The War of the Worlds* by Orson Welles' Mercury Theatre of the Air **panics** the nation.

1939 With Japan at war with China, and Hitler's Germany having merged with Austria, the growing **international crisis** dominates the political agenda. In January, Roosevelt asks Congress for $1.3 billion for defence. After Germany invades Czechoslovakia in March, he receives no response when he asks Hitler and Mussolini to guarantee no further aggression.

World War II breaks out in September, when Britain and France react to the German invasion of Poland on September 1 by declaring war on Germany on September 3. Roosevelt issues an official proclamation of **US neutrality** on September 5.

The administration now finally persuades Congress to modify the Neutrality Act, the embargo provisions of which have encouraged aggression by preventing assistance to its victims. A new **Neutrality Act** in November allows arms to be exported to belligerents who pay cash and ship them away in their own vessels. While Roosevelt promotes this so-called **cash and carry** policy as the best means to avoid war – in that German submarines will have no reason to target American shipping – it's clearly intended to help the future Allies.

1940 When France falls to the Germans in June, Roosevelt seeks to boost national unity by appointing two Republicans to his cabinet: **Henry L. Stimson** as Secretary of War and **Frank Knox** as Secretary of the Navy. He also negotiates a deal that gives the British fifty 'overaged' US destroyers in return for 99-year leases on naval and air bases throughout the Western hemisphere. In September, for the first time ever, Congress introduces **conscription** in peacetime. Steady increases in **defence spending** amount to $17 billion by October.

Without explicitly stating his intention to break with precedent by running for a third term of office, Roosevelt accepts the Democratic presidential nomination. His Republican opponent, the popular lawyer **Wendell Wilkie**, seems to oppose the implementation of the New Deal rather than the actual programmes, and although he's against war he openly sympathizes with the Allies. Assuring voters that 'your boys are not going to be sent into any foreign wars', Roosevelt is comfortably **re-elected**, by 27million to 22 million popular votes, and 449 to 82 electoral ones.

1941 In his annual message to Congress on January 6, Roosevelt spells out the **Four Freedoms** cherished by the world's democracies – freedom of speech, freedom of worship, freedom from want, and freedom from fear. In March, despite the charge from one isolationist Senator that it 'will plow under every fourth American boy', Congress passes the **Lend–Lease Act**. Prompted by the British inability to continue paying for arms, this entitles the president to sell, lend, lease or otherwise supply goods and services to nations whose defence he 'deems vital to the defense of the US'. Roosevelt sells this policy to the country by using the analogy of lending a garden hose to a neighbour whose house is on fire. In May, he declares an unlimited state of **national emergency**.

The USS **West Virginia** and the USS **Tennessee** attacked at Pearl Harbor on December 7, 1941

The attack on Pearl Harbor

On November 27, 1941, the US government issued secret 'war warnings', reading: 'Japanese future action unpredictable but hostile action possible at any moment. If hostilities cannot . . . be avoided the United States desires that Japan commit the first overt act.' A few days earlier, a 33-strong **Japanese fleet**, including six aircraft carriers, had sailed from Japan. Although it was assumed to be heading for the Philippines, in fact it followed an icy, seldom used northerly course towards a different target: Hawaii's **Pearl Harbor**, headquarters of the US Pacific Fleet. The Japanese did not expect to achieve complete surprise, but their approach was not detected. At 6am on December 7, the first wave of planes took off. Within four hours the US Navy lost eighteen warships – including eight battleships, three light cruisers, and three destroyers – and 87 planes. A total of 2403 military personnel were killed, and 1178 wounded.

No evidence supports revisionist assertions that Roosevelt knew the attack was coming, but allowed it to happen in order to join the war, or that the British knew, and didn't warn the Americans for the same reason. The best explanation is probably found in statements by two leading protagonists. The Japanese commander reported a fortnight later that 'good luck, together with negligence on the part of the arrogant enemy, enabled us to launch a successful surprise attack'. US Admiral Husband E. Kimmel, asked informally why he had left his ships exposed, replied, 'I never thought those little yellow sons-of-bitches could pull off such an attack, so far from Japan.'

In the long run, the Japanese decision to provoke the US into all-out war proved suicidal. Even the actual vessels that were damaged or sunk returned for the most part to active service. In 1945, the **West Virginia**, risen from the waters, was in Tokyo Bay to witness the Japanese surrender.

In August, Roosevelt meets British Prime Minister **Winston Churchill** in Newfoundland. Their **Atlantic Charter** amounts to a joint declaration of war aims. Echoing Wilson's Fourteen Points of 1918, and forming a blueprint for the United Nations, it rejects any territorial aggrandizement and calls for self-determination for all peoples, with equality of economic opportunity and access to raw materials, so that 'all the men in all the lands may live out their lives in freedom from fear and want'. Thirteen other nations, including **Russia** – invaded by Germany in June – sign up within a month.

Orson Welles directs the movie *Citizen Kane*, widely interpreted as a thinly veiled depiction of newspaper magnate William Randolph Hearst.

The autumn sees several German attacks on US shipping in the North Atlantic, including the sinking of the US destroyer *Reuben James* off Iceland on October 30.

On December 7, while still negotiating in Washington, the **Japanese** launch a surprise attack on the US naval base at **Pearl Harbor**, Hawaii, killing 2403 American personnel. On December 8, with the nation in a state of shock and outrage, President Roosevelt denounces the attack as 'a day that will live in infamy', and Congress **declares war** on Japan. The other **Axis** powers, **Germany** and **Italy**, enter the war three days later.

8
From World War to Cold War

1942–60

O nce President Franklin D. Roosevelt had committed the US to **World War II** in 1941, American manpower and economic muscle made a crucial impact on the global conflict. US forces eventually swept all before them, in both the Pacific and Europe. Much like Lincoln at the end of the Civil War, however, Roosevelt died just as victory was about to be secured, with the Nazis in retreat and the foundations for the postwar carve-up with Stalin and Churchill already laid at **Yalta**. He was thus spared the fateful decision, made by his successor **Harry Truman**, to end the war against Japan by using the newly developed **atomic bomb** on Hiroshima and Nagasaki.

With the war won, Americans were in no mood to revert to the isolationism of the 1930s. Amid much hopeful rhetoric, Truman enthusiastically participated in the creation of the **United Nations**, and set up the **Marshall Plan** to speed the recovery of Europe – a task in which it was far more successful than any of the corresponding attempts made 25 years earlier. However, as Winston Churchill announced in Missouri in 1946, an '**Iron Curtain**' had descended upon Europe, and Joseph Stalin was transformed from ally to enemy almost overnight.

The ensuing **Cold War** lasted for more than four decades, at times fought in ferocious combat (albeit often by proxy) in scattered corners of the globe, and during the intervals diverting colossal economic resources towards the stockpiling of ever more destructive arsenals. Some of its ugliest moments came in its earliest years: Truman was still in office in 1950 when war broke out in **Korea**. A dispute over the arbitrary division of the Korean peninsula into two separate nations, North and South, soon turned into a standoff between the US and China (with Russia, in theory at any rate, lurking in the shadows). Two years of a bloody stalemate ended, with little to show for it, except that Truman had by now been replaced by the genial **Dwight D. Eisenhower**, the latest war hero to turn president.

The Eisenhower years are often seen as an era characterized by bland complacency. Once Senator **Joseph McCarthy**, the 'witch-hunting' anti-Communist scourge of the State Department and Hollywood, had finally discredited himself by attacking the army as well, middle-class America seemed to lapse into a wilful suburban stupor. Great social changes were starting to take shape, however. World War II had introduced vast numbers of women and members of ethnic minorities to the rewards of factory work, and it had shown many Americans from less prosperous regions the lifestyle that was attainable in other parts of their own country. The development of a **national highway system**, and a huge increase in automobile ownership, encouraged people to pursue the American Dream wherever they chose. Combined with increasing mechanization on the cotton plantations of the South, this led to another **mass exodus** of blacks from the rural South to the cities of the North, and to a lesser extent the West. The cities of **California** entered a period of rapid growth, with the aeronautical industries of Los Angeles in particular attracting thousands of prospective workers.

It was also during the 1950s that **television** reached every home in the country. Together with the long-playing record, it created an entertainment industry that at first served to promote mass conformity but which swiftly showed itself capable of addressing the needs of consumers, such as **teenagers**, who had previously been barely identified. **Youth culture** burst into public prominence from 1954 onwards, spearheaded in music by **Elvis Presley** and other rock'n'roll artists, and in the movies by 'rebel' actors such as **Marlon Brando** and **James Dean**.

Racial segregation of public facilities, which had remained the norm in the South ever since Reconstruction, was in 1954 finally declared illegal by the Supreme Court ruling on *Brown v Board of Education of Topeka*. Just as a century before, however, the Southern states saw the issue more in terms of states' rights than of human rights, and attempting to implement the law, or even to challenge the failure to implement it, required immense courage. The action of Rosa Parks in refusing to give up her seat to a white man on a bus in **Montgomery**, Alabama, in December 1955, triggered a successful mass boycott of the city's transportation network, and pushed the 27-year-old **Rev. Dr Martin Luther King, Jr**, to the forefront of the civil rights campaign. Further confrontation took place at the Central High School in **Little Rock**, Arkansas, in 1957, when the reluctant Eisenhower found himself forced to call in federal troops to counter the state's unwillingness to integrate its education system.

'Ike' himself remained personally popular, and aided perhaps by the fact that as a victorious general he felt no need to prove himself further as a fighter, presided over an era of relative peace. As he came to the end of his second term, however, relations with the Russians began to deteriorate once again, and the US suffered the twin humiliations of being seen as losing the **Space Race**, and being caught lying about a **U-2** spy plane downed in Soviet airspace. The election of the photogenic, charismatic **John F. Kennedy** to the presidency in 1960 came as a breath of fresh air to American politics. He won his narrow victory, however, largely by making spurious allegations about a nonexistent 'missile gap'; the Cold War was about to heat up again.

1942 In the immediate aftermath of Pearl Harbor, the British surrender **Singapore** on February 15, while General **Douglas MacArthur** withdraws from the **Philippines** on March 11, promising 'I shall return'. The Japanese advance across the Pacific is finally halted by two American victories. The **Battle of the Coral Sea** on May 7 and 8 – the first naval battle in which the opposing fleets never actually see each other, as all the fighting is done by planes taking off from aircraft carriers – thwarts a Japanese landing on southern New Guinea, and a potential invasion of Australia. Then, in the **Battle of Midway** on June 4 to 6, the Japanese, hoping to lure the entire US Pacific Fleet to its destruction, attack Midway Island in the central Pacific. Admiral Chester Nimitz's fleet does indeed respond, but thanks to the cracking of Japan's secret naval code succeeds in devastating the Japanese forces, and destroying all four Japanese aircraft carriers.

General MacArthur now launches his own offensive in the Pacific, with an amphibious landing on **Guadalcanal** in the Solomon Islands on August 7. Over the next six months, subsequent naval battles inflict massive casualties on both sides, but give the Americans control of the island.

In the **Atlantic**, during the early months of the year, German **submarines** sink almost four hundred American vessels just off the East Coast. Improved US defences, and a nightly blackout of coastal towns, progressively bring the problem under control.

Britain and the US agree to conduct joint military operations, with their top priority being to defeat **Germany** before Japan. Major General **Dwight D. Eisenhower** is appointed to command US forces in **Europe** in June. However, the British resist both Russian and American pressure for an invasion of the continent, so American military involvement in Europe remains minimal throughout the year.

In **North Africa**, the German General **Erwin Rommel** sweeps into Egypt, but British forces halt his progress in the first battle of **El Alamein** in July and then, under General **Bernard L. Montgomery**, drive him out in the second battle of **El Alamein** in late October. Both to support Montgomery, and in response to Russian calls to divert at least some of Germany's attention from the titanic struggle for **Stalingrad**, Eisenhower leads a joint Anglo-American landing in **Morocco** and **Algeria** in November.

At home, the US **economy** quickly moves onto a war footing. The **War Production Board**, created to oversee the manufacture of armaments, halts all nonessential construction work, while price controls and tax increases are imposed, most wages are frozen, and gasoline is rationed. In addition, from February onwards, upwards of 100,000 American citizens of Japanese origin, predominantly living in Western states, are **interned** for the duration of the war.

1943 President **Franklin Roosevelt** meets British Prime Minister **Winston Churchill** and other Allied leaders at the **Casablanca Conference** in January. They make their goal the **unconditional surrender** of the Axis powers, as opposed to the armistice that ended World War I.

The last German attackers surrender at **Stalingrad** in February, while the surrender of German and Italian forces in **Tunisia** in May leaves the Allies in control not only of **North Africa**, but also of the **Mediterranean**.

General Eisenhower's successful invasion of **Sicily** in July leads to the resignation of **Mussolini**, and is followed by an invasion of **Italy** in September. Although the Italian government surrenders on September 8, and declares war on Germany in October, the war against the German occupiers of Italy continues.

In the **Pacific**, MacArthur pursues a strategy of '**island-hopping**', seeking to avoid major confrontations by pinpointing smaller islands on which Japanese defences are weak. Casualties are nonetheless high.

At home, the **Office of War Mobilization** takes on the task of co-ordinating the war effort. The construction of munitions plants, combined with conscription, greatly increases labour opportunities for women and blacks, and triggers a **mass migration** to the cities of the West in particular. Announcing that 'Dr Win-the-War' has replaced 'Dr New Deal', Roosevelt tightens price and wage controls.

In November, Roosevelt and Churchill rendezvous in **Cairo** with the Chinese Nationalist leader **Chiang Kai-shek**, and agree that Japan will be forced to evacuate all Chinese territory as well as its Pacific conquests. They then continue to **Tehran** for their first joint meeting with **Stalin**, to plan an invasion of Europe.

1944 On June 6, **D-Day**, the Allies **invade Europe** along a forty-mile stretch of France's Normandy coast, under the overall command of General Eisenhower. In the ten weeks of bloody fighting before they reach Paris on August 25, 124,400 American soldiers, along with 82,300 from Britain and Canada, lose their lives. Allied forces then press east towards Germany, meeting stiff resistance during the **Battle of the Bulge** in the Ardennes Forest from December 16 onwards.

In the **Pacific**, a huge victory won by US aircraft carriers in the **Battle of the Philippine Sea** on June 19 clears the way for MacArthur to land on the Philippine island of

Leyte on October 20, proclaiming 'I have returned'. Enemy fleets converge, but despite the first use of kamikaze suicide pilots, Japanese naval resistance is crushed on October 25 in the largest-ever naval battle, the **Battle of Leyte Gulf**.

The **Bretton Woods** conference, in New Hampshire in July, establishes the blueprint for the postwar financial structure of the capitalist world by creating the **International Monetary Fund** and the **World Bank**.

In the first wartime **presidential election** for eighty years, some isolationist Republicans flirt with nominating MacArthur, but June's Republican convention picks New York Governor **Thomas E. Dewey**. Roosevelt, running despite ill health for an unprecedented fourth term, replaces Vice President Henry Wallace with **Harry S. Truman** of Missouri as his running mate. Campaigning on his most radical platform yet, pledging to use victory in the war as the springboard to eradicate hunger, homelessness and unemployment, he is **re-elected** once more, by virtually the same margin as in 1940: 25.6 million to 22 million popular votes, and 432 to 99 electoral ones.

1945 Meeting at **Yalta** in the Crimea in February, Roosevelt, Churchill and Stalin plan the final defeat and occupation of Germany, and discuss the postwar world, sketching out a vision for the **United Nations**. With Russian forces already occupying much of **Eastern Europe**, Stalin is able to insist that the US recognizes the Communist government he has set up in **Poland**. His verbal commitment to free elections elsewhere in the region proves almost immediately to be worthless. He also promises to enter the war against Japan once the German defeat is complete. Roosevelt subsequently comments: 'I didn't say the result was good. I said it was the best I could do.'

On April 12, President **Roosevelt dies** suddenly of a cerebral hemorrhage at Warm Springs, Georgia, and **Harry S. Truman** becomes president.

On April 25, representatives from fifty Allied nations meet in San Francisco to agree a charter for the **United Nations**, which will have an eleven-member **Security Council** of which five members are permanent: Britain, France, Russia, China and the US. That same day, Allied troops heading east across Germany meet Russian forces heading west at the **Elbe River** on April 25. The Russians enter **Berlin** on May 2. The German surrender on May 7, which ends the war in Europe, is celebrated on **V-E Day**, May 8.

On June 5, both **Germany** and **Berlin** are divided into four zones under American, British, Russian and French occupation.

In the **Pacific**, US marines land on **Iwo Jima** on February 19, and **Okinawa** on April 1; the capture of Okinawa, completed by June 21, costs 80,000 American lives. As Japan comes within bombing range, **incendiary attacks** devastate Tokyo, Osaka and other cities from March onwards, causing hundreds of thousands of casualties.

In July, President Truman has his only meeting with Stalin, together with Churchill – replaced in mid-conference by a newly elected British prime minister, **Clement Attlee** – at **Potsdam**. Truman's primary aim is to secure Russian intervention against Japan, but the conference bogs down in fruitless wrangling over the future of Germany.

Following a successful test in New Mexico on July 26, an **atomic bomb** is dropped on **Hiroshima** on August 6, killing somewhere between 50,000 and 100,000 people. A second atomic bomb, dropped on **Nagasaki** on August 9, claims another 36,000 lives. On August 14, Emperor Hirohito of Japan accepts US surrender terms, prompting

Wartime poster preparing the US public for the invasion of Japan that never came

The atomic bomb and the decision to use it

It was Albert Einstein, in 1939, who first impressed the urgency of constructing the **atomic bomb** upon President Roosevelt. In 1942, by now desperate to build one before the Germans, the American and British governments set up the **Manhattan Project** at Los Alamos, New Mexico. It took just over two years for the bomb to become a reality; the first successful test took place in the New Mexican desert on July 16, 1945. Witnessing the explosion, team leader **J. Robert Oppenheimer** recalled a line from the Bhagavad Gita: 'I am become Death, the shatterer of Worlds'.

The news reached **President Truman** at Potsdam; before he even knew why, Winston Churchill spotted an immediate change in Truman's confidence in handling Stalin. Within a month, Truman had authorized the dropping of two bombs – on **Hiroshima** on August 6, and on **Nagasaki** on August 9 – and a complete **Japanese surrender** had brought an end to World War II.

Debate has centred ever since over Truman's decision to use the bomb. Truman argued that only the bomb could convince the Japanese emperor that his country faced obliteration. By removing the need to invade Japan, it thus saved perhaps half a million American servicemen. General Marshall pointed out that the Japanese had not surrendered despite losing 100,000 lives in a single night's bombing of Tokyo.

On the other hand, several physicists petitioned Truman that June to demonstrate the bomb on 'a barren island' rather than actually use it, while Eisenhower later claimed that he told Secretary of War Henry L. Stimson that 'the Japanese were ready to surrender and it wasn't necessary to hit them with the awful thing'. Some historians suggest that Truman's primary interest lay in demonstrating the bomb to the Russians, and in denying them the chance to enter the war in Asia and seize Japanese-held territories.

Perhaps the simplest explanation is that Truman didn't make a 'decision' so much as inherit a military programme with unstoppable momentum. Churchill recalled that whether or not to drop the bomb 'was never an issue'; he never heard 'the slightest suggestion that we should do otherwise'.

celebrations of **V-J Day** in the US. General MacArthur arrives in Japan as Supreme Commander of Allied Powers, and a formal **Japanese surrender** is signed on September 2.

Truman sets out a postwar programme on September 6 that amounts to a continuation and expansion of the New Deal. When his calls for wage increases in major industries go unheard, the United Auto Workers at General Motors' Detroit plant go on **strike** in November.

In December, General **George C. Marshall** is sent to **China** to negotiate peace between Chiang Kai-shek and Mao Zedong.

1946 Further **strikes** during the winter include walkouts by miners, steelworkers and railroad employees. Truman is forced to relax price controls in order to fund wage increases, and inflation starts to rise. His administration is blamed by employers and workers alike, and in the November elections the **Republicans** gain control of both houses of Congress.

The **United Nations General Assembly** holds its first meeting in London in January, and convenes again in New York City, which will be its permanent home, in October.

Relations with **Russia** are deteriorating fast. Speaking in Fulton, Missouri, in March, former British Prime Minister **Winston Churchill** declares that 'from Stettin in the Baltic to Trieste in the Adriatic an **iron curtain** has descended across the Continent', and proposes that the English-speaking nations should exploit the power of the atomic bomb and combine to free Eastern Europe. By the end of the year, however, **demobilization** has reduced the US army from 8 million men to 1 million, and the navy from 3.5 million to fewer than 1 million.

The Marshall Plan

In March 1947, former General **George C. Marshall**, President Truman's new Secretary of State, travelled to Moscow to meet the Council of Foreign Ministers. This inconclusive conference highlighted the fact that, while the Americans and the British saw a reunited Germany, restored to full economic strength, as essential for European stability, the Russians were so determined that Germany should never again pose a military threat, that they were prepared to envisage a continent-wide economic collapse. Marshall's trip convinced him that postwar Europe was in very dire straits, and that 'the patient is sinking while the doctors deliberate'.

On June 5, Marshall therefore invited European nations to apply for American aid, proclaiming that his **Marshall Plan** was 'directed not against any country or doctrine but against hunger, poverty, desperation and chaos'. European representatives duly assembled in Paris that same month, and eventually proposed a **$28 billion** package in August. The Russian foreign minister, V. M. Molotov, stormed out after the first few days, charging that the scheme would split Europe, and promptly announced a **Molotov Plan** to aid Russian satellite nations in Eastern Europe.

1947 On January 7, former General Marshall is appointed Secretary of State. In a speech at Harvard on June 5, he announces what will become known as the **Marshall Plan**, to provide economic aid to Europe (see above).

On March 12, addressing a joint session of Congress, President Truman makes the new direction of US foreign policy explicit by spelling out the **Truman Doctrine**: wherever an anti-Communist government is under threat, America will provide economic and military aid. The impending British withdrawal of aid to **Greece** and **Turkey** having prompted fears of a Russian takeover, Congress responds by appropriating a $400 million package to the two countries.

Acknowledging the Marshall Plan and the Truman Doctrine as 'two halves of the same walnut' – the economic and military components of his strategy to contain Russian expansion – Truman asked Congress for $17 billion, for what was officially the **European Recovery Program**, in December. As the European situation deteriorated following a Russian-backed coup in Czechoslovakia, Congress finally consented to an initial $4 billion package in March 1948.

In all, **$13 billion** was pumped into Europe between 1948 and 1951, with individual countries largely free to decide where it ended up. Humanitarian concerns certainly played their part, but the aid also staved off a potential domestic slump by enabling European governments to buy American imports; meant they could provide their own military protection; and helped to restore West Germany as a bastion against Russia. On the downside, as Molotov had predicted, it did indeed serve to solidify the division of the continent into rival camps.

In June, despite Truman's veto, the new Republican Congress passes the **Taft–Hartley Act**. Among many other restrictions, what union leaders call the '**slave-labor act**' forbids strikes by federal employees; entitles the president to intervene in strikes he considers to jeopardize national health or safety; outlaws closed-shop agreements under which only union members may be hired to particular jobs; forbids the use of union funds for political purposes; and obliges union leaders to swear they are not Communists.

July's **National Security Act** makes permanent the wartime creation of the Joint Chiefs of Staff, and establishes the **Central Intelligence Agency**, of which Truman will

> **❝** At the present moment in world history nearly every nation must choose between alternative ways of life . . . I believe that it must be the policy of the United States to support free peoples who are resisting attempted subjugation by armed minorities or outside pressures. **❞**
>
> President Harry S. Truman sets out his Truman Doctrine, March 12, 1947

much later observe: 'I never had any thought when I set up the CIA that it would be injected into peacetime cloak-and-dagger operations.'

On December 29, **Jackie Robinson** joins the Brooklyn Dodgers, and becomes the first black player in major league baseball since 1889.

1948 On May 14, as the British mandate expires in **Palestine**, pressure on the Arab states from America and Russia, working through the United Nations, enables the state of

> **❝** [Russian] political action is a fluid stream which moves constantly, wherever it is permitted to move, toward a given goal. Its main concern is to make sure that it has filled every nook and cranny available to it in the basin of world power. [US foreign policy should consist of] . . . the adroit and vigilant application of counterforce at a series of constantly shifting geographical and political points, corresponding to the shifts and maneuvers of Soviet policy. **❞**
>
> State Department official George Kennan, proposing 'containment' as a new direction for US foreign policy, in an anonymous article published in July 1947

Israel to declare its independence. It is recognized within minutes by the US, and soon afterwards by the Russians. Both countries spring to Israel's support when the Arab nations subsequently invade, and Russian military assistance ensures Israel's immediate survival. From now on, America's **Jewish** community will remain a powerful influence on US policy in the Middle East.

In late June, after the American, British and French zones of Germany are amalgamated into what will become **West Germany**, and the equivalent sectors in Berlin into **West Berlin**, the Russian occupiers of the fourth zone block all traffic to Berlin. Truman instigates the **Berlin Airlift** to supply the city by air.

In August, as scare stories of Communist subversion in the US begin to rise, State Department official **Alger Hiss** denies to the House Un-American Activities Committee that he is a Communist. The charge has been made by former associate **Whittaker Chambers**, encouraged by a young Congressman from California, **Richard Nixon**. The allegations, and the climate that surrounds them, divide the nation. Hiss will be jailed for perjury in 1951.

In the presidential election, the Republicans again choose **Thomas E. Dewey** as their candidate. Anticipating an easy victory, and proclaiming 'to err is Truman', he promises to tidy up the mess left by sixteen years of Democrat rule, but declines to indulge in Red-baiting. Truman goes on the offensive, calling Congress back into session during the summer to pass further New-Deal-style legislation, and telling voters that 'you're a bunch of damn fools and ingrates if you vote Republican'. His expressed support for **civil rights** prompts some Southern Democrats to break away, and put up South Carolina Governor **Strom Thurmond** as a States' Rights Democratic candidate. The result is so close that some early editions report a Dewey victory, but in one of the greatest upsets in presidential history

Truman is re-elected, winning 24.2 million popular votes to Dewey's 22 million and Thurmond's 1.2 million.

1949 President Truman launches his second administration by calling for a **Fair Deal**. Although the Democrats now have majorities in Congress, conservative Southern Democrats combine with Republicans to prevent him doing much more than extending pre-existing New Deal programmes. His request that they repeal the Taft–Hartley Act is rejected, and legislation on civil rights and national health insurance also fails.

Secretary of State Marshall resigns due to poor health, and is succeeded by **Dean Acheson**. In April, the US and Canada join with European powers including Britain and France to sign the North Atlantic Treaty, which will result in 1950 in the creation of the North Atlantic Treaty Organization,

Harry Truman celebrates his election as president in December 1948 – whatever the papers might say

> All middle-class citizens of education have a common belief that the tendencies towards centralization and paternalism must be halted and reversed. No one who voices these opinions can be elected . . . Consequently we must look around for someone of great popularity and who has not frittered away his political assets by taking positive stands against national planning, etc, etc. Elect such a man to Presidency, *after which* he must lead us back to safe channels and paths.

Dwight D. Eisenhower's summary, written in 1949, of Republican Thomas E. Dewey's attempt to persuade him to run for president

NATO. In May, the Russians abandon their blockade in Germany.

On September 23, Truman announces that the Russians have tested their own **atomic bomb**. The news triggers frantic US efforts to develop the more powerful **hydrogen bomb**.

On October 1, Mao Zedong proclaims the foundation of the **People's Republic of China**. As Truman has spent $2 billion supporting Chiang Kai-shek's defeated Nationalists, he's widely seen as having 'lost China'.

1950 On February 9, Wisconsin Senator **Joseph McCarthy** announces that he has a list of 205 Communist sympathizers in the State Department (see p.286).

President Kim Il Sung of **North Korea** launches an invasion of **South Korea** on June 25. Truman notes in his diary that 'it looks like **World War III** has come'. General **Douglas MacArthur** lands in Korea on June 29, the day after the fall of Seoul, and is appointed on July 8 to lead **United Nations** forces in the country, by which time

American troops are already in combat. Despite early set-backs, including three thousand US casualties in the first week, the North Koreans are pushed back to the previous border, the 38th parallel, on September 29.

On October 7, MacArthur – privately referred to by Truman as 'Mr Prima Donna' – takes the fateful decision to continue north, and invade **North Korea**. This provokes a massive **Chinese** intervention; the Red Army drives UN forces back amid devastating carnage. Secretary of State Acheson will later recall 'we sat around like paralyzed rabbits while MacArthur carried out this nightmare'. Truman declares a state of **national emergency** on December 16.

BETTMANN/CORBIS

Senator Joseph McCarthy confers with aide Roy Cohn during Senate committee hearings

November's **McCarran Internal Security Act** bars Communists from working in defence industries, from using their passports if they are citizens, and from naturalizing as citizens if they are aliens. Truman vetoes it for putting 'the Government into the business of thought control', but it passes anyway.

1951 In January, UN forces halt the Chinese counterattack in **Korea**, and by March the front line returns approximately to the 38th parallel. When Truman proposes peace negotiations to restore that as the frontier, MacArthur undermines him by pressing for war against China, declaring 'there is no substitute for freedom'. On April 11 Truman therefore **dismisses MacArthur**. Though Truman is supported by the military, it's an unpopular move: when MacArthur presents his case to a joint session of Congress on April 19, former President Hoover hails him as 'the reincarnation of St Paul' while Truman growls that it was nothing but 'a bunch of damn bullshit'. Nonetheless Senate hearings accept the assessment of General Omar Bradley, Chairman of the Joint Chiefs of Staff, that open conflict with China would represent 'the wrong war at the wrong place at the wrong time with the wrong enemy'. **Peace talks** open on July 10, although a truce will only finally be agreed in July 1953, by which time 33,000 US soldiers will have been killed.

On February 26, the **Twenty-Second Amendment** to the Constitution, a belated slap for Roosevelt, restricts future presidents to two terms in office.

On March 12, a Senate committee chaired by Democrat **Estes Kefauver** of Tennessee opens nationally televised hearings that produce a fortnight of sensational disclosures about **organized crime**, and reveal considerable corruption in major Democrat-run cities.

On April 5, **Julius and Ethel Rosenberg** are sentenced to death for passing nuclear secrets to the Russians. They will be **executed** in June 1953.

The rise and fall of Joseph McCarthy (1908–57)

The most notorious 'Red-baiter' of the 1950s, **Joseph McCarthy** was born in Wisconsin in 1908. Aided by his fanciful embroidering of his Pacific war record, he was elected first a district judge, and then in 1946 a Republican Senator, the country's youngest. His career was faltering when he announced in Wheeling, West Virginia, on February 9, 1950, that he had in his pocket a list of **205 Communist sympathizers** in the State Department. If any such list existed, it was probably based on a House report of 1946, identifying employees who might be further investigated. McCarthy never produced his list, and neither then nor in his entire career did he ever unmask any federal employee as a Communist. Instead, he repeatedly changed the overall number and specific names of his targets, simply moving on to new allegations as each charge was proved false.

McCarthy's testimony to subsequent Senate hearings did much to fuel a national panic about 'Communist subversion', affecting far more lives than simply those that came under direct investigation. He even accused current and former Secretaries of State Dean Acheson and George Marshall of belonging to 'a conspiracy on a scale so immense as to dwarf any previous such venture in the history of man'.

Once his smears against the Democratic administration had helped to propel Dwight D. Eisenhower to the presidency in 1952, however, McCarthy's usefulness was over. As Chairman of the Senate's Subcommittee on Investigations, he went on **'witch-hunting'** in 1953, but with the Republicans now in government he was far less popular among his colleagues. The end came in 1954, when McCarthy was accused before his own committee of permitting his staff to blackmail the army. The hearings culminated on June 9, when army lawyer Joseph Welch lambasted him with 'Have you left no sense of decency?' Censured by the Senate that December for 'conduct unbecoming a member', McCarthy died a broken man, aged 48, in May 1957.

> **“** The only possible means left to MacArthur to regain his lost pride and military reputation was now to inflict an overwhelming defeat on those Red Chinese generals who had made a fool of him. In order to do this he was perfectly willing to propel us into all-out war with Red China, and possibly with the Soviet Union, igniting World War III and a nuclear holocaust. **”**
>
> General Omar Bradley, Chairman of the Joint Chiefs of Staff, assessing General Douglas MacArthur's 1951 strategy in Korea

J. D. Salinger publishes *The Catcher in the Rye*, encapsulating the feelings of suburban middle-class youth in his portrait of teenager Holden Caulfield.

1952 On June 2, the **Supreme Court** restricts presidential powers by ruling a federal takeover of steel mills in Ohio, ordered by Truman in April to avert a strike, to be unconstitutional. 600,000 steel workers then go out on strike, in a dispute ended by wage and price increases in July.

Douglas MacArthur hopes for the Republican presidential nomination, but July's convention in Chicago instead chooses **Dwight 'Ike' Eisenhower**, who has only revealed himself as a Republican within the past year, and resigned as commander of Allied forces in Europe in April. On September 23, his running mate, **Richard Nixon**, responds to charges that he has a 'secret slush fund' by making an emotional televised appeal, known as his **Checkers speech** for its mention of his dog Checkers.

Truman having decided not to run again, the Democratic candidate is Governor **Adlai E. Stevenson** of Illinois. Thanks to the unpopularity of both Truman and the

Korean War, **Eisenhower wins** an easy victory in November, by 33.9 million to 27.3 million popular votes, and 442 to 89 in the electoral college. The Republicans also gain narrow majorities in Congress.

The first successful **hydrogen bomb** test takes place on Eniwetok Atoll in the Pacific on November 1.

1953 Joseph **Stalin dies** in Moscow on March 5. After much political jockeying in the Kremlin, **Nikita Khrushchev** will emerge as his successor.

In July, thanks to Senator Joseph McCarthy, the former leader of the Manhattan Project, **J. Robert Oppenheimer**, is deemed to be a security risk and barred from access to classified material.

In August, a CIA-sponsored coup deposes the democratically elected government in **Iran**, toppling Prime Minister Mohammed Mossadegh and enabling **Muhammad Reza Shah** to introduce autocratic rule.

1954 On January 12, Secretary of State **John Foster Dulles** announces a new doctrine for US defence policy, promising '**massive retaliation**' against foreign aggression.

On March 1, a **hydrogen bomb** is exploded for the first time at **Bikini Atoll** in the Marshall Islands.

Also in March, the **Vietminh** – Vietnamese nationalists led by Ho Chi Minh, and backed by both the Russians and the Chinese – besiege the crucial French military garrison at **Dien Bien Phu** in Indochina. Asked for his reaction in April, Eisenhower puts forward the **domino theory**: 'You have a row of dominoes set up, you knock over the first one, and what will happen to the last one is the certainty that it will go over very quickly'. Countries he sees as potentially falling to Communism include Australia, New Zealand and Japan. After the French are humiliatingly defeated in May, despite receiving over $500 million in aid from the US, Vietnam is divided into two separate nations, with Communists in the north and anti-Communists in the South.

On May 17, in a landmark decision on *Brown v Board of Education of Topeka*, the **Supreme Court** declares **racial segregation** in schools to be unconstitutional: 'in the field of public education the doctrine of "separate but equal" has no place. Separate educational facilities are inherently unequal.' Its unanimous ruling, masterminded by **Earl Warren** – appointed Chief Justice by Eisenhower in October 1953 – finally overturns the 1896 *Plessy v Ferguson* decision. The court will follow up in 1955 by decreeing that public schools must be integrated 'with all deliberate speed'. Eisenhower himself proves at best lukewarm in his support; he will later allege that the decision 'set back progress in the South at least fifteen years'.

In June, a CIA-backed invasion of **Guatemala**, supported by US bombers, overthrows the democratic government, which has attempted to reduce the United Fruit Company's hold on the national economy, and imposes a military dictatorship.

Nowhere is the prosperity of postwar America more conspicuous than in the spending power of a newly emergent demographic group – **teenagers**. **Elvis Presley** cuts his first single at Memphis' Sun Studio, *That's All Right*, on July 5. **Marlon Brando**, who starred as a leather-jacketed motorcycle rebel in 1953's *The Wild One*, reappears in *On the Waterfront*, while his disciple **James Dean** will be seen in *East of Eden* and *Rebel Without a Cause* in 1955. Actress **Marilyn Monroe** marries baseball star **Joe Di Maggio** in January, films *The Seven Year Itch* in the summer, and divorces by the end of the year.

After November's Congressional elections produce Democrat majorities in both houses, the Senate censures **Joseph McCarthy** and ends his witch-hunting career (see p.286). President Eisenhower, who has justified his failure to do

Elvis Presley (1935–77)

Looking now at footage of the young **Elvis Presley**, in his 1950s' prime, he seems an impossibly alien creature. Even his backing band appear bemused by his outlandish appearance, flamboyant clothes and raw sexual energy. And yet Elvis didn't descend fully fledged from the skies. Born in Tupelo, Mississippi, on January 8, 1935, he was raised such a poor piece of 'white trash' that even the segregation of the South failed to shield him from black culture. He thus absorbed every available musical influence, including blues and gospel as well as country, pop and light opera.

Having moved as a teenager to **Memphis**, Tennessee, Elvis cut a demo at **Sun Studio** in 1953. When owner Sam Phillips invited him back to make a commercial recording, Elvis tore into *That's All Right* with a fresh, heady exhilaration far removed from the muted resignation of bluesman Arthur Crudup's original. A raw acetate, played on the radio before a record even existed, made the song an instant local smash. No one knew how to define this new music – was it black or white, blues or country? – but the new **teenage** audience just didn't care.

Over the next sixteen months, Elvis and Phillips crafted the template for **rock'n'roll**. While popular myth has it that Elvis 'stole' from unsung black musicians, he transformed his sources. Subtle changes to lyrics, and the lip-smacking relish of his intonation, turned the world-weariness and all-too-adult boasting of the blues into epics of youthful exuberance and optimism.

Phillips eventually sold Presley's contract to major label RCA for $40,000 in 1955. Within a year, Elvis was a global phenomenon, releasing hits like *Heartbreak Hotel*; bursting onto national **television**; and starting his **movie career** in the critically lauded *Love Me Tender*. If his physical decline over the next twenty years is indisputable – there was not a shred of dignity in his bloated, drug-addled 1977 death – his often-imputed artistic decline is arguably less so. After all, his enduring iconic status owes as much to the overblown splendour of his 1970s' Las Vegas incarnation as it does to his explosive early impact.

more than disapprove from the sidelines by saying 'I refuse to get down in the gutter with that guy', jokes that McCarthyism has become McCarthywasm.

1955 In January, President Eisenhower responds to Red Chinese shelling of the offshore islands of **Quemoy** and **Matsu**, held by Chiang Kai-shek's Nationalists, by persuading Congress to grant him the authority to use US armed forces to defend Taiwan (Formosa). His threats soon draw the Chinese to a peace conference with Taiwan.

On July 17, Walt Disney opens **Disneyland** in California.

On August 27, a 14-year-old black visitor from Chicago, **Emmett Till**, is brutally murdered in Tallahatchie County, Mississippi, after he allegedly disrespects a white woman (stories vary as to his precise 'offence', but it seems likely that he simply said 'hello baby' as a dare). The overt racism displayed during the subsequent trial, in which his killers – who later sell their confessions to a journalist – are found not guilty, attracts worldwide media attention.

In November, the Interstate Commerce Commission orders that **racial segregation** on buses and trains that cross state lines must cease by January 10, 1956.

On November 22, the Russians test their first **hydrogen bomb**.

On December 1, **Rosa Parks**, a black seamstress in Montgomery, Alabama, is arrested for refusing to move from her seat on a segregated bus. Her action starts the **Montgomery bus boycott**, which brings **Rev. Martin Luther King, Jr**, to national prominence (see p.318).

1956 Abstract expressionist painter **Jackson Pollock**, who has become famous for his 'drip' canvases, is killed in a car crash in August.

In October, Israeli forces invade the Sinai Peninsula, acting in concert with the British and the French against

The Montgomery bus boycott

Tired after a long day working as a tailor's assistant, **Rosa Parks** boarded a bus in **Montgomery**, Alabama, on December 1, 1955. Under the city's racial segregation policy, the front ten rows were reserved for whites, and the back 26 for blacks. However, once the white section was filled, whites could use the black section as well. When the arrival of an extra white passenger meant that Rosa Parks and her companions in the eleventh row were ordered to vacate their seats, she refused. The police were called, and she was arrested.

As the local secretary of the **NAACP** (National Association for the Advancement of Colored People), Rosa Parks had previously discussed the possibility of **boycotting** the city's buses. Now the moment had arrived. A one-day boycott was called for December 5, and a meeting that day formed the **Montgomery Improvement Association** (MIA). The recently appointed minister of the Dexter Avenue Baptist Church, the little-known 26-year-old **Rev. Martin Luther King, Jr**, was chosen as its leader. That same night, addressing a crowd of thousands, he called for the boycott to continue, in a Christian, nonviolent campaign that would 'fight until justice runs down like water and righteousness like a mighty stream'.

Despite personal hardships, bombings and jailings, the boycott lasted for a full year, and involved a total of forty thousand black citizens. Many walked to work, while black-owned taxis carried those who lived further afield for the same 10¢ fare as the buses, and car-pools used every available vehicle. Meanwhile, the laid-off white bus drivers were employed as temporary police officials, issuing countless tickets to black drivers for minor violations. By April, the bus company had lost so much money that it announced it was going to stop enforcing segregation. However, the city government insisted that the laws continue to be imposed. When the US District Court ruled against it, it appealed to the **Supreme Court**, which finally responded, in November 1956, by declaring segregation on public transportation to be illegal. On December 21, Reverend King boarded the first non-segregated bus in Montgomery.

President Nasser of Egypt, who has nationalized the **Suez Canal**. After both the US and Russia declare their support for the United Nations charter, and thus effectively for Arab nationalism, the invaders are forced to back down. On October 31, the day after British and French bombing of Egypt begins, the Russians invade **Hungary** to impose a regime more to their liking.

Defeating **Adlai Stevenson** once again, but this time by an even wider margin, President Eisenhower is **re-elected** in November. **Richard Nixon**, despite an initial attempt to drop him from the ticket, remains vice president, while the Democrats win majorities in both houses of Congress.

1957 With Egypt appearing to gravitate towards Russian domination, the president proclaims his **Eisenhower Doctrine** in January, promising arms to any Middle Eastern country that requests US aid to resist Communism. It's approved by Congress in March.

When nine black students attempt to enrol in the newly de-segregated Central High School in **Little Rock**, Arkansas, in September, State Governor Orval Faubus orders the Arkansas National Guard to keep them out. After three weeks, President Eisenhower sends in the **101st Airborne Division** to enable the students to get past the redneck mob that has been controlling Little Rock. Televised nightly, the ongoing confrontation appals the nation and the world.

On October 4, the Russians send the first artificial satellite into orbit – **Sputnik**. Although US officials publicly deride it as a 'useless hunk of iron' and a 'silly bauble', the launch follows a Russian announcement that, unlike the Americans, they now possess **intercontinental ballistic missiles**, and triggers a frantic attempt to catch up – the **Space Race**.

1958 A team led by former German rocket scientist Wernher von Braun launches the first US **satellite**, *Explorer 1*, on

January 31. In July, the creation of the National Aeronautics and Space Administration, **NASA**, unites the rival space programmes being developed by the army, navy and air force.

Tensions rise in the **Middle East**, where President Nasser briefly combines Egypt with Syria, and a leftist coup overthrows the pro-US government in **Iraq**. Eisenhower sends five thousand US **marines** into Lebanon in July, but they withdraw in October.

1959 After a three-year guerrilla war, **Fidel Castro** takes power in **Cuba** on January 1.

Alaska becomes the 49th state of the Union on January 3, and **Hawaii** the fiftieth on August 21.

Vice President Richard Nixon confronts Soviet premier Nikita Khrushchev in Moscow, July 1959

Detroit Ford worker and part-time songwriter **Berry Gordy, Jr**, borrows $800 from his family to set up record label **Tamla Motown**. From his first hit onwards – the prophetic *Money (That's What I Want)* – he sets out to create a crossover pop style that will appeal to black and white consumers alike.

During an impromptu '**kitchen debate**' with Vice President **Nixon**, as they tour a showpiece kitchen at a US trade exhibition in Moscow in July, Russian leader **Nikita Khrushchev** promises the Soviet Union will overtake the US within seven years. Khrushchev then visits the US in September. His talks with Eisenhower produce little of substance, but appear to herald a thaw in relations.

1960 A major international summit, which Eisenhower hopes will result in a **test ban treaty** to halt nuclear proliferation, is scheduled for **Paris** in May. However, since 1956, secret American **U-2** spy planes have been flying high over Russia, taking photos that have helped to convince Eisenhower that the Soviet military threat is being exaggerated by scaremongers. On May 1, during the last such mission before the summit, a U-2 is shot down. Khrushchev tricks the US administration into lying about the flight, before revealing that its pilot, **Francis Gary Powers**, has been captured alive. The Paris summit is an angry affair, and Khrushchev, who feels himself humiliated at home for his previous willingness to trust Eisenhower, withdraws an invitation for 'Ike' to visit Moscow.

On February 1, four black college students refuse to leave after being denied service at a 'whites-only' *Woolworth* lunch counter in Greensboro, North Carolina. Such '**sit-ins**' swiftly spread to other Southern cities.

November's presidential election pits Vice President **Richard Nixon** against the 43-year-old junior Democratic Senator from Massachusetts, **John F. Kennedy**. A

Catholic of Irish descent – both of which characteristics would traditionally be expected to alienate Southern voters in particular – and the son of an immensely wealthy former US ambassador to Britain, Kennedy vows to increase military spending to close a supposed '**missile gap**' with the Soviet Union. Crucial turning points in the campaign include four **televised debates** between the candidates, in which the photogenic JFK outshines the sweaty, unshaven Nixon, and Kennedy's call to the wife of Martin Luther King, Jr, after King is jailed for a traffic violation. **Kennedy wins** in the popular vote by just 118,574 votes out of 68 million, but by 303 to 219 in the electoral college. Allegations of corruption in Chicago, where Mayor Richard Daley manages to give Illinois to Kennedy rather than Nixon, are almost certainly true, but that alone would not have changed the overall result.

9
From Kennedy to Carter

1961–80

The 43-year-old **John F. Kennedy** became the youngest man ever elected to the presidency in 1960 by projecting a wholesome, vigorous image that bore little relation to the true picture of chronic ill health and even more chronic promiscuity. He hurtled into office with apparently boundless energy; he was prepared literally to reach for the moon, pledging the US to victory in the **Space Race** in which it had thus far lagged humiliatingly behind the Soviet Union. The two decades that lay ahead, however, were to be characterized by disillusion, defeat and despair. If the Eisenhower years had been dull, the 1960s in particular were far too interesting for almost everybody's liking.

Kennedy's sheer glamour made him a popular president during his lifetime, while his assassination suffused his administration with the romantic glow of 'Camelot'. His one undisputed success, however, came with the **Cuban Missile Crisis** of 1962, when the US military fortunately spotted Russian bases in Cuba before any actual missiles were ready to use, and Kennedy faced down premier Khrushchev to insist they be withdrawn. On the other hand, he'd had rather less success the previous year, in launching the abortive **Bay of Pigs** invasion of Cuba, and he also managed to embroil America deeper in the ongoing war against Communism in Vietnam, by sending more 'advisers', including Green Berets, to Saigon.

Although a much publicized call to the wife of Rev. Martin Luther King, Jr, during one of King's many sojourns in Southern jails, was a factor in Kennedy's election success, he was rarely keen to identify himself with the **civil rights** movement. The campaign nonetheless made headway, given added momentum by the global television coverage of such horrific confrontations as the onslaught by Birmingham police on peaceful demonstrators in 1963. The movement's defining moment came when Rev. King delivered his electrifying 'I Have a Dream' speech during the March on Washington later that summer. King was subsequently awarded the Nobel Peace Prize for his unwavering espousal of Gandhian principles of nonviolence. Perhaps an equally powerful factor in middle America's recognition that the time had come to address racial inequalities, however, was the not-so-implicit threat in the rhetoric of **Malcolm X**, who argued that black people had the right to defend themselves against aggression. After Kennedy's assassination in November 1963, his successor **Lyndon B. Johnson** pushed through legislation that enacted most of the civil rights campaigners' key demands. Even then, violent white resistance in the South continued, and only the long, painstaking and dangerous work of registering Southern black voters en masse eventually forced Southern politicians to mend their ways.

Johnson won re-election by a landslide in 1964, but his vision of a '**Great Society**' soon foundered. Instead, he was brought low by the war in **Vietnam**, where US involvement escalated beyond all reason or apparent control. Broad-based popular opposition to the conflict grew in proportion to the American death toll, and the threat of the draft heightened the mood of youthful rebellion. San Francisco in particular responded to psychedelic prophet Timothy Leary's call to 'turn on, tune in, drop out'; 1967's 'Summer of Love' saw the lone beatniks of the 1950s transmogrify into an entire generation of hippies.

In 1968, the very social fabric of the US reached the brink of collapse. Shortly after his plummeting popularity forced Johnson to withdraw from the year-end elections, Martin Luther King was gunned down in a Memphis motel. Next, JFK's brother Robert, now redefined as spokesman for the nation's dispossessed, was fatally shot just as he emerged as Democratic frontrunner. Four crucial young leaders had now been assassinated within five years: King and Malcolm X had both died at 39, the two Kennedys in their forties. It didn't take a conspiracy theorist to see that the spate of deaths reflected a malaise in the soul of America.

Somehow – perhaps because the brutally suppressed riots at the Chicago Democratic convention raised the spectre of anarchy – the misery of 1968 resulted in the election of Republican **Richard Nixon** as president. Nixon had famously told the press after failing to become governor of California in 1962 that 'you won't have Richard Nixon to kick around any more'. Now he was back, and it soon became apparent that he had scores to settle with his countless perceived enemies, above all in the media. Nixon's impeccable conservative credentials enabled him to bring the US to a rapport with China, but the war in Vietnam dragged on, to claim a total of 58,000 American lives. Attempts to win it included the secret and illegal bombing of **Cambodia**, which raised opposition at home to a new peak, but ultimately it was simpler to abandon the original goals in the name of 'peace with honor'. The last US ground forces were withdrawn from Vietnam in 1973 – when Henry Kissinger and Le Duc Tho were awarded the Nobel Peace Prize for negotiating a treaty, and Tho at least had the grace to decline – but the war truly ended in 1975, when Saigon finally fell.

During Nixon's first term, many of the disparate individuals politicized by the events and undercurrents of the 1960s coalesced into **activist groupings**. Feminists united to campaign for abortion rights and an Equal Rights Amendment; gay men in New York's *Stonewall* bar fought back after one police raid too many; Native Americans formed the American Indian Movement; and even prisoners attempted to organize themselves, resulting in such bloody debacles as the storming of Attica prison in 1971. Nixon directed various federal agencies to monitor the new radicalism, but his real bugbear was the antiwar protesters. Increasingly ludicrous covert operations against real and potential opponents culminated in a botched attempt to burgle Democratic National Headquarters in the **Watergate** complex in 1972. It took two years of investigation for Nixon's role in the subsequent cover-up to be proved, but in 1974 he **resigned**, one step ahead of impeachment by the Senate, to be succeeded by **Gerald Ford**, his own unelected appointee as vice president.

With the Republicans momentarily discredited, former Georgia Governor **Jimmy Carter** was elected president as a clean-handed outsider in the bicentennial year of 1976. His victory showed how far the US had come in a decade, let alone two centuries; a crucial constituency for this new-style Southern Democrat was the recently enfranchised black population of the South. However, Carter's enthusiastic attempts to put his Baptist principles into practice on such issues as global human rights were soon perceived as naive, if not un-American. Misfortune followed misfortune. He had to break the news that the nation was facing an **energy crisis**, following the formation of the OPEC cartel of oil producers. Worse still, the Shah of Iran was overthrown, and staff at the US embassy in Tehran were taken hostage by Islamic revolutionaries. Carter's failed attempts to arrange

JFK campaign poster

their release were seized upon by the Republicans as a sign of his weak leadership, and all but destroyed his hopes of winning re-election in 1980. Instead he was replaced by a very different figure, the former Hollywood movie actor **Ronald Reagan**.

1961 In his farewell address on January 17, **President Eisenhower** warns the nation that 'the conjunction of an immense military establishment and a large arms industry is new in the American experience . . . we must guard against the acquisition of unwarranted influence, whether sought or unsought, by the **military–industrial complex**'.

Three days later, **President John F. Kennedy** is inaugurated, and proclaims a **New Frontier**.

On April 17, in a plan instigated under Eisenhower but inherited and authorized by Kennedy, 1400 CIA-trained Cuban exiles launch the '**Bay of Pigs**' invasion of **Cuba**. Determined to conceal US involvement, Kennedy does not allow US bombing before or during the invasion. A parallel CIA scheme to assassinate Fidel Castro having failed, the invasion is a disaster; an anticipated uprising fails to materialize, and 114 of the exiles are killed, and 1189 taken prisoner. Kennedy accepts responsibility for the fiasco, but blusters 'Let the record show our restraint is not inexhaustible', and continues plotting to overthrow Castro.

Student **sit-ins** having all but ended segregation in Southern restaurants, the New York-based Congress of Racial Equality (**CORE**) decides to target segregation on interstate transportation. It recruits a racially mixed group of **Freedom Riders**, who set off on May 4 to travel from Washington, DC, to New Orleans. Attacked and beaten in South Carolina and Alabama, by white mobs with police connivance, they fail to complete the journey. Another group, organized by the Student Nonviolent Coordinating Committee (**SNCC**), is similarly assaulted in Alabama. Attorney General **Robert F. Kennedy**, the president's younger brother, who regards the Freedom Riders as providing 'good propaganda for America's enemies', reluctantly steps in. Rather than guaranteeing their right to travel, however, he agrees to let Mississippi police arrest them so long as they protect the riders from violence. Over three hundred riders are arrested in Mississippi, but on November 1 the Interstate Commerce Commission formally **bans segregation** on interstate buses and travel facilities.

On May 5, **Alan Shepard** becomes the first American **astronaut**, by making a short suborbital flight in a Mercury capsule. Soviet cosmonaut **Yuri Gagarin** has, however, beaten him to it, becoming the first man in space on April 12.

US military '**advisers**' have been present in **South Vietnam** since 1955. Kennedy increases their number, and also sends four hundred Special Forces troops into Laos, Cambodia and North Vietnam in May.

> **"** Let the word go forth from this time and place, to friend and foe alike, that the torch has been passed to a new generation of Americans . . . Let every nation know, whether it wishes us well or ill, that we shall pay any price, bear any burden, meet any hardship, support any friend, oppose any foe, to assure the survival and the success of liberty . . . And so, my fellow Americans: ask not what your country can do for you – ask what you can do for your country. **"**
>
> President John F. Kennedy in his inaugural address, January 20, 1961

The Space Race

On April 12, 1961, President Kennedy reacted to the news that the first Russian cosmonaut had gone into orbit by pleading: 'If somebody could just tell me how to catch up. Let's find somebody – anybody. I don't care if it's that janitor over there.' Kennedy had never been a space enthusiast. Three weeks earlier, he had decided to stop funding the development of manned space flight, in the **Apollo** programme. However, it was unthinkable for the Communist Russians to be seen as more technologically advanced than the Americans. The failure of the Bay of Pigs invasion three days after Gagarin's flight made it even more urgent to raise US international prestige.

The nucleus of the team that won the ensuing **Space Race** were the German scientists who developed the V-2 military rocket during World War II, and then fled westwards in 1945. Assured by their leader, **Wernher von Braun,** that he had a 'sporting chance' of success, and heartened by Alan Shepard's fifteen-minute sub-orbital flight on May 5, Kennedy made an extraordinary announcement to Congress on May 25: 'I believe this nation should commit itself to achieving the goal, before this decade is out, of landing a man on the moon and returning him safely to earth.'

Many balked at the **expense:** Dwight D. Eisenhower commented that 'anyone who would spend $40 billion in a race to the moon for national prestige is nuts'. However, fulfilling the pledge became a matter of honour after Kennedy's death, and President **Johnson** was in any case a space nut, responsible while in the Senate for the creation of NASA. By 1966, the programme employed over 400,000 people, and was absorbing one percent of American GDP.

While the world watched – and Kennedy's old opponent Richard Nixon hogged the limelight – **Neil Armstrong** of *Apollo 11* finally made his 'giant leap for mankind' on July 20, 1969. Then, somehow, the Space Race seemed to fade into history. Although ten more Americans, including Shepard, followed in Armstrong's footsteps before the Apollo missions ended in 1972, more than half the world's population has now been born since a man walked on the moon.

In **Vienna** in June, Soviet premier **Nikita Khrushchev** tests President Kennedy's nerve in summit discussions on Taiwan, Berlin and nuclear disarmament. Kennedy's private verdict is that 'he beat the hell out of me'.

To combat mass emigration to the West, and in violation of international agreements, Communist forces start to build the **Berlin Wall** on August 13.

The **Twenty-Third Amendment** entitles citizens of Washington, DC, to vote in presidential elections.

In his novel *Catch-22*, **Joseph Heller** provides a cynical take on World War II that will be read as an eerily accurate vision of US entanglement in Vietnam.

1962 In January, US aircraft start spraying the defoliant **Agent Orange** on the Ho Chi Minh jungle trail in Vietnam, to diminish the cover available to **Viet Cong** guerrilla fighters.

On February 20, **John Glenn,** the first American astronaut to go into orbit, circles the earth three times. In July, a collaboration between the government and AT&T launches the first communications satellite, **Telstar**.

Pop Art captures the public imagination. **Andy Warhol** has his first solo exhibitions in Los Angeles and New York, displaying painted cans of Campbell's soup, and also produces his first silkscreen prints, depicting Marilyn Monroe and Elvis Presley among others. **Roy Lichtenstein** starts to paint and exhibit acrylic renditions of scenes from war comics, including *Whaam!*

On September 20, Governor Ross Barnett of Mississippi defies a federal court order by refusing to let black student **James Meredith** enrol at the University of Mississippi. Meredith is eventually admitted after Robert Kennedy sends in federal troops; two people die in the accompanying riots.

The Cuban Missile Crisis

Early in 1962, Soviet premier **Nikita Khrushchev** concluded a secret deal to install nuclear missiles on Cuba. Since the Bay of Pigs landing in 1961, **Fidel Castro** was sure another US invasion was imminent. Whether he actually wanted Soviet missiles, or accepted them in return for more general aid, is however unclear. When an American U-2 spy plane spotted the launch sites on October 14, 36 medium-range missiles (range 1020 miles), were already in Cuba, while 32 intermediate-range ones (range 2200 miles) were on their way by sea.

The ensuing **Cuban Missile Crisis** is generally acknowledged as the closest approach to nuclear war the world has seen since Hiroshima and Nagasaki. To the Americans, whose radar systems all faced north, a threat from ninety miles south was unconscionable. Tape recordings from the crucial White House meeting of October 16 reveal **President Kennedy** struggling to understand Khrushchev's motivation – was he hoping to bargain over Berlin, or over US missiles in Turkey, or over Cuba itself? Kennedy initially favoured a surprise all-out attack on Cuba, but

In late October, President Kennedy faces down the Russians in the **Cuban Missile Crisis**; see above.

1963 A major year of **civil rights** campaigning, designed in part to mark the centenary of Emancipation, begins in the segregated city of **Birmingham**, Alabama, in April. On Good Friday, April 12, fifty black leaders are arrested, including Rev. **Martin Luther King, Jr**, who writes a widely publicized *Letter from Birmingham Jail*, calling for further action. In May, schoolchildren join the demonstrations; televised images of the brutal response of police commissioner Eugene 'Bull' Connor, who uses dogs and water cannon against the protesters, cause national outrage. More than two thousand children are jailed before city business leaders agree to integrate facilities and hire blacks.

he finally opted to go public, and order a blockade of ships approaching Cuba. After a week of excruciating tension, Russian vessels turned back rather than face the US Navy; in the terminology of the time, it was the Russians who 'blinked'.

Although no formal agreement ended the crisis, it was defused after Khrushchev wrote two successive letters to Kennedy on October 26 and 27. The first offered to withdraw the missiles if the US promised not to invade Cuba, the second to 'exchange' them for American missiles in Turkey. So far as the public was told, the Americans simply ignored the second, and agreed to the first, and the Soviet missiles were indeed withdrawn. In fact, it has since emerged, a secret agreement was struck over Turkey, and the US missiles there were also removed.

World and national opinion saw Kennedy, the cool, unflinching statesman, as the victor; Khrushchev, despite claiming he had saved Cuba from the US, was deposed for his humiliating climbdown two years later. As far as Castro was concerned, what really saved Cuba was the diversion of US attention towards Vietnam.

On June 11, **President Kennedy** sends in the National Guard to force Governor **George Wallace** to allow two black students to enrol at the University of Alabama. He then announces that he will ask Congress to pass a Civil Rights Bill. That same night, in Jackson, Mississippi, black civil rights leader **Medgar Evers** is assassinated outside his home. He is buried a week later in Arlington National Cemetery.

On June 26, visiting **West Berlin**, President Kennedy expresses his solidarity with the people of the city by announcing '**Ich bin ein Berliner**.'

250,000 blacks and whites gather on August 28 for the **March on Washington**, a massive civil rights demonstration

> **❝** I have a dream that one day this nation will rise up and live out the true meaning of its creed – we hold these truths to be self-evident, that all men are created equal . . . With this faith we will be able to work together, to pray together, to struggle together, to go to jail together, to stand up for freedom together, knowing that we will be free one day. **❞**
>
> Rev. Martin Luther King, Jr, addressing the March on Washington,
> August 28, 1963

that represents the fruition of a plan originally proposed by black leader **A. Philip Randolph** in 1941. Some black groups, notably the SNCC, decline to participate, charging that the civil rights movement has been co-opted by the Kennedy administration to support its own limited goals. However, the march is an enormous success, culminating in the passionate 'I Have a Dream' speech by Rev. **Martin Luther King**, **Jr**.

Two weeks later, on September 15, a **bomb** at a Birmingham church kills four young black girls attending Sunday school.

On the basis that the corruption, brutality and anti-Buddhist repression of the regime led by the Catholic President Ngo Dinh Diem may make it difficult to justify US military support of **South Vietnam**, Kennedy gives his tacit consent to **Diem's assassination** on November 1. However, the coup that brings General Minh to power is merely the first of many.

In *The Fire Next Time*, gay, black novelist and essayist **James Baldwin** delivers a searing 'sermon' on black alienation in the US. Betty Friedan's *The Feminine Mystique* becomes a bestseller; see p.310.

On November 22, President Kennedy is **assassinated** while visiting Dallas, Texas. The suspected assassin, **Lee Harvey Oswald** – a former marine who has returned after emigrating to Russia – is himself shot by nightclub owner Jack Ruby two days later. The subsequent **Warren Commission** concludes that Oswald acted alone, but conspiracy theories surround Kennedy's murder to this day, suggesting connections with organized crime and/or Cuban emigres.

Vice President **Lyndon B. Johnson** of Texas, Senate majority leader between 1954 and 1960, is sworn in as president. Shortly before his death, Kennedy has indicated plans to withdraw US forces from Vietnam, but Johnson immediately assures Republican leaders that 'I am not going to lose Vietnam. I am not going to be the President who saw Southeast Asia go the way China went.'

1964 In January, the **Twenty-Fourth Amendment** becomes law. It tackles black disenfranchisement in the South by forbidding states to use payment of poll or other taxes as a requirement to vote in federal elections.

On February 25, **Cassius Clay** defeats Sonny Liston to become world heavyweight boxing champion. He promptly announces that he has joined the Nation of Islam, and changes his name to **Muhammad Ali**. Also in February, the **Beatles** visit America for the first time.

President Johnson, known as **LBJ** in conscious homage to FDR, makes domestic issues his top priority. On March 16, he tells Congress that 'this administration here and now declares unconditional **war on poverty** in America', and announces social welfare programmes including Head Start for pre-schoolers and the Job Corps for older youth. On May 22, he gives his vision a name – the **Great Society**.

Betty Friedan (b.1921) and the Women's Movement

In 1957, the author and labour activist **Betty Friedan** circulated a questionnaire among the women who had graduated with her fifteen years earlier from Smith College. Of the two hundred who replied, all but six were married, and all but 22 were housewives. The majority echoed the dissatisfaction that Friedan noted in herself: 'a strange discrepancy between the reality of our lives as women and the image to which we were trying to conform'.

Friedan failed to persuade any magazine to accept an article on 'the problem that has no name', highlighting women's desire to pursue their education and careers, and the lack of fulfilment felt by many in the much vaunted role of motherhood. Instead she wrote a book, *The Feminine Mystique*, which became a multi-million-selling sensation in 1963. She argued that while World War II had been a time of great promise and hope for women, in terms of opportunities, the years since had seen a retreat into an unreal, and inevitably unsatisfying, fantasy of domesticity: 'somehow, somewhere, someone must have figured out that women will buy more things if they are kept in the underused,

Kennedy's proposed civil rights legislation has been stalled in Congress by Southern Democrats, but Johnson now pushes through a much more radical **Civil Rights Bill**. Passed on June 19, it bans racial discrimination in all public places and federal programmes, and also in employment and union membership. It even bans **sexual discrimination** in employment for the first time, after what conservatives intend to be a 'wrecking' amendment is passed along with the rest, but that provision is not taken seriously and is barely enforced.

On August 4, Johnson announces that North Vietnamese torpedo ships have launched 'unprovoked' attacks on two

nameless-yearning, energy-to-get-rid-of state of being housewives'.

As a national figure, Friedan set out to persuade the government to enforce the equal rights provision of the 1964 Civil Rights Act. That frustrating quest led her to found the National Organization for Women (**NOW**) in 1966, and campaign for an **Equal Rights Amendment** to the Constitution – agreed by Congress in 1972, but never ratified by the states – and for **abortion rights**, which were eventually secured by the Supreme Court's *Roe v Wade* decision of 1973. Friedan herself remained rooted in a traditional political approach, advocating legislation as the means to improve women's economic condition, and came to believe that NOW was neglecting the needs of ordinary working women. Out of tune with what she called the 'bedroom war' waged by younger **women's liberationists**, as exemplified by Kate Millett's *Sexual Politics* in 1970, she continued to champion economic empowerment, this time for the **elderly**, by publishing *The Fountain of Age* in 1993.

US destroyers in the **Gulf of Tonkin**. In fact only one such attack has taken place, and it was against a vessel in disputed waters that was covertly monitoring a US-sponsored attack by South Vietnamese troops. Nonetheless, the incident becomes the pretext for the **Tonkin Gulf Resolution** of August 7. In a crucial moment for the escalation of the undeclared war on North Vietnam, Congress all but unanimously authorizes Johnson to undertake 'all necessary measures to repel any armed attack against the forces of the United States and to prevent further aggression'.

During the **Mississippi Freedom Summer**, a drive to register black voters in Mississippi recruits several hundred white student volunteers from the North. On June 21, three young participants (two white, one black) disappear after being arrested in Neshoba County; Johnson sends in the **FBI**, and their bodies are discovered on August 4. Two days later, newly registered black voters hold a convention of the **Mississippi Freedom Democratic Party** and elect delegates to the national Democratic convention. However, fearful of embarrassment, Johnson insists that the convention seat delegates from Mississippi's all-white traditional Democratic Party instead.

In September, a returning Mississippi volunteer, **Mario Savio**, reacts to a ban on political activity on the **Berkeley** campus of the University of California by founding the **Free Speech Movement**, which will become a major influence on student protests across the nation.

In October, Rev. **Martin Luther King, Jr**, is awarded the **Nobel Peace Prize**, and premier **Khrushchev** is deposed in Moscow.

Meanwhile, the Republicans have nominated Arizona Senator **Barry Goldwater** as their most right-wing

> **❝** We believe all men are entitled to the blessings of liberty. Yet millions are being deprived of those blessings – not because of their own failures, but because of the color of their skin . . . We can understand – without rancour or hatred – how this happened, but it cannot continue . . . Our Constitution, the foundation of our Republic, forbids it. The principles of our freedom forbid it. Morality forbids it. And the law I will sign tonight forbids it. **❞**
>
> President Lyndon B. Johnson, signing the Civil Rights Act in 1964

Malcolm X, as leading spokesman for the Nation of Islam, visits Hartford, Connecticut in 1963

presidential candidate of the century. Though later hailed as a hero by Ronald Reagan, he's widely perceived as likely, indeed even keen, to precipitate nuclear war with Russia. Pronouncements such as 'extremism in the defense of liberty is no vice' strike no chord with voters still mourning Kennedy, and **Johnson** wins a **landslide** victory in November, winning 61 percent of the popular vote and by 486 to 52 in the electoral college.

1965 The focus of the **civil rights** movement shifts in January to **Selma**, Alabama, a majority black city where only one percent of blacks are registered to vote. By February 1, Rev. **Martin Luther King, Jr**, and three thousand other demonstrators are in jail. After police shoot a black youth during a night-time demonstration in nearby Marion on February 18, a protest march from **Selma to Montgomery** on March 7 is violently broken up by state troopers. They

Malcolm X (1925–65)

Born in Omaha, Nebraska, **Malcolm Little** moved to Lansing, Michigan, when he was 4. The death of his activist father soon afterwards, hit by a streetcar, was later regarded by Malcolm as a lynching rather than an accident. The only black child in his class (and its president), Malcolm left school after a teacher told him 'you've got to be realistic about being a nigger'. At 15, he was a hustler on the streets of New York and Boston.

While jailed for burglary in the early 1950s, Malcolm joined the **Nation of Islam**, also known as the Black Muslims. The movement had been led since 1934 by **Elijah Muhammad**, whose advocacy of strict self-discipline and sobriety transformed the lives of many disaffected and criminalized urban blacks. Malcolm abandoned his 'slave name' to become **Malcolm X**, and characterizing himself as 'the angriest black man in America' became the Nation's most prominent spokesman, denouncing whites as 'blue-eyed devils'. A spellbinding orator, he rejected the nonviolence of Martin Luther King – whom he only met once, by chance – and called the 1963 March on Washington a 'circus' and a 'sellout'. He insisted that American blacks should resist oppression **'by any means necessary'**.

Malcolm subsequently became disenchanted with the Nation's lack of a political and economic programme, while his own hajj to Mecca convinced him that it was indeed possible – if in traditional Islam, then conceivably in the US as well – for different races to live in equality. His estrangement from Elijah Muhammad was completed in 1964, after Elijah suspended him for commenting of President Kennedy's assassination that 'chickens coming home to roost never did make me sad'.

In his final months, he changed his name again, to El-Hajj Malik El-Shabazz, and set up the Organization of Afro-American Unity. Before his new vision could be articulated, he was gunned down in Harlem, almost certainly by Nation of Islam members. Current leader **Louis Farrakhan** acknowledges a degree of complicity, but blames 'manipulation and stimulation of our own pettiness and weakness by . . . the government of America'.

also stop King leading another march on March 9. Prompted by these events, President Johnson presents a new **Voting Rights Bill** to Congress on March 15, then federalizes the Alabama National Guard and sends in the army to protect a third march, which completes the 54-mile route from Selma to Montgomery between March 21 and 25.

On February 21, **Malcolm X** is assassinated in New York (see opposite).

After the **Viet Cong** kill eight Americans during an attack on the Plei Ku air base on February 5, US aircraft start to **bomb** North Vietnam. These retaliatory strikes are formalized in March as **Operation Rolling Thunder**, the largest bombing campaign in history, which will continue until October 1968. Also in March, the first US **combat troops** arrive in Vietnam. During the first half of the year, the US military presence increases from 23,000 to 75,000, while on July 28 Johnson announces a further build-up that will amount to an additional 175,000 soldiers.

At the **Newport Folk Festival** in July, **Bob Dylan**, who has made his name as the troubadour of the protest movement, stuns purists by 'going electric' – playing with an amplified back-up band. During the year, he releases two albums, *Bringing It All Back Home* and *Highway 61 Revisited*, and the single *Like A Rolling Stone*, that pioneer what is about to become known as **rock music**.

On July 30, LBJ signs the **Medicare** Bill, under which healthcare for the elderly will be financed from Social Security funds. Former President Truman, on hand for the ceremony, declares 'I am glad to have lived this long'. A week later, on August 6, Johnson signs the **Voting Rights Act**, which abolishes literacy and other tests that have been used to disenfranchise blacks.

For six days following August 11, the **Watts Riot**, which starts as a protest against police brutality, engulfs a black

BETTMANN/CORBIS

Rev. Martin Luther King, Jr, in jail in Birmingham, Alabama

district of Los Angeles; 34 die and over a thousand are injured. Coming so soon after major civil rights victories, it's read as a sign by the movement's leaders that they should shift their attention from the rural South towards the urban ghettoes.

In October, the **Immigration Act** replaces quotas for individual nations by sanctioning an annual influx of 120,000 persons from the western hemisphere and 170,000 from the rest of the world.

On December 24, President Johnson **suspends the bombing** of North Vietnam. His hopes of prompting negotiations come to nothing, however, and bombing **resumes** on January 31, 1966.

During the year, the oral **contraceptive pill** becomes widely available in America and across the world.

1966 In May, **Stokely Carmichael**, who espouses separation rather than integration and advocates the new philosophy of 'black power', becomes the leader of the SNCC.

Andy Warhol is by now presiding over a multimedia studio, **The Factory**, in New York, where projects during the year include making several movies and producing a rock band, the **Velvet Underground**.

Ruling on *Miranda v Arizona* in June, the **Supreme Court** declares that arrested individuals must be advised of their rights to silence and counsel.

On June 6, **James Meredith**, leading his own march from Memphis to Jackson, Mississippi, to encourage voter registration, is shot and wounded. During the summer, further **race riots** hit Chicago, Brooklyn, Atlanta, Cleveland and other cities.

Protest against the Vietnam War is growing. 6400 professionals and academics demand an end to hostilities in the

Rev. Martin Luther King, Jr (1929–68)

Martin Luther King, Jr, was born in Auburn Avenue, the middle-class black district of Atlanta, Georgia, on January 15, 1929. Both his father and grandfather served as pastor of **Ebenezer Baptist Church.** Ordained at 19, young Martin studied at Crozer Theological Seminary in Pennsylvania, where he encountered the ideas of Karl Marx and Gandhi, and at Boston University.

Returning to the South, King became pastor of Dexter Avenue Baptist Church in **Montgomery,** Alabama, in 1954. A year later, his leadership during the bus boycott (see p.292) brought him to national prominence. As president of the **Southern Christian Leadership Conference,** founded in 1957, he subsequently became the figurehead for the **civil rights** struggle, planning strategy for future campaigns, flying into each new trouble spot, and commenting to the news media on every latest development. His apotheosis in that role came in August 1963, when he addressed the **March on Washington** with his 'I Have a Dream' speech.

Despite King's passionate espousal of nonviolence, J. Edgar Hoover's **FBI** branded him 'the most dangerous and effective Negro leader in the country', and persistently attempted to discredit him over his personal life. King himself became more overtly politicized in his final years. Challenged by the stridency of Malcolm X and the radicalism of urban black youth, he came to see the deprivation and poverty of the cities of the North as affecting black and white alike, and only solvable by tackling 'the triple evils of racism, extreme materialism, and militarism'. In the South, he had always been able to appeal to the federal government as an (albeit often reluctant) ally; now, having declared his opposition to the war in **Vietnam,** he faced a sterner and lonelier struggle. In the event, his **Poor People's Campaign** had barely got off the ground before King was assassinated in Memphis on April 4, 1968.

Many former associates argue that King's posthumous quasi-deification has served to obscure two points they see as crucial: firstly that for all his pacifism King was a fiery political being, and secondly that the movement created King, not King the movement.

New York Times in June; in July, the CORE convention encourages resistance to the draft, endorses black power, rejects nonviolence, and demands US withdrawal from Vietnam; and demonstrators in Washington in November chant for the first time 'Hey, hey, LBJ, how many kids did you kill today?'

1967 On January 15, in football's first-ever **Superbowl**, the NFL's Green Bay Packers defeat the AFL's Kansas City Chiefs by 35–10.

On January 27, three US **astronauts die** in a launch-pad fire as their *Apollo 1* spacecraft is being tested at Cape Kennedy, Florida.

On February 10, the **Twenty-Fifth Amendment** becomes law, clarifying the arrangements for the succession should the president die, become incapacitated, or leave office.

Speaking in Congress on March 12, **Robert Kennedy**, now a Senator for New York, denounces LBJ's conduct of the Vietnam War, and calls for an end to the bombing. The two men have become increasingly estranged. Several hundred thousand antiwar protesters demonstrate in New York City – where they're joined by Rev. **Martin Luther King, Jr** – and San Francisco on April 15. Two weeks later, **Muhammad Ali**, who has been called up to serve in Vietnam, refuses on

> ❝ The picture of the world's greatest superpower killing or injuring 1000 noncombatants a week, while trying to pound a tiny backward nation into submission on an issue whose merits are hotly disputed, is not a pretty one. ❞
>
> Secretary of Defense Robert McNamara, considering the war in Vietnam, May 1967

religious grounds to be inducted into the US armed forces. His earlier remark that 'I ain't got no quarrel with them Viet Cong' has polarized national opinion; he's stripped of his world heavyweight title, and will be refused permission to fight again until October 1970.

In June's **Six-Day War**, Israel launches a pre-emptive attack against massing Arab forces, and extends its borders to include the Sinai Peninsula, the West Bank and the Golan Heights. US military and financial support for Israel will earn lasting enmity from Arab and Muslim nations.

Race riots during the summer include major disturbances in Newark and Detroit. In San Francisco, however, this will be remembered as the **Summer of Love**, as long-haired '**hippies**' take over the city's Haight-Ashbury district.

In August, **Thurgood Marshall** becomes the first black judge to be appointed to the **Supreme Court**.

On October 21 and 22, fifty thousand **antiwar** marchers converge on Washington, DC, and attempt to 'levitate' the Pentagon. During December's **Stop the Draft Week**, the six hundred protesters arrested in New York include child-care expert Dr Benjamin Spock and poet Allen Ginsberg.

1968 On January 31, the **Viet Cong** ignore the customary informal truce for the Vietnamese New Year by launching the **Tet Offensive**, in which they capture the city of Hué and penetrate deep into Saigon. They're driven back with heavy casualties, but it's a massive blow for US confidence, and convinces many commentators, including the much respected Walter Cronkite, that the war is unwinnable. The US military presence in Vietnam will peak during the year, at 549,000 troops.

On March 12, leading what's called the 'Children's Crusade' because his campaign attracts so many student volunteers, an antiwar candidate, Minnesota Senator

BETTMANN/CORBIS

President John F. Kennedy confers with his brother, Attorney General Robert F. Kennedy, at the White House in 1962

John F. Kennedy (1917–63) and Robert F. Kennedy (1925–68)

The aura of martyrdom that surrounds the two murdered Kennedy brothers makes it all but impossible to separate myth from reality. **John F. Kennedy** is still regularly ranked among the greatest of all presidents, his brief spell in office remembered as a 'Thousand Days' of high, if ill-defined, achievement. **Robert F. Kennedy** has been eulogized as a tragic lost hope, though it's impossible to know whether he would have even have secured the 1968 Democratic nomination, let alone whether his apparent transformation into the champion of the underdog would have lasted beyond the election.

Both boys were raised in a fiercely competitive atmosphere. Their father, **Joseph Kennedy, Sr**, was an extremely wealthy businessman whose bootlegging past, and disastrous spell as ambassador to Britain before World War II, stymied his own political ambitions. Instead he dreamed of his eldest son, **Joseph Kennedy, Jr**, becoming president; after Joseph Jr died in the war, he focused on John instead.

Aided by his war record, rescuing survivors after a Japanese destroyer sank his patrol boat, *PT-109*, **JFK** was elected as both Representative (1947–53) and Senator (1953–61) from Massachusetts. Though he did little to distinguish himself in

Eugene McCarthy, wins a creditable 42 percent of the vote to LBJ's 48 percent in New Hampshire's Democratic primary. That encourages **Robert Kennedy** to declare his own candidacy on March 16, proposing to 'end the bloodshed in Vietnam and in our cities'. In a televised broadcast on March 31, the exhausted President Johnson announces a partial end to the bombing of North Vietnam and new initiatives towards a cease-fire, and reveals that he **will not stand** for re-election.

Congress, he wrote the Pulitzer Prize-winning *Profiles in Courage*, and his good looks and indefinable 'charisma', plus his father's money, propelled him into the White House. His numerous sexual conquests, said to have ranged from Marilyn Monroe to gangsters' molls, and his crippling illnesses, which included severe back pain that required constant medication and often necessitated the use of a wheelchair, remained hidden from the public, who saw instead a firm-jawed Cold Warrior who doted on his glamorous wife Jackie.

A pugnacious aide during the 1950s to Joseph McCarthy's witch-hunts and investigations into union corruption, **Robert** was John's campaign manager, and later his **Attorney General** and closest confidant. Devastated by his brother's death, he swiftly fell out with LBJ, and in 1964 became a Senator for New York. Though both brothers had appeared lukewarm towards civil rights, 'Bobby' was radicalized by his exposure to poverty and black alienation, and spurred to build a new coalition of the downtrodden. That mission acquired a new urgency after the slaying of Martin Luther King, but his own death just two months later left the promise forever unfulfilled.

Meanwhile, although details will not emerge until late 1969, US soldiers led by Lieutenant William Calley **massacre** around five hundred Vietnamese civilians in the village of **My Lai**, on March 16.

On April 4, Rev. **Martin Luther King, Jr**, is **assassinated** in Memphis, Tennessee, sparking riots across America. Gunman James Earl Ray is arrested two months later at London's Heathrow Airport, and convicted of the murder,

> The original plans for the March on Washington had been far from polite: the original plan had been to lie down on airport runways, to block the streets and offices. To immobilize the city completely, and to remain as long as we had to, to force the government to recognize the urgency and the justice of our demands. Malcolm [X] was very caustic about the March on Washington, which he described as a sell-out. I think he was right. Martin, five years later, was five years wearier and five years sadder, and still petitioning . . . five years later, it was very hard to believe that the frontal assault, on the capitol, could possibly have produced more bloodshed, or more despair.

James Baldwin on meeting Rev. Martin Luther King, Jr, in 1968, five years after the March on Washington

but suspicions will endure, including among King's family, that he did not act alone.

On June 3, **Andy Warhol** is shot, but not killed, at the Factory by Valerie Solanis, the founder of SCUM (the Society for Cutting Up Men).

The tense struggle between McCarthy and Kennedy in the race for the Democratic nomination appears to be decided on June 4, when Kennedy, now widely regarded as the spokesman for America's underprivileged, wins the crucial California primary. At his Los Angeles victory celebration that night, however, **Robert Kennedy is assassinated** by Sirhan Sirhan, for his perceived support for Israel.

The subsequent **Democratic convention**, in Chicago in August, is a fiasco. Inside the hall, there's fierce antagonism between supporters of McCarthy and of the eventual nominee, Johnson's vice president, **Hubert Humphrey**, a relative war 'hawk'. Outside, chaotic demonstrations by the **Yippies** – members of the Youth International Party, who nominate a pig for president – and other antiwar radicals are brutally repressed by police.

The Republicans nominate **Richard Nixon** as their presidential candidate, who intimates that he has a secret plan to end the Vietnam War and provide 'peace with honor', while Alabama's Democrat Governor **George Wallace**, an advocate of racial segregation, stands as an independent. On November 5, **Nixon wins** a narrow victory, with 31.8 million votes – two million fewer than he received when losing to JFK in 1960 – to Humphrey's 31.3 million, and Wallace's 9.9 million. The Democrats keep their majorities in both houses.

Over Christmas, the **Apollo 8** astronauts successfully orbit the moon, and return safely to earth.

1969 In March, President Nixon authorizes a campaign devised by Henry Kissinger, and the secret, illegal, **bombing**

> 66 Like anybody, I would like to live a long life. Longevity has its place. But I'm not concerned about that now. I just want to do God's will. And He's allowed me to go up to the mountain, and I've looked over, and I've seen the promised land. I may not get there with you. But I want you to know tonight that we, as a people, will get to the promised land. And so I'm happy tonight. I'm not worried about anything. I'm not fearing any man. Mine eyes have seen the glory of the coming of the Lord. 99
>
> Rev. Martin Luther King, Jr, speaking in Memphis on April 3, 1968, the night before his assassination

of Communist positions in **Cambodia** begins After meeting South Vietnamese President **Thieu** on Midway Island on June 8, Nixon announces the first **withdrawal** of US troops from **Vietnam**. 110,000 will leave by the end of the year. Nixon's strategy is for South Vietnamese soldiers to bear the brunt of the fighting, supported by US bombing.

Police in New York City raid a male gay bar, the *Stonewall Inn*, on June 17. The resultant **Stonewall Riots** spark the creation of the **Gay Liberation Front**.

On July 18, **Edward Kennedy**, Massachusetts Senator and younger brother of John and Robert, drives off a bridge at Chappaquiddick Island, and his passenger Mary Jo Kopechne drowns. His failure to report the accident for ten hours damages his standing.

On July 20, **Neil Armstrong** becomes the first man to walk on the **moon**, after the **Apollo 11** mission lands at Tranquillity Base. An excited Richard Nixon speaks to the astronauts on the lunar surface, and greets them on their return by saying 'this is the greatest week in the history of the world since the Creation'.

In August, the **Woodstock Music Festival** attracts almost half a million young people in upstate New York. However, the **murders** of actress Sharon Tate and others, by members of **Charles Manson**'s so-called 'Family', during the same month in Los Angeles, are widely seen as marking the end of the hippie dream.

Also in August, President Nixon's National Security Adviser, **Henry Kissinger** – who has more influence over foreign policy than Secretary of State William Rogers – opens secret **peace talks** in Paris with Le Duc Tho of North Vietnam.

On September 24, the **Chicago Eight** go on trial, accused of conspiring to incite riots during the 1968

The Stars and Stripes flutter on the moon, July 1969

Democratic convention. Amid courtroom disorder, **Bobby Seale**, leader of the militant separatist **Black Panthers**, is bound and gagged; in November, he is sentenced to four years' imprisonment for contempt. Another Black Panther leader, **Fred Hampton**, is killed during a police raid on his Chicago apartment on December 4.

Antiwar protests continue throughout the year, culminating on November 15, when 250,000 demonstrators march in Washington, and 150,000 in San Francisco.

1970 In February, seven of the **Chicago Eight** are acquitted of conspiracy, but five of them are jailed for five years for crossing state lines with intent to incite a riot.

In April, the **Apollo 13** lunar mission is jeopardized by a sudden loss of power, but the astronauts manage to steer their crippled spacecraft back to earth.

On April 30, little more than a week after announcing a further reduction of 150,000 troops in Vietnam, President Nixon reveals that US troops have **invaded** 'neutral' **Cambodia** to 'clean out' Viet Cong bases; the 'incursion' will last until the end of June. This escalation of a war he has promised to end spurs angry protests, especially among students. On May 4, Ohio National Guardsmen open fire on student demonstrators at **Kent State** University, killing four. The country is increasingly polarized; counter-demonstrations against the peace movement also take place, and construction workers break up a protest in New York City on May 8.

On June 24, the Senate votes by a large majority to **repeal** the Tonkin Gulf Resolution of 1964, the original basis for US involvement in Vietnam. Six days later, it passes the **Cooper–Church Amendment**, which by specifying that Nixon cannot act further in Cambodia without Congressional approval marks the first time that limits have been imposed on any president's ability to wage war.

In July, the independent **Environmental Protection Agency** is established, to oversee control of air and water pollution and toxic waste.

On August 26, the National Organization for Women calls a **national strike of women** to mark the fiftieth anniversary of the Nineteenth Amendment, which gave women the vote.

1971 On June 3, the *New York Times* starts to publish the '**Pentagon Papers**', leaked State Department documents that reveal details of the secret decision-making processes that led to the Vietnam War. After the Supreme Court refuses to suppress the material on June 30, it greatly contributes to public disenchantment with the war .

Also on June 30, the **Twenty-Sixth Amendment** comes into force, lowering the **minimum voting age** to 18.

On July 15, in the wake of a secret visit by Kissinger to Beijing, President Nixon makes the startling announcement that he will **visit the People's Republic of China** in 1972.

On August 15, responding to inflation, unemployment and the first US trade deficit since 1894, Nixon announces his '**new economic policy**'. He imposes a ninety-day freeze on wages and prices, a ten percent additional tax on imports, and replaces the 1944 Bretton Woods system by suspending the convertibility of the dollar into gold. Within a month the Organization of Petroleum Exporting Countries (**OPEC**) takes action to maintain the real value of its ever-increasing oil exports to the US. Nixon hails a wholesale revaluation of major world currencies on December 17, in which the dollar is devalued by eight percent, as 'the most significant monetary agreement in the history of the world', but it will result in **stagflation**, a previously unknown phenomenon that combines high inflation with economic stagnation.

In September, four guards and 39 inmates die when state troopers storm the **Attica** Correctional Facility in upstate New York, ending a prisoners' revolt against racial mistreatment.

1972 Between February 21 and 25, President Nixon meets with Mao Zedong and Foreign Minister Zhou Enlai in Communist **China**. The US has until now insisted that the Taiwanese government is the only legitimate Chinese authority, and refused to recognize 'Red' China. Now Nixon agrees that the People's Republic and not Taiwan will represent China in the United Nations. A major motivation is his hope that by playing China and Russia off against each other, both may stop supporting North Vietnam.

President Richard Nixon meets Mao Zedong in Beijing, February 1972

In March, Congress approves the **Equal Rights Amendment**, which as the Twenty-Seventh Amendment would outlaw sex discrimination. However, conservative opposition will ensure that it is only ever ratified by 35 of the necessary 38 states, and it will expire in 1982.

In response to a large-scale North Vietnamese offensive, the US resumes its **bombing** of North Vietnam, after a three-year gap, in April, and mines and blockades North Vietnamese ports in May.

During a ground-breaking trip to **Russia** in May, Nixon signs two treaties with Leonid Brezhnev. The **ABM** Treaty restricts the number of antiballistic missiles each side will build, while the first Strategic Arms Limitation Treaty – **SALT I** – freezes the construction of many kinds of offensive nuclear weapons. However, by exempting Multiple Independent Re-entry Vehicles (**MIRVs**), which enable Inter-Continental Ballistic Missiles (**ICBMs**) to deliver multiple warheads, it does little to control the arms race.

On June 17, five men are arrested during a break-in at the Democratic National Committee offices in the **Watergate** complex in Washington, DC. On June 22, Nixon denies any involvement.

On October 26, **Henry Kissinger**, who has resumed his closed meetings with North Vietnam's Le Duc Tho, declares that '**peace is at hand**'. Thanks largely to his high-profile achievements in foreign policy, President Nixon is triumphantly **re-elected** a week later, although his ineffectual antiwar Democratic opponent, South Dakota Senator **George McGovern**, pleads 'don't let this man fool you again'. Nixon wins the largest-ever Republican victory, with over sixty percent of the popular vote and a margin of 520 to 17 in the electoral college. However, the peace talks break down again immediately afterwards, and Nixon resumes intensive bombing of North Vietnam over Christmas.

Watergate

The **Watergate** saga began with the arrest on June 17, 1972, of five burglars in the Democratic National Committee's offices in Washington's Watergate complex. One, **James McCord**, worked for **CREEP**, the Committee to Re-Elect The President – Richard Nixon's campaign organization for that year's election. Three others were Cuban veterans of the Bay of Pigs invasion; one carried the phone number of **E. Howard Hunt**, the CIA operative responsible. With former FBI man **G. Gordon Liddy**, Hunt had the previous year set up the '**Plumbers**', a White House task force designed to stem leaks of information. The White House connection led to immediate suspicions of conspiracy, but both CREEP's chief, former Attorney General **John Mitchell**, and Nixon himself, denied all knowledge.

With the election safely won, Hunt, Liddy and the five men were found guilty of conspiracy in January 1973. However, suspecting the burglars had been paid hush money, Judge John Sirica delayed sentencing. In March, McCord cracked, saying that the White House had known in advance, and Mitchell was in charge. A '**cover-up**' had clearly taken place; a Senate Committee, along

Movie director **Francis Ford Coppola** releases *The Godfather*, hailed by critic Pauline Kael as 'the greatest gangster picture ever made', which will be followed by *The Godfather Part II* in 1974.

1973 Ruling on *Roe v Wade* on January 22, the **Supreme Court** declares that states cannot forbid voluntary **abortions** during the first three months of pregnancy.

On January 27, US military involvement in the **Vietnam War ends** when Henry Kissinger signs a pact in Paris with the North and South Vietnamese. An immediate cease-fire is followed on March 29 by the withdrawal of the last US combat forces, and the release of American POWs. Over

with reporters like Bob Woodward and Carl Bernstein of the *Washington Post* (guided by the anonymous **Deep Throat**), set out to establish who knew what, when.

Although administration officials fell thick and fast, Nixon continued to deny all knowledge, proclaiming 'I am not a crook'. On July 16, however, it emerged that he had secretly **taped** Oval Office conversations. Despite Nixon's frantic ensuing attempts to avoid handing over the tapes, they emerged bit by bit, eroding his credibility – his foul-mouthed tirades brought the phrase '**expletive deleted**' into common currency – until the Supreme Court ruled in July 1974 that he must release them all. With impeachment proceedings about to begin, Nixon **resigned** on August 8 rather than face the ultimate humiliation. A month later, President **Gerald Ford** pardoned him for all offences 'he has committed or may have committed'. Ford had himself been appointed by Nixon in October 1973 to replace disgraced Vice President Spiro Agnew, some allege in return for the promise of just such a pardon.

58,000 Americans have lost their lives since Johnson committed the US to war, 20,000 of them during Nixon's presidency. Vietnamese casualties are estimated at over one million.

The trial of the **Watergate** burglars ends on January 30. Four of those who carried out the actual break-in have pleaded guilty – charges that there has been a '**cover-up**' centre initially on the judge's suspicion, later proved correct, that they have been paid to do so, to avoid incriminating anyone else. In addition, two White House employees, **E. Howard Hunt** and **G. Gordon Liddy**, are convicted of burglary and conspiracy. On February 7, the **Senate** establishes a Select Committee to investigate the affair.

On April 23, James McCord, one of the convicted Watergate burglars, names former Attorney General **John Mitchell** as 'the overall boss' of the operation. The director of the FBI, Patrick Gray, resigns over his part in the cover-up on April 20, as do White House counsel **John Dean**, and top aides **John D. Ehrlichman** and **H. R. Haldeman** – both later jailed – on April 30. John Dean testifies to the Senate committee on June 25 that Nixon was directly involved in the cover-up.

The occupation of **Wounded Knee**, South Dakota, by members of the radical American Indian Movement (**AIM**), who take hostages to highlight the ongoing grievances held by the Sioux against the government, ends on May 8 in a **shoot-out** with FBI agents and federal marshals, in which one Indian is killed.

On July 16, White House aide Alexander Butterfield reveals to the Senate committee that Nixon has been **tape-recording** all his Oval Office and telephone conversations.

Salvador Allende, the democratically elected socialist president of **Chile**, is killed during a military coup on September 11, backed by the CIA and Henry Kissinger, which brings General Augusto Pinochet to power.

Following an investigation not linked to Watergate, Vice President **Spiro Agnew resigns** on October 10; he's suspected of taking bribes, but admits only to a specimen charge of income tax evasion.

In the '**Saturday Night Massacre**' of October 20, both Attorney General **Elliott Richardson** and his deputy resign rather than follow Richard Nixon's order to dismiss Watergate special prosecutor **Archibald Cox**, who is insisting that Nixon hand over the White House tapes. Cox is fired anyway. Faced by public hostility, Nixon then agrees to start releasing the tapes, but mysterious gaps and omissions damage his credibility still further.

Also in October, following the **Yom Kippur War** in which Israel drives back concerted attacks by Egypt and Syria, the Arab states punish the US for its support of Israel by imposing an embargo on **oil** exports, which remains in force until March 1974.

Overriding Nixon's veto, Congress passes the **War Powers Act** on November 7, which hopes to prevent another Vietnam by limiting the president's power to wage war without Congressional consent.

On December 6, **Gerald R. Ford**, Michigan Congressman and former House minority leader, is sworn in as **vice president**. Appointed by Nixon but confirmed by Congress, he concedes 'I am a Ford, not a Lincoln', but pledges that he will not pardon Nixon of any criminal offences: 'I do not think the public would stand for it'.

1974 On February 4, **Patricia 'Patty' Hearst**, granddaughter of newspaper magnate William Randolph Hearst, is **kidnapped** in Berkeley, California, by the obscure Symbionese Liberation Army, which demands ransom payments of food to the poor. In April, Hearst announces that she has joined her kidnappers, and is later filmed participating in a San Francisco bank robbery. She will finally be arrested in September 1975.

In June, the **Supreme Court** rules that employers must pay women **equal wages** for doing the same work as men.

Congress tells Nixon in May that his failure to hand over the White House tapes constitutes an impeachable offence. On July 24, the **Supreme Court** unanimously orders him to do so, and **impeachment** proceedings start three days later. Newly released tapes make it clear that six days after the original break-in, Nixon ordered the FBI to stop its investigations. With his Congressional support almost completely eroded, **Nixon resigns** in an emotional televised speech on August 8.

On September 8, new **President Gerald Ford**, citing the need for the nation to move on, **pardons Nixon**, and declares 'our long national nightmare is over'. Eight days later, he also announces an amnesty for Vietnam **draft dodgers** and deserters.

Ford's unwillingness to act decisively on the weakening economy – he refuses to increase federal spending, cut taxes, or impose wage or price freezes – dooms his 'Whip Inflation Now' programme to failure, and the Democrats add to their majorities in both houses of Congress in the mid-term elections. Among the many bills Ford vetoes is an augmentation of the **Freedom of Information Act**, which nonetheless passes on November 21 and increases the public's right of access to government files.

1975 In March, in defiance of the 1973 peace agreement, the North Vietnamese invade South Vietnam. As the US declines to intervene, **Saigon is captured** and renamed Ho Chi Minh City on April 30; televised images of the desperate scramble to board the last American helicopters leaving the city make it even harder to argue that the US has achieved the promised 'peace with honor'.

Also in April, the Communist **Pathet Lao** take power in **Laos**, while the Communist **Khmer Rouge** capture Phnom Penh in **Cambodia** on April 16. After the Cambodian navy seizes the US merchant ship *Mayaguez* on May 12, 41 American marines die on May 15 in an attempt to rescue its crew – whom it later transpires the Cambodians have already agreed to release.

A Congressional loan enables **New York City**, hard hit by the ongoing economic crisis, to escape **bankruptcy** in June. The president's initial refusal to help prompts the headline: 'Ford to New York: Drop Dead'.

In July, **Jimmy Hoffa**, the former president of the International Brotherhood of Teamsters, disappears in Detroit; he's presumed murdered by the Mafia.

On August 1, the US, Russia and 31 other countries sign the **Helsinki Accords**, which guarantee Europe's national borders as 'inviolable', promise trade and cultural exchanges, and pledge respect for human rights.

The success of *Jaws*, about a man-eating shark, launches a run of hits from director **Steven Spielberg** that will soon include *Close Encounters of the Third Kind* (1977) and *ET* (1982). It also, arguably, ends a golden era for individual directors by turning Hollywood's attention towards the production of big-budget 'blockbuster' movies.

1976 Presenting himself as a humble peanut farmer, political outsider, and born-again Christian, a little-known former governor of Georgia, **Jimmy Carter**, wins the Democratic nomination in July. **President Ford** sees off a strong challenge from **Ronald Reagan** to become the Republican candidate. In October's televised debates, Ford stumbles by saying there is 'no Soviet domination of Eastern Europe'. In November, with a low turnout but aided by strong Southern support, especially from blacks, **Carter is elected** by a narrow margin – 41 million to 39 million in the popular vote, 297 to 241 in the electoral college. Carter thus becomes the first president from the Deep South since Andrew Jackson.

1977 On January 3, murderer **Gary Gilmore** faces a firing squad in Utah, and becomes the first person executed in the US since 1967. This follows a 1976 Supreme Court ruling that **capital punishment** is not 'cruel and unusual', and is thus permitted by the Constitution.

In June, the US and **Cuba** agree to exchange diplomatic representatives.

Reflecting his concern with energy conservation, President Carter establishes the **Department of Energy** on August 4.

Alex Haley's television series **_Roots_**, tracing his slave ancestry back to Africa, is a national sensation.

Under September's **Panama Canal Zone Treaty**, the US agrees that the canal will revert to Panamanian control by 2000.

1978 A Russian-backed Marxist government takes over **Afghanistan** on April 30, prompting US fears of Soviet expansion in Central Asia.

The success of **Proposition 13**, a California state referendum to limit local taxes, on June 6, prompts similar initiatives to reduce federal and state taxation across the nation.

Thirteen days of talks between President Carter, Anwar El-**Sadat** of Egypt, and Menachem **Begin** of Israel culminate on September 17 with the **Camp David Agreement**, in which Israel agrees to withdraw from the Sinai Peninsula in return for recognition by Egypt. The resultant estrangement of Egypt from the rest of the Arab world will thwart hopes of a more extensive Middle Eastern peace settlement.

In October, Carter finally succeeds in getting an **Energy Bill** passed, but it's an inept compromise that satisfies no one and does little to address the energy problem he has characterized as 'the moral equivalent of war'.

On November 28, San Francisco Mayor **George Moscone** and Supervisor **Harvey Milk** – the first openly **gay** city official to be elected in the US – are assassinated by Dan White, a former supervisor and ex-cop. San Francisco's gay community hail Milk as a martyr, and react in fury when in May 1979, White is sentenced to seven years and eight months' jail for manslaughter, after he pleads in the so-called '**Twinkie defense**' that too much junk food had driven him temporarily insane.

1979 Civil unrest causes the **Shah** to flee **Iran** in January. The **Ayatollah Khomeini** returns from exile in February and establishes an Islamic fundamentalist regime; demonstrators briefly occupy the US embassy in Tehran on February 14.

A near-cataclysmic meltdown at Pennsylvania's **Three Mile Island** on March 28 effectively ends the construction of nuclear power plants in the US.

In June, a new Strategic Arms Limitation Treaty – **SALT II** – is signed in Vienna, restricting both the US and Russia to 2250 bombers and missiles apiece, and placing limits on other weapons systems. Owing to the **Soviet invasion of Afghanistan** in December, it's never ratified by the Senate, but both sides will more or less adhere to its terms.

In July, following extensive uprisings and the withdrawal of US support, President Somoza of **Nicaragua** is deposed, and a Marxist **Sandinista** regime comes to power.

As **oil prices** steadily rise, due to the policies of both OPEC and the new Iranian government, President Carter appeals to Americans to restrain their use of energy. Congress rejects his proposal to introduce **gasoline rationing** in May, but agrees in October that he can do so if the world fuel crisis deepens.

After the exiled **Shah** of Iran arrives for cancer treatment in New York in October, Iranian students take over the US embassy in Tehran on November 4 and seize around a hundred of its occupants. Once women, blacks and non-US citizens have been released, they hold 52 **American hostages**, and demand that the US hand over the Shah for trial. Carter responds with a freeze on Iranian assets and an embargo on Iranian oil.

On December 25, in response to tribal uprisings that seem set to topple the Communist regime, the Russians **invade Afghanistan**.

1980 In January, the president calls the invasion of Afghanistan 'the gravest threat to peace since World War II', and warns that if necessary force will be used to protect oil shipping lanes in the Persian Gulf.

When the Shah, who has first moved to Panama, takes refuge in Egypt in March, Carter expects the **hostage crisis** to end. The Iranians, however, who by now also demand the return of the Shah's assets and an apology for past US interference, remain inflexible. Carter expels Iranian diplomats and imposes a complete economic embargo on April 7, and then attempts a disastrous **rescue mission** on April 25. Eight Americans die after their planes crash in the desert, causing **Cyrus Vance** to resign as Secretary of State.

On May 18, **Mount St Helens** in Washington state explodes, killing 34 people, in the fiercest **volcanic eruption** in US history.

Jimmy Carter sees off a challenge from **Edward Kennedy** to secure the Democratic nomination, while the Republicans finally choose the 69-year-old **Ronald Reagan** as their candidate, with **George Bush** as his running mate.

Although Carter devotes all his attention to the hostage crisis rather than to the presidential campaign, and offers to normalize relations and lift all sanctions and embargoes if the hostages are released, no deal is forthcoming. It will later emerge that Reagan has made a **secret deal** with Khomeini, agreeing that if the Iranians keep the hostages until after the election, he will supply them with much-needed arms for the war with **Iraq** that has started in September.

In November, with inflation running at around thirteen percent, unemployment at 7.5 percent, and interest rates at twenty percent, Carter suffers the **worst defeat** ever inflicted upon an incumbent president. **Ronald Reagan**, as a former actor especially comfortable on television, beats him by 50.7 percent to 41 percent in the popular vote (an independent liberal Republican, John Anderson, picks up the rest), and by 489 to 49 in the electoral college.

On December 8, former Beatle **John Lennon** is assassinated in New York City.

10
The US since 1981

1981–2003

Ronald **Reagan** was a new kind of president. Unlike his workaholic predecessor, Jimmy Carter, he made a virtue of his hands-off approach to the job, joking that 'they say hard work never killed anybody, but I figured why take the risk?' That laissez-faire attitude was especially apparent in his domestic economic policies, under which the rich were left to get as rich as they could. The common perception that Reagan was barely aware of what went on around him allowed his popularity to remain undented by a succession of scandals, including the labyrinthine **Iran-Contra** affair, under which illegal arms sales to Iran were used to fund support for the Contra rebels in Nicaragua.

Reagan's most enduring achievement came during his second term, when, with his credentials as a Cold Warrior beyond question, the electorate allowed him greater leeway than a Democrat might have received to negotiate **arms-control** agreements with **Mikhail Gorbachev**, the new leader of what he had previously called the 'evil empire'. On the downside, his successors were left to cope with the explosion in the **national debt** that followed the combination of extensive **tax cuts** alongside the deregulation of the financial markets, the collapse of the Savings and Loans system, and above all, the enormous increases in defence spending that funded such pet projects as the Strategic Defense Initiative ('**Star Wars**').

In 1988, **George Bush** became the first vice president in 150 years to be immediately elected to the presidency. Despite his unusually broad experience in foreign policy (which included a spell as director of the CIA), Bush did little more than sit back and watch in amazement as the domino theory suddenly went into reverse. One after another, the Communist regimes of Eastern Europe collapsed, until finally even the Soviet Union crumbled away. Bush was also president when **Operation Desert Storm** drove the Iraqis out of Kuwait in February 1991, an undertaking that lasted a hundred hours and in which virtually no American lives were lost. At the moment of triumph in Kuwait, Bush's soaring popularity seemed certain to guarantee his re-election.

And yet the much anticipated '**peace dividend**' – the dramatic injection of cash into the economy that voters expected to follow the end of the arms race – never materialized. As one Democrat contender for the 1992 presidential nomination, Paul Tsongas, succinctly put it, 'the Cold War is over and Japan won'. Between 1980 and 1990, the US had gone from being the world's largest creditor to being the world's largest debtor. The national debt had trebled from $908 billion to $2.9 trillion, and much of the borrowing came from Japan, spared from incurring military expenditures on anything like the same scale. With the 1992 campaign focusing on domestic affairs rather than what was happening overseas, twelve years of Republican government were ended by the election of Arkansas Governor **Bill Clinton**.

Clinton's first two years were characterized by his failure to deliver on specific promises – most obviously, to reform the healthcare system. That enabled the Republicans to sweep to power in Congress in 1994, and resulted in two years of legislative gridlock. Displaying a better grasp of the popular mood, Clinton blamed the mess on the

Republicans, and was elected to a second term. However, the 'Comeback Kid' found holding on to office more of a challenge, when his adulterous affair with Monica Lewinsky was exposed in 1998. Special Prosecutor Kenneth Starr's exhaustive probing led to the disgrace of **impeachment**, but the Senate ultimately failed to convict, sensing perhaps that the American people did not feel Clinton's indiscretions were serious enough to merit removal. Clinton had lost his moral if not his actual authority, however, and the nation limped into the twenty-first century devoid of effective leadership.

As Clinton left the presidency, however, the economy was **booming**, coming to the end of a record ten-year burst of sustained growth that had seen the budget deficit eradicated far ahead of even the most optimistic schedule, and the Dow Jones rise by over 260 percent since the day Clinton came to office. Seeming too ashamed of his boss's character failings to bring himself to campaign on his economic record, Clinton's vice president, **Al Gore**, managed to lose the **2000 election** – with a short delay, and a little help from the Supreme Court, not to mention questionable voting practices in Florida – to Republican **George W. Bush**. A **recession** was probably due whoever was in the White House, as the bursting of the dot.com bubble drove hundreds of high-tech companies into bankruptcy. However, during his first months in office Bush showed little sign of halting the slide, and also seemed alarmingly indifferent to the concerns of America's friends and neighbours abroad.

Then the atrocity of **September 11, 2001**, abruptly made matters infinitely worse, inflicting a devastating blow to both the nation's economy and its pride. Bush found himself confronting a new, changed world where the costs of maintaining vigilance and military preparedness seemed incalculable, and yet the costs of not doing so might prove even higher.

Far from balking at the challenge, he has rewritten the traditional rule-book of diplomacy and international law, declaring that the US has a right to launch **pre-emptive attacks** in order to stop potential enemies from reaching the point where they might pose a threat. By the summer of 2003, US-led invasions had taken control of both **Afghanistan** in 2001, and **Iraq** in 2003, but neither of the prime targets, **Osama Bin Laden** and **Saddam Hussein**, were anywhere to be seen, and there was no clear sense of where the **war on terror** would be directed next. We live in dangerous times.

1981 On January 20, just as **President Ronald Reagan** concludes his inaugural address, the American **hostages** are finally released in Tehran.

Reagan has come to office advocating '**supply-side**' economics, arguing that cuts in taxes and federal spending will encourage saving and investment. The greater the benefit to rich Americans, the more wealth will '**trickle down**' to the rest, and the overall boost to the economy will pay for increased defence spending. At first, his plans are rejected by Congress.

On March 30, **Reagan is shot** by John Hinckley (who hopes to impress actress Jodie Foster) in Washington, DC. He survives, badly wounded; Press Secretary James Brady suffers permanent brain damage.

In May, the *New York Times* reports an as-yet unexplained health crisis under the headline 'Rare Cancer Seen in 41 Homosexuals'. In June, the federal **CDC** (Centers for Disease Control) describes the disease that next year it will name **AIDS** (Acquired Immune Deficiency Syndrome). 152 cases have been identified in the US by the end of 1981, with 128 deaths.

The arrest of **Wayne Williams** in Atlanta, Georgia, on June 21, signals the end of investigations into 28 **child murders** that have plagued the city's black population. Although he will be convicted of two killings in 1982, many feel he is a scapegoat.

Reagan's courage having lifted his popularity, Congress agrees in August to the **Economic Recovery Tax Act**, which reduces income tax by a quarter.

Also in August, Reagan tackles a strike of **air traffic controllers** by dismissing those who refuse to return to work, and replacing them with military personnel.

On September 21, **Sandra Day O'Connor** becomes the first woman member of the **Supreme Court**.

On December 1, former child star **Michael Jackson** releases *Thriller*, which will become the bestselling album of all time. Lavish promotional **videos** for songs such as *Billie Jean*, *Beat It* and *Thriller* itself help shift the focus of the popular music industry towards cable TV stations such as **MTV**, which starts this year.

On December 29, the US imposes limited **sanctions** on the **Soviet Union**, which has forced the **Polish** government to implement martial law to repress the trade union **Solidarity**. However, the NATO allies refuse to join any economic blockade.

1982 After Argentinian forces invade the **Falkland Islands** in April, provoking war with Britain, Reagan gives the British secret military and intelligence assistance.

On May 26, Secretary of State **Alexander Haig** calls for 'international action' to end a civil war in the **Lebanon**, which has become a major base for the Palestine Liberation Organization. This is widely read as a coded message to the **Israelis**, who invade Lebanon on June 6; following an international outcry when they bombard PLO camps in

August, Haig resigns and is succeeded by **George Schulz**. An international **peacekeeping** force is sent in, which includes US marines.

Almost all the nation's **Savings and Loan** banks (**S&Ls**), created under the 1930s New Deal to help Americans to save to buy their own homes, are being driven into insolvency by the requirement to offer inexpensive home loans at a time when interest rates are otherwise soaring. In October, with Reagan's ardent support, Congress **deregulates** the industry by allowing S&Ls to invest forty percent of their assets in other real-estate deals. States such as California go even further, permitting S&Ls to invest all their funds anywhere they choose, while still remaining guaranteed by the federal government. Over the coming decade, foolish investments, greed and a slump in the real-estate market will cause the S&Ls to **collapse**, costing taxpayers $500 billion.

Under November's **Boland Amendment**, Congress forbids aid to the **Contras**, guerrilla fighters who oppose the Marxist Sandinista regime in **Nicaragua**. The ban will come into force in October 1984, and last until 1986.

On November 13, the **Vietnam Veterans Memorial**, a black granite wall inscribed with the names of 58,156 dead or missing US personnel, is inaugurated on the Mall in Washington, DC.

1983 On March 23, two weeks after denouncing the Soviet Union as an '**evil empire**', President Reagan announces the **Strategic Defense Initiative** (SDI), an antimissile defence system known colloquially as **Star Wars**.

A South Korean Boeing 747 is **shot down** after straying into Soviet airspace near Sakhalin on September 1; the CIA denies Russian charges that it was carrying spying equipment.

On October 23, **suicide bombers** attack the US marine compound in **Beirut**, killing 241 marines and 58 French peacekeepers.

After the army seizes control in a left-wing military coup in **Grenada** on October 19, and execute Prime Minister Maurice Bishop, US marines **invade** Grenada on October 25, with help from six other Caribbean states, and swiftly restore order. Three days later, the US vetoes a UN resolution deploring the invasion.

On November 2, President Reagan signs legislation to honour Rev. **Martin Luther King, Jr's birthday**, on January 15, as a federal holiday.

Despite large-scale protests throughout Western Europe, US **cruise missiles** are deployed in the UK and West Germany on November 23, in a programme originally authorized by President Carter.

On December 29, the US announces that it will withdraw from **UNESCO** – the United Nations Educational, Scientific and Cultural Organization – at the end of 1984, because it 'exhibits hostility towards the basic installations of a free society.'

1984 In a pivotal year in the development of **personal computers**, the **Apple Macintosh** is launched with a dramatic TV advert shown only once, during the Superbowl on January 22, while **Microsoft** issues the first version of its **Windows** operating system, which will only acquire a significant market share when version 3.1 is released in 1992.

President Reagan announces the 'redeployment' of US marines from **Beirut** on February 7; all are withdrawn within three weeks.

In July, **Walter Mondale**, formerly President Carter's vice president, wins the Democratic presidential nomination.

His running mate **Geraldine Ferraro** becomes the first **woman** to run for vice president for a major party, but questions about her husband's finances soon tarnish her image.

On September 20, **suicide bombers** kill 25 people by detonating a truck in the US embassy in **Beirut**.

With falling oil prices helping the economy, President Reagan is easily **re-elected** on November 6, winning 59 percent of the popular vote and defeating Mondale by 525 electoral votes to 13.

On December 22, white 'vigilante' **Bernard Goetz** shoots and wounds four black youths who he claims have threatened him on the New York subway.

1985 On March 1, Reagan hails the **Contras** as 'the moral equal of our Founding Fathers'. Two months later, the US bans all trade with **Nicaragua**.

In Moscow, on March 11, following the deaths since 1982 of Leonid Brezhnev, Yuri Andropov and Konstantin Chernenko, **Mikhail Gorbachev** is elected First Secretary of the Soviet Communist Party. Over the next five years, his policies of *glasnost* (openness) and *perestroika* (reconstruction) will transform the Soviet Union, Eastern Europe, and the world.

Police in **Philadelphia** attempting to dislodge members of a black separatist group, **MOVE**, bomb their house from a helicopter on April 13, killing twelve people and leaving three hundred homeless.

On July 8, President Reagan brands Iran, Libya, Cuba, Nicaragua and North Korea as '**terrorist states**'.

On October 7, **Palestinian** terrorists hijack an Italian cruise liner, the *Achille Lauro*, and kill an elderly American passenger. Three days later, US fighters intercept a plane

The Iran-Contra Affair

From the day of his inauguration in 1981, when Iran fulfilled a secret deal by releasing the hostages in Tehran, there was always a contradiction between Ronald Reagan's public insistence that he would never negotiate with terrorists, and the behind-the-scenes reality. When the **Iran-Contra Affair** finally lifted the lid, the revelations almost destroyed Reagan's presidency.

On July 8, 1985, Reagan denounced the Iranian government as 'Murder Incorporated'. That very month, however, 96 US antitank missiles were shipped via Israel to Iran, in the hope of securing the release of William Buckley, the CIA chief in **Lebanon**, one of seven Americans held by Islamic militants in **Beirut**. Buckley having been tortured to death, another hostage was released. A pattern was established, on the premise that the Iranians both could and would arrange more such releases in return for more arms. National Security Adviser **Robert McFarlane** and his aide Lieutenant Colonel **Oliver North** secretly flew to Tehran to confirm the details in May 1986. The plot thickened when $12 million from that month's second shipment was diverted to buy weapons for the **Contra** fighters in **Nicaragua**, although Congress had prohibited such aid in 1982.

carrying the hijackers from Egypt, where they have surrendered, to Tunis, and force it to land in Sicily. Although President Reagan warns terrorists everywhere '**you can run but you can't hide**', the Italians release the ringleader on October 12.

In his first face-to-face encounter with a Russian leader, Reagan meets **Gorbachev** in Geneva in November. Differences over **Star Wars** stall any treaty on arms control, but they agree to meet annually from now on.

1986 On January 28, the **space shuttle** *Challenger* **explodes**

The story came to light in a Lebanese magazine in November 1986, just as the Democrats gained control of the Senate for the first time in six years. Subsequent investigations, including Congressional hearings, revealed an administration in disarray. Within weeks, McFarlane's successor, Admiral **John Poindexter**, resigned, while North was dismissed for 'serious questions of impropriety' but nonetheless praised by Reagan as 'an **American hero**'. Secretary of State George Schulz and Defense Secretary Caspar Weinberger both said they'd known of, and objected to, the operation; the president, who at first denied all knowledge, eventually accepted moral responsibility.

While Oliver North's defiant (and perjured) testimony to Congress in July 1987 made him a conservative icon, Reagan may only have escaped impeachment because he was so near the end of his second term. The scandal formally ended on December 24, 1992, when President George Bush pardoned six White House officials, including Weinberger, who had been indicted for lying to Congress. As for the Beirut hostages, three were indeed released during the Iran-Contra affair, but seven more were taken.

on takeoff in Florida, killing seven astronauts including schoolteacher Christa McAuliffe. With NASA's credibility severely damaged, the future of the space programme is thrown into doubt.

On April 14, in retaliation for suspected **Libyan** involvement in the bombing of a Berlin discotheque a week earlier, in which two US servicemen die, US aircraft **bomb** Tripoli and Benghazi, killing a daughter of Libyan leader Colonel Qaddafi. Within three days, kidnappers in Lebanon execute three hostages, one American and two Britons.

BETTMANN/CORBIS

Oliver North takes the oath at the Iran-Contra hearings, July 1987

On October 2, the Senate overrides a presidential veto and imposes sanctions on **South Africa**, in the hope of weakening the apartheid system of racial segregation.

A week later, Reagan and Gorbachev meet again in **Reykjavik**, Iceland. Reagan initially agrees to Gorbachev's proposal that both sides halve their nuclear arsenals immediately, and eliminate them completely within a decade, but the talks founder when Reagan refuses to abandon Star Wars.

On November 3, a report in a Lebanese magazine that the US has sold arms to Iran to secure the release of American hostages in Beirut sparks what will become known as the **Iran-Contra Affair** (see pp.350–351).

In **Congressional elections** the next day, the Democrats capture control of the Senate, for the first time during Reagan's presidency.

> **“** In spite of the wildly speculative and false stories of arms for hostages and alleged ransom payments, we did not – repeat did not – trade weapons or anything else for hostages nor will we. **”**
>
> President Ronald Reagan, November 13, 1986

> **“** A few months ago I told the American people I did not trade arms for hostages. My heart and my best intentions still tell me that's true, but the facts and the evidence tell me it is not . . . What began as a strategic opening to Iran deteriorated, in its implementation, into trading arms for hostages. This runs counter to my own beliefs, to administration policy, and to the original strategy we had in mind. There are reasons why it happened, but no excuses. It was a mistake. **”**
>
> President Reagan, March 4, 1987

1987 On May 17, in what the US agrees to regard as an accident, an **Iraqi** Exocet missile hits the USS *Stark* in the Persian Gulf, killing 37 naval personnel.

At a fund-raising dinner on May 31, President Reagan for the first time addresses the issue of **AIDS**, which has by now killed almost 21,000 Americans.

Speaking in front of the **Berlin Wall** on June 12, Reagan challenges: 'Mr Gorbachev, tear down this wall!'

Also in June, US aid to **Panama** is suspended after General Manuel **Noriega** – a longtime associate of US intelligence services, and of former CIA director George Bush in particular – incites anti-US demonstrations.

In early July, **Oliver North** testifies to the Congressional Select Committee investigating the **Iran-Contra Affair** (see p.350–351).

With the national debt, and the trade deficit, soaring, the Dow Jones Industrial Average starts to slide in October, then plunges 508.32 points, or almost 23 percent, in a single day – **Black Monday**, October 19. Similar crashes follow around the world. Reagan asserts that the 'underlying economy remains sound', but agrees to a lukewarm rescue programme that includes small tax increases.

In Washington, DC, on December 9, Reagan and Gorbachev sign the Intermediate Nuclear Force (**INF**) treaty, a major breakthrough in **arms control** that provides for the elimination of intermediate-range missiles, and entitles each side to inspect the other's missile sites for verification.

President Ronald Reagan and Soviet leader Mikhail Gorbachev sign the INF treaty in December 1987

1988 On February 5, the US indicts Panama's General **Noriega** on charges of drug-trafficking.

After the US and Russia guarantee the Geneva Agreement in April, Soviet forces start to withdraw from **Afghanistan** on May 15. All will leave within a year.

In April, in the **Persian Gulf**, the US Navy responds to the damaging by a mine of a US frigate by destroying two **Iranian** oil platforms and attacking several Iranian ships.

On July 3, the USS *Vincennes* **shoots down** an Iranian airbus over the Persian Gulf, killing 290 passengers and crew. Reagan later apologizes and pays compensation. A truce ends the eight-year **Iran–Iraq War** soon afterwards.

During the early months of the year, **Jesse Jackson**, an aide during the 1960s to Rev. Martin Luther King, Jr, appears to have a genuine chance of winning the Democratic presidential nomination and becoming the first black candidate of a major party. His '**Rainbow Coalition**' founders, however, and Massachusetts Governor **Michael Dukakis** is chosen instead in July.

Accepting the Republican nomination in August, Vice President **George Bush** kick-starts his campaign by promising to authorize '**no new taxes**'. He swiftly turns around his initial opinion-poll deficit, taunting Dukakis with the '**L-word**' and thus branding him as a liberal. **Bush wins** on November 8, with 54 percent of the popular vote and a margin of 426 to 111 in the electoral college.

In October, the **Indian Gaming Regulatory Act** legalizes casino gambling on Indian reservations. Certain tribes, especially in California, Florida and Massachusetts, will gain enormous financial benefits in the coming years; one leader hails gambling as the 'third great equalizer', along with horses and guns, to enable Native Americans to survive the European invasion.

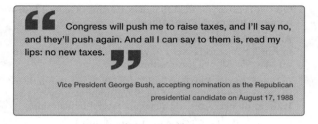

On December 7, **Mikhail Gorbachev** tells the UN General Assembly in New York that he will drastically reduce the Soviet military presence in **Eastern Europe**.

1989 **President George Bush** is inaugurated on January 20, promising 'to make kinder the face of the nation and gentler the face of the world'. In February, he visits **China** – where he was once US envoy – to meet premier **Deng Xiaoping**.

On March 24, the tanker *Exxon Valdez* hits a reef in Prince William Sound, Alaska; the largest **oil spill** in US history causes a 45-mile slick.

On June 4, the Chinese Army crushes pro-democracy demonstrations in **Tiananmen Square**, Beijing. Although the US imposes limited trade sanctions on China in response, these are soon lifted in the interests of American business.

With the **Savings and Loan** banks in desperate trouble, Congress agrees to Bush's $300 billion bail-out plan in August; the total estimated cost will be revised in 1990 to $500 billion.

Also in August, Major General **Colin Powell**, the first black chairman of the Joint Chiefs of Staff, takes command of US armed forces.

The installation by the **Solidarity** movement in August of **Poland**'s first non–Communist government since World War II is followed on November 9 by the breaching of the **Berlin Wall**, which heralds the collapse of Communist regimes throughout Eastern Europe.

In a hasty response to developments in Eastern Europe, President Bush holds his first **summit** with Mikhail **Gorbachev** off the coast of **Malta** on December 2 and 3. They announce that the **Cold War has ended**, and agree to discuss arms control in 1990.

After General **Noriega** declares a 'state of war' with the US on December 15, US troops **invade Panama** on December 20, in **Operation Just Cause**. Noriega seeks asylum in the Papal Nunciature, then surrenders on January 3, 1990, and is flown to Miami where he's charged with drug-trafficking. He'll be convicted in 1992.

1990 On February 11, the imprisoned leader of the African National Congress, **Nelson Mandela**, is freed from jail in South Africa.

After elections on February 25 in **Nicaragua**, where US sanctions have devastated the economy, Daniel Ortega's Sandinista government peacefully cedes power to a US-backed coalition led by Violeta Chamorro.

In Washington, DC, on June 1, **Bush** and **Gorbachev** agree to reduce stocks of long-range nuclear weapons by thirty percent and chemical weapons by eighty percent, but large-scale US aid to Russia is not forthcoming.

With the US economy in chaos, and the deficit soaring, President Bush fails to manoeuvre the Democrat-dominated Congress into proposing tax rises. On June 26, he finally puts forward a rescue package that includes '**tax revenue increases**' as well as spending cuts; he will later call this 'a mistake', but he's seen, not least by conservative Republicans, as having broken his 'no new taxes' pledge.

On August 2, **Iraq invades Kuwait**. Iraqi leader **Saddam Hussein** resents the fact that increased Kuwaiti production has depressed oil prices, making it harder to pay off debts from the Iran–Iraq War, and expects his US allies to turn a blind eye. However, President Bush condemns the invasion, and, in **Operation Desert Shield**, secures UN backing to send US troops to **Saudi Arabia**, which he believes may be the next target, from August 7.

The **Democrats** gain seats in both the House and Senate in November's mid-term elections.

In late November, Secretary of Defense **Dick Cheney** declares that **Iraq** is likely to develop **nuclear** weapons within months.

By the end of 1990, over 100,000 Americans have died of **AIDS**, and former President Reagan has apologized for his administration's neglect of the issue.

1991 Pressure and sanctions from the entire international community, including Russia, fail to produce an Iraqi withdrawal from **Kuwait**. On January 12, the Senate votes by 52 to 47 to authorize Bush to use force. On January 17, the **Gulf War** begins with a massive, multinational bombing campaign against Iraq.

Once Iraqi air defences have been destroyed, **Operation Desert Storm** continues with a **land invasion** on February 24. Allied forces outflank Iraqi defenses in Kuwait and penetrate deep into Iraq. However, with one fifth of the country occupied, Bush announces that 'Iraq's army is defeated and Kuwait is liberated', and calls a **cease-fire** on February 28. Despite the expectations raised by his demonization of Saddam Hussein as another Hitler, Bush respects the limits of his authorization by the UN and declines to advance on **Baghdad**. Iraqi casualties are conservatively estimated at 100,000; 79 US soldiers are killed, and 213 wounded. Saddam remains in power, free to crush internal opposition; Bush's popularity rating at home reaches an unprecedented ninety percent.

On March 3, the television transmission of video footage showing white Los Angeles policemen beating a black motorist, **Rodney King**, causes national outrage.

In Moscow on July 31, Bush and Gorbachev sign the Strategic Arms Reduction Treaty (**START**), specifying limits for launching systems, warheads and cruise missiles, and cutting total arsenals by thirty percent. Three weeks later, an attempted **military coup** fails to re-establish Communist authority in the Soviet Union, but fatally impairs Gorbachev's authority. As individual Soviet republics declare their independence, **Boris Yeltsin** becomes the most powerful figure in Russia.

To succeed the retiring Supreme Court Justice Thurgood Marshall, Bush names another black judge, the relatively inexperienced **Clarence Thomas**. After his former assistant, law professor **Anita Hill**, accuses him of sexual harassment, Thomas's appointment is eventually narrowly confirmed by the Senate in October. However, the vilification of Hill during the hearings incenses women across America, and prompts an upsurge in the numbers of women who stand for election in 1992.

Around one in five of the American labour force, 25 million people in all, are **unemployed** at some point in the year. Corporate '**downsizing**' costs 100,000 jobs at General Motors, IBM and Xerox in December alone.

On December 25, the **Soviet Union disintegrates** into fifteen separate republics.

1992 Arkansas Governor **Bill Clinton** emerges so early as the frontrunner for the Democratic presidential nomination that by February 18 he has already, with the help of his wife **Hillary**, faced down allegations of an extramarital affair and of dodging the Vietnam draft, and is able to present coming second with 25 percent of the vote in that day's New Hampshire primary as a victory for the '**Comeback Kid**'.

Several days of **riots** in south-central Los Angeles, at the end of April and into May, follow the acquittal by an all-white jury in suburban Simi Valley of the four LAPD policemen accused of beating **Rodney King**. Forty-four die and 1800 are injured.

The **Twenty-Seventh Amendment**, ratified on May 7 but first mooted in 1789, declares that any **pay rise** that members of Congress vote for themselves can only become effective after another Congressional election.

Visiting a school in Trenton, New Jersey, on June 15, Vice President **Dan Quayle** tells a 12-year-old who has written 'potato' on the blackboard that 'you're close, but you left a little something off'. By insisting on the spelling '**potatoe**', Quayle permanently damages his political career.

On August 24, **Hurricane Andrew** hits Florida, killing 38, leaving 250,000 homeless, and causing damage estimated at $30 billion.

A maverick **independent** candidate, Texan software billionaire **H. Ross Perot**, enters, withdraws from and re-enters the presidential campaign, proclaiming that his business background equips him to take the kind of hard-nosed decisions needed to reduce the deficit and stimulate the national economy. His eventual nineteen percent share of the popular vote reveals widespread disenchantment with the two major-party candidates, Bush and Clinton. Nonetheless, insisting that 'it's the economy, stupid', **Clin-**

ton is elected in November, with 43 percent of the popular vote and by 370 to Bush's 168 in the electoral college. The Democrats retain control of Congress, and more women than ever before are elected to the Senate, including **Carol Moseley Braun** of Illinois as the first female black Senator.

On November 11, in his first press conference as president-elect, Clinton alienates conservative sentiment by announcing that he will allow **gays** to serve openly in the US military.

On December 17, the US, Canada and Mexico sign the North American Free Trade (**NAFTA**) treaty, which is strongly opposed by Perot and consumer rights advocate Raph Nader, but supported by both Bush and Clinton.

Also in December, President Bush authorizes US leadership of **Operation Restore Hope**, a UN programme to police food aid to war-torn **Somalia**.

Bill and Hillary Clinton on the campaign trail, 1992

PETER TURNLEY/CORBIS

1993 On January 3, President Bush and Boris Yeltsin sign the second Strategic Arms Reduction Treaty, **START II**, which cuts the US and Russian nuclear arsenals by two-thirds.

On February 26, seven people are killed, and a thousand injured, in a terrorist **bombing** of the **World Trade Center** in New York City. The 'mastermind' behind the attack, Ramzi Yousef, will be arrested in Pakistan in 1995, then tried in the US and sentenced to 240 years' imprisonment in 1998; he's said to have entered the US on an Iraqi passport, and to have associations with Osama Bin Laden.

On February 28, four federal agents die during a raid on a compound occupied by members of the Branch Davidian religious cult in **Waco**, Texas. The ensuing 51-day siege ends on April 19, when an FBI assault authorized by Attorney General **Janet Reno** leaves 81 dead.

Despite his campaign promises to cut taxes, President Clinton is convinced by Federal Reserve chairman **Alan Greenspan** among others to make **reducing the deficit** his top priority. His attempts to do so are stymied in Congress until August, when the Republican minority abandons its previous 'filibuster' tactics of prolonging debate to block legislation, and a $500 billion package of tax increases and spending cuts is finally passed.

A suspected **Iraqi** plot to kill former President Bush during a visit to Kuwait in April is foiled.

On May 13, the Strategic Defence Initiative – **Star Wars** – is cancelled.

President Clinton has pledged during his campaign to reform the national **healthcare** system and introduce comprehensive health insurance for all citizens. **Hillary Clinton** is appointed to head a Task Force, which reports to Congress in September. What's widely seen as an immensely overcomplicated plan fails to win Republican support, and after the president threatens to veto any proposal that doesn't offer one hundred percent coverage, any hope of compromise disappears. The plan will finally be dropped in September 1994.

On September 13, Israeli Prime Minister **Yitzhak Rabin** and PLO leader **Yasser Arafat** shake hands at the White House, and sign a draft peace agreement negotiated in secret in Oslo, Norway.

In **Somalia**, on October 3, eighteen US soldiers are killed when during bloody attempts to capture a so-called 'warlord' a US Black Hawk helicopter is shot down by armed militia. A humiliated Clinton will withdraw all US forces in March 1994.

Black American novelist **Toni Morrison**, best known for her searing examination of slavery in *Beloved* (1987), is awarded the **Nobel Prize** for Literature on October 7.

1994 The **NAFTA** agreement, approved by Congress after much debate on November 17, 1993, comes into force on January 1, creating a single common market between the US, Canada and Mexico.

Also in January, the **Trilateral Statement** between the US, Russia and the Ukraine ordains the dismantling of all the former Soviet Union's nuclear weapons in the **Ukraine**.

In May, President Clinton imposes an economic blockade on **Haiti**, where the US has been trying to restore President Jean-Aristide Briand, deposed in a 1991 military coup, to power. In September, US representatives including former President Carter and former General Colin Powell persuade General Cédras to step down, and US troops land unopposed as part of a multinational force.

The trials and tribulations of Bill Clinton

Even Hillary Clinton, who charged that a 'great right-wing conspiracy' was out to sabotage **Bill Clinton**, would have to accept that his own behaviour did the most damage to his presidency. Clinton was obsessed with his 'place in history'; he may be best remembered as the second president to be impeached, and the first to confess to lying under oath.

Well before his election, Clinton weathered charges of committing adultery, dodging the draft and smoking marijuana. The truth of such allegations was seldom the issue; the **'Comeback Kid'** dismissed them as unimportant or malicious, or sidestepped them with such arguments as that he 'didn't inhale'. Each time his supporters stood by him, his appalled opponents resolved to dig deeper.

More sexual allegations emerged during Clinton's first year in office, when **Paula Jones** told of being propositioned by Governor Clinton back in Arkansas. Rumours then surfaced that Bill and Hillary had profited from 'sweetheart' investments in Arkansas's **Whitewater** resort. Hoping to clear his name, Clinton asked Attorney General Janet Reno to appoint a special prosecutor, only for Republicans to divert the job to the tenacious **Kenneth Starr**.

Former President Carter has also visited **North Korea** in June, paving the way for an agreement signed in October under which the US agrees to recognize the country and finance modernization of its civil nuclear industry, so long as it submits to inspections to ensure that it is not developing **nuclear weapons**.

In a stunning repudiation of President Clinton's failure to deliver reform on healthcare or welfare, or to cut taxes, the **Republicans seize control** of both houses of Congress in November's mid-term elections.

Despite several years' probing and a $50 million budget, Starr found no evidence of criminal wrongdoing over Whitewater. However, he was still beavering away in January 1988, when the story broke of Clinton's affair with a young White House intern, **Monica Lewinsky**. On January 26, accused of lying about his relationship with Lewinsky during testimony for Paula Jones' lawsuit, Clinton declared '**I did not have sex with that woman**'.

Sordid details then emerged, including the positive testing of semen discovered on Lewinsky's cocktail dress. Clintonian equivocations extended to quibbling over whether oral sex counts as sex, and 'that depends on what your definition of "is" is'. No one, least of all Hillary, was impressed. Starr triumphantly delivered a 36-box report to Congress, recommending **impeachment**. And yet the country didn't seem to care; Clinton's popularity remained unimpaired, and the Democrats did well in the November elections. The House voted for impeachment in December 1998, on charges of perjury and obstruction of justice, but in February 1999, the Senate failed to deliver a simple plurality, let alone the two-thirds majority necessary to convict, on either count.

1995 When the new Congress assembles on January 4, Georgia's **Newt Gingrich** becomes the first Republican **Speaker** since 1954. For the first few months of the year, as he sets about enacting the **Contract with America** that formed the basis of the Republican programme in the recent elections, he appears to be the virtual 'prime minister' of the United States. By April, nine out of ten items of the Contract have been passed by the House, including measures that cut taxes and prohibit the federal government from obliging states to carry out programmes without also funding them. However, many falter in the Senate, including proposed

> **❝** I say this to the militias and all the others who believe that the greatest threat to freedom comes from the government . . . If you say violence is an acceptable way to make change, you are wrong. If you say government is a conspiracy to take your freedom away you are just plain wrong . . . How dare you suggest that we in the freest nation on earth live in a tyranny? How dare you call yourselves patriots and heroes? I say to you, all of you . . . there is nothing patriotic about hating your country, or pretending that you can love your country but despise your government. **❞**
>
> President Bill Clinton at Michigan State University on May 5, 1995, two weeks after the Oklahoma City bombing

Constitutional amendments to restrict Congressional term limits, and to oblige the balancing of the budget by 2002.

Meanwhile, other than guaranteeing loans totalling $50 billion to rescue **Mexico** from bankruptcy in January, President Clinton suggests almost no policy initiatives of his own. On April 18, with his standing at perhaps its lowest ebb, he is reduced to insisting on national TV that 'the president is **relevant**'.

The next day, a **truck bomb** devastates the Alfred P. Murrah Federal Building in **Oklahoma City**, killing 168 and injuring more than four hundred. Though initially assumed by many to be the work of Islamic terrorists, home-grown anti-government extremists, seeking to revenge the killings at Waco in 1993, are in fact responsible. President Clinton's empathy for the bereaved strikes a chord with the nation, as, to a lesser extent, does his rhetorical linkage between the Republicans' anti-government stance and the climate that has made the bombing possible.

The situation in the former Yugoslav republic of **Bosnia-Herzegovina**, which has been the scene of vicious fighting since it declared its independence in 1992, deteriorates still further in July, when Serbs ruthlessly carry out the '**ethnic cleansing**' of the Moslem population of the supposed 'safe area' of Srbrenica. President Clinton establishes a cease-fire in October and hosts talks at Dayton Air Force Base, Ohio, in November, which result in the signing of the **Dayton Accords** peace settlement in Paris in December.

On October 3, black former football star **O.J. Simpson** is acquitted of the 1994 murder of his wife, Nicole Brown Simpson, and Ronald Goldman. The verdict divides America on racial lines; opinion polls reveal that almost ninety percent of blacks believe Simpson is innocent, as opposed to barely a third of whites.

On October 16, an estimated 837,000 black Americans participate in the **Million Man March** in Washington, organized by Nation of Islam leader **Louis Farrakhan** as a day of pride and solidarity.

In late October, Congress agrees a spending plan to cut taxes and **balance the budget**, only for Clinton to **veto** it on the grounds that it would hit health, education and the environment too hard. Rather than compromise, Gingrich forces a brief, partial **government shutdown** when federal funds run out in mid-November. After six days, the Republicans seem to have won when Clinton agrees to balance the budget within seven years, but the two sides still fail to agree on a concrete plan, and a **second shutdown** begins on December 16. This time it lasts for three weeks, but national opinion turns against the Republicans, while Clinton emerges as the staunch protector of popular programmes such as **Medicare** and **Medicaid**.

1996 In the absence of any challenge for the presidency from within the Democratic Party, Bill Clinton follows an approach his strategist Dick Morris calls '**triangulation**', in which he manoeuvres as far as he can towards the Republican position on any issue without alienating too many Democrats. He also raises unprecedented amounts of **money** for his campaign; allegations of illegal practices will later be made against both Clinton and his Vice President Al Gore, but no charges brought. His Republican opponent is the 72-year-old **Bob Dole**, who resigns his position as Senate leader in May.

A **terrorist** attack on US barracks in **Saudi Arabia** on June 25 kills nineteen Americans.

On July 27, two die and more than a hundred are injured when a **bomb** explodes in Centennial Park during the **Olympic Games** in Atlanta. The suspected perpetrator will not be arrested until 2003.

In August, Clinton signs, and takes the credit for, three new bills approved by the Republican Congress. One raises the **minimum wage** by 21 percent, to $5.15 per hour; another guarantees continued **health insurance** for workers who change or lose their jobs; and the **Welfare Reform Bill** restricts welfare payments to two years at a time, and five years in a lifetime, all predicated on a willingness to work.

Rap and **hip-hop** are becoming the bestselling music genres in the US. The murder of **Tupac Shakur** in Las Vegas on September 7 is widely blamed on rivalry between record companies, and will be followed by the killing of his New York rival **Notorious B.I.G.** in March 1997.

On November 5, **Bill Clinton** becomes the first Democratic president since Franklin Roosevelt to be **re-elected**, receiving 49 percent of the popular vote, and 379 electoral votes to Dole's 159. **Ross Perot**, this time running as the **Reform Party** candidate, makes less impact, and receives just 8.4 percent. The Republicans retain control of Congress.

On December 5, **Madeline Albright** is the first woman to become **Secretary of State**.

1997 In January, **Newt Gingrich** is re-elected Speaker despite allegations of corruption, but then fined $300,000 by the House for using tax-exempt donations for political purposes, and submitting false evidence to the House Ethics Committee.

On June 20, US **tobacco** companies negotiate immunity from further legal action by agreeing to pay $368.5 billion over 25 years to settle outstanding claims by smokers and state health authorities who have sued for compensation over tobacco-related illnesses.

On July 1, President Clinton announces a bipartisan scheme to encourage the burgeoning area of **e-commerce** – business conducted over the **internet**. The proposal that online purchases will be **tax-free** is rapidly adopted all over the world.

During the summer, the president and Congress agree to draw up legislation, which will include tax cuts, aimed at **balancing the budget** by 2002.

As part of an ongoing attempt by the Clinton administration to break up software giant **Microsoft**, which it believes enjoys an unfair monopoly, the Justice Department first fines it $1 million per day for forcing computer manufacturers to 'bundle' its web browser with its operating software, and then orders it to sell the browser separately. The case will drag through the courts until 2001.

On December 11, at a summit on **global warming** in **Kyoto**, Japan, US representatives join an accord calling for industrialized nations to cut 'greenhouse emissions' by around seven percent below 1990 levels by 2012. Even before the agreement is signed, however, Senate Republicans announce they will not ratify it, and declare the treaty 'dead on arrival'.

1998 On January 26, President Clinton dismisses allegations of an affair with **Monica Lewinsky** by proclaiming 'I did not have sex with that woman' (see pp.364–365).

On February 2, three years ahead of schedule, Clinton presents Congress with the first **balanced budget** since 1969.

On August 7, terrorists **bomb** the US embassies in **Kenya** and **Tanzania**. Holding Saudi millionaire **Osama Bin Laden** responsible, Clinton orders cruise missile strikes on an alleged terrorist training camp in **Afghanistan**, and what he identifies as a chemical weapons plant connected with Bin Laden in **Sudan** – but will turn out to be probably an ordinary pharmaceutical factory – on August 20. Four members of Bin Laden's **Al-Qaeda** network will be convicted of the bombings in May 2001.

On October 29, astronaut **John Glenn**, aged 77 and about to retire as Democratic Senator for Ohio, returns to space in the shuttle *Discovery*.

The Republicans present November's **mid-term elections** as a chance for voters to show their disapproval of Bill Clinton. In an unexpected verdict, the Democrats make gains instead, although the Republicans keep their Congressional majorities. **Newt Gingrich** subsequently resigns as Speaker and leaves the House.

On December 16, following the latest in a series of refusals to co-operate with UN weapons inspectors, US and British forces carry out four days of air strikes against **Iraq** in **Operation Desert Fox**.

On December 19, after considering a report from special prosecutor Kenneth Starr, the House votes to **impeach** President Clinton on charges of perjury and obstruction of justice; see p.365.

1999 On January 19, Clinton delivers his annual **State of the Union** address to Congress, continuing with 'business as usual' by making no mention of the impeachment proceedings under way in the Senate.

On February 12, the Senate votes on largely partisan lines on the two **impeachment** charges. On the perjury count, the vote is 55 not guilty, 45 guilty; on obstruction of justice, it's 50–50. As a two-thirds majority is necessary to convict, President Clinton is therefore **acquitted**.

In March, following repeated UN attempts to halt depredations against the Albanian population of **Kosovo** by the Serbian government of **President Milosevic**, **NATO** authorizes the most extensive military campaign in Europe since World War II. Known as **Operation Allied Force**, air strikes continue until June 8, and include the accidental bombing of the **Chinese embassy** in Belgrade (for which the US will later pay $28 million compensation). The Serbs then withdraw from Kosovo.

On April 20, two students shoot fifteen students and staff at **Columbine** High School in Littleton, Colorado, then commit suicide.

On September 30, the US offers to write off **debts** owed to it by Third World countries, so long as they spend the money on reducing poverty instead.

On October 13, the Senate narrowly votes not to ratify the **Comprehensive Nuclear Test Ban treaty** negotiated by Clinton in 1996.

Talks held by the World Trade Organization in **Seattle** in November are disrupted by thousands of **anti-globalization** protesters.

On November 25, a 5-year-old Cuban boy, **Elian González**, is rescued off Florida after his mother has drowned while fleeing to the US. Cuban exiles in **Miami** petition the courts to allow him to stay, while demonstrations in Cuba demand his return. He will eventually be sent back to Cuba in June 2000.

On December 14, former President Carter represents the US at ceremonies to mark the handing over of the **Panama Canal Zone** to Panama.

2000 On January 14, the Dow Jones index peaks at 11722.98, having stood at 3241.95 when Bill Clinton took office.

A **terrorist** attack on the **USS** *Cole*, off Yemen, kills seventeen American sailors on October 12.

After a strong challenge from Senator John McCain, Texas Governor **George W. Bush**, son of the 41st president, is selected as Republican candidate for the presidency, with his father's former Secretary of State **Dick Cheney** as his running mate. The Democrats choose Vice President **Al Gore**, who runs a lacklustre campaign, deliberately distancing himself from Bill Clinton.

On November 7, in an extremely close national contest, Gore receives a total of 50,988,442 votes, and Bush 50,449,494. However, the result is officially 'too close to call' in **Florida**, where victory would secure Bush enough votes in the all-important electoral college to win the presidency. After five weeks of re-counts, controversy, and legal wranglings – see pp.374–375 – a **Supreme Court** ruling on December 12 eventually ensures a Republican triumph in Florida, and thus **George W. Bush is elected presi-**

dent. Some disgruntled Democrats blame Gore's defeat on the 2.2 million votes picked up nationally by consumer activist **Ralph Nader**, the Green Party candidate.

The **Congressional** elections are equally close. The Republicans keep hold of the House, while the **Senate**, which now includes **Hillary Clinton** as a Democratic Senator for New York, is split 50–50. As the vice president has the casting vote in the Senate, the decision to award the election to Bush produces the rare situation in which not only is there a Republican president and a Republican majority in both houses of Congress, but also a conservative majority on the Supreme Court.

2001 Rather than adopt a conciliatory approach, **President George W. Bush** pushes a conservative agenda in his first months in office, cutting taxes and federal spending, alienating environmentalists by rejecting US compliance with the 1997 **Kyoto** agreement on global warming, and announcing that he hopes to open the **Arctic National Wildlife Refuge** (ANWR) to oil and gas development.

This aggressive strategy backfires on May 24, when Republican Senator **Jim Jeffords** of Vermont announces that he will henceforth be independent but vote with the Democrats. The Democrats thus regain majority control of the Senate; they will thwart Bush's energy plans in particular, and protect the ANWR.

Convicted Oklahoma City bomber **Timothy McVeigh** receives a lethal injection on June 11, making him the first federal prisoner to be executed in 38 years.

On September 6, the Justice Department announces that it will no longer attempt to break up **Microsoft**; see p.369.

On **September 11**, over three thousand people die in the worst **terrorist attack** in US history. Two hijacked planes are flown into the **World Trade Center** in New York

Bush v Gore 2000: the disputed election

Bill Clinton is generally agreed to have won the 1996 presidential election via 'triangulation', adopting elements of his opponents' agenda to scoop up middle-ground voters. Arguably, both candidates in 2000, Al Gore and George W. Bush, followed Clinton's example so well, and so precisely targeted the centre of the political spectrum, that the result was inevitable: a tie.

As the results came in on election night, Gore and Bush were running neck-and-neck across the country. It became clear that whoever captured Florida's 25 electoral-college votes would be the next president. The television networks first 'gave' the state to Gore, then switched to Bush. However, his final margin, of 1200 votes out of almost six million, was so small that a re-count was mandatory.

When the re-count began, anomalies began to emerge. Many black Floridians had been unable to vote, after being wrongly disenfranchised in a sweep of convicted felons. Thanks to a confusing 'butterfly ballot' in Palm Beach County, three thousand elderly Jewish voters had mistakenly voted for right-wing Republican Pat Buchanan rather than Gore. And in several predominantly black areas, antiquated machinery had failed to punch the proper holes, leaving thousands of ineligible ballots with so-called 'pregnant' or 'hanging' chads.

City, and one into the **Pentagon**; a fourth crashes in **Pennsylvania** after its passengers and crew attempt to regain control.

On September 20, addressing a joint session of Congress, President Bush blames **Osama Bin Laden**, and the **Taliban** regime in Afghanistan that is harbouring him. 'Our war on terror begins with **Al-Qaeda**, but it does not end there. It will not end until every terrorist group of global reach has been found, stopped and defeated.' He tells 'every nation, in every region' that 'either you are with us, or you are with the terrorists'.

The Constitution has traditionally been interpreted to make contested elections a **political** rather than a judicial issue; thus Congress decided the 1876 impasse by creating an electoral commission (see p.197). However, perhaps partly because the Florida official responsible for overseeing elections, **Katherine Harris**, was also joint chairwoman of Bush's campaign, while **Al Gore** himself, as vice president, would have the casting vote if the issue reached the Senate, the 2000 presidential race became embroiled in the **courts**. Gore had many powerful moral arguments on his side, including his majority in the national popular vote, but fewer legal ones; it made little sense to impose new standards of legitimacy when re-counting votes.

Re-counts started and stopped with successive court rulings, before the conservative **Supreme Court** decided on December 12 that there was no longer time to hold a full re-count, and the existing figures should stand. Bush therefore won the presidency by 271 votes to 267 in the electoral college. At the time, the charge that he had '**stolen**' the election was expected to seriously impair his presidency, while the authority of the **Supreme Court** was also threatened by the perception of its ruling as partisan. Since September 11, 2001, however, both issues have receded into the background.

After the Taliban refuse to hand over Bin Laden, US troops, with widespread international support, lead a joint **invasion of Afghanistan** on October 7. The capital **Kabul** falls on November 13, but military operations continue in several parts of the country until December 16, with the **Tora Bora** region near the border with Pakistan, where **Osama Bin Laden** is suspected to be hiding, as a principal target. However, neither Bin Laden nor **Mullah Omar**, the Taliban leader, is captured.

October also sees a national panic when five people die as a result of mailings of **anthrax** spores. Although initially

CHRIS COLLINS/CORBIS

New York City, September 11, 2001

September 11, 2001

During his first year in office, **President George W. Bush** set about withdrawing America from its international treaties and commitments, and appeared to be steering the nation towards a new era of isolationism. Then came **September 11, 2001**.

That morning, nineteen **hijackers**, including fifteen Saudi Arabians, armed with knives, took over four passenger planes shortly after takeoff from East Coast airports. The crews assumed they would be forced to fly to some new destination; instead, the planes themselves, laden with fuel for their cross-country flights, became guided missiles. At 8.46am, American Airlines flight 11 from Boston to Los Angeles was piloted by one of the terrorists, using skills acquired at a US flight school, into the North Tower of the **World Trade Center**. For sixteen minutes, it seemed like a tragic accident; then United Airlines 175 hit the South Tower, which the occupants had been advised not to evacuate. Forty minutes later, with all US air traffic now grounded by unprecedented federal order, a third plane struck the **Pentagon**. By now, the hijackers' suicide tactic had lost the element of surprise; the passengers on the fourth plane, having heard what was happening via cellular phones, made a desperate attempt to overpower the hijackers, causing it to crash in rural Pennsylvania at 10.10am. It was later said to have been heading for the White House or Capitol.

By 10.28am, both of the Twin Towers had **collapsed**. Most of the occupants below the points of impact survived; all who were higher up, along with hundreds of rescue workers, were killed. For several days, anxious relatives surrounded the site known as **Ground Zero**, appealing for news of their missing loved ones, but no survivors emerged from the rubble. The death toll was **2666** in the World Trade Center; **125** in the Pentagon; and **266** on the four planes.

Within hours, official sources were blaming the terrorist network known as **Al-Qaeda** ('the base'), led by Saudi millionaire **Osama Bin Laden** and based in **Afghanistan**. President Bush found himself confronted with a new mission, one that appeared set to dominate at least the first decade of the twenty-first century – the open-ended campaign against world terrorism he called the **'war on terror'**.

assumed to be the work of Islamic terrorists, they're later attributed by the FBI to some unknown domestic source.

On December 2, the Texas-based energy conglomerate **Enron**, the seventh largest corporation in the US and a major donor to Republican and Democrat politicians alike, files for **bankruptcy**. Amid allegations of accounting fraud, criminal investigations soon follow.

2002 On January 11, the first prisoners from Afghanistan arrive to be detained at **Camp Zero**, in the US base at **Guantanamo Bay** in Cuba.

Speaking at the bicentennial celebrations of West Point Military Academy on June 1, President George W. Bush outlines a new doctrine of **pre-emptive action** for US foreign policy. From now on, America will 'confront the worst threats before they emerge'.

Turning his attentions to his father's major piece of unfinished business, President Bush asks the UN General Assembly on September 12 to confront the 'grave and gathering danger' of **Iraq**, its **'weapons of mass destruction'**, and its 'continuing to shelter and support terrorist organizations'. He also refers to an Iraqi attempt to assassinate a 'former American president' – his father – and announces that the US will rejoin **UNESCO**.

Congress authorizes Bush on October 2 to use US forces as he considers appropriate.

In a triumph for President Bush that's seen as reflecting popular support for the 'war on terror', November's **midterm elections** restore Republican control of both houses of Congress.

On November 8, the UN Security Council unanimously supports a joint US and British resolution requiring **Iraq** to allow weapons inspectors to return after a four-year absence.

> **"** For much of the last century, America's defense relied on the Cold War doctrines of deterrence and containment. In some cases, those strategies still apply. But new threats also require new thinking . . .We cannot defend America and our friends by hoping for the best . . . If we wait for threats to fully materialize, we will have waited too long . . . We must take the battle to the enemy, disrupt his plans, and confront the worst threats before they emerge . . . our security will require all Americans . . . to be ready for preemptive action when necessary to defend our liberty and to defend our lives. **"**
>
> President George W. Bush, speaking at the bicentennial celebrations of West Point Military Academy on June 1, 2002

On December 20, Mississippi Senator **Trent Lott** resigns as **Senate Republican leader**, after remarking at a party to celebrate the hundredth birthday of South Carolina Senator **Strom Thurmond** that the nation would have been better off if the segregationist Thurmond had won his campaign for the presidency in 1948. First elected to the Senate as a Democrat in 1954, Thurmond has been a Republican since 1964. He will retire in January, and die in June 2003.

2003 On February 1, the **space shuttle** *Columbia* **disintegrates** as it re-enters the earth's atmosphere, killing seven astronauts.

President Bush and British Prime Minister **Tony Blair** argue that **Iraq** has failed to comply with UN weapons inspections, or to disarm. On March 17, faced with opposition from China, France and Russia, the US and Britain abandon hope of obtaining Security Council support for a

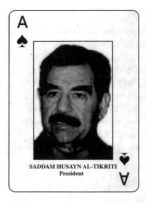

A ♠

SADDAM HUSAYN AL-TIKRITI
President

further resolution authorizing war on Iraq.

On March 20, **war with Iraq** begins anyway, with US air strikes against Baghdad and other targets. The **land invasion** by British and American troops that follows captures **Baghdad** on April 9, and **Tikrit**, the home town of Iraqi leader **Saddam Hussein**, on April 14. There is no sign of Saddam himself, however, and neither are any weapons of mass destruction discovered.

On May 22, the UN Security Council votes 14–0 (with Syria abstaining) to lift sanctions against Iraq, and accepts that as 'occupying powers' the US and Britain now have control of the country. Demonstrations and isolated attacks against the US and British military presence continue.

In June, the **Supreme Court** belies its conservative reputation with two landmark rulings on **civil rights**. The first upholds the principle of **affirmative action** by declaring that the University of Michigan law school is entitled to consider race in its admissions policy; the second, by striking down a Texas state law that forbids sodomy, for the first time enshrines a Constitutional right to **sexual privacy**.

books

books

I t would be impossible, in the space available here, to provide a comprehensive bibliography of American history. Instead, most of the books listed below are simply those that were especially useful in the writing of this volume, and are recommended for further reading.

Most of the titles listed are currently available in paperback. Those that are out of print (o/p) may be found online, or secondhand. Publishers are detailed with the UK publisher first, and the US publisher second. If the book is available in only one market, the words 'UK' or 'US' have been added, while if the same publisher handles both, it is simply listed once.

General histories

Daniel J. Boorstin, *The Americans* (Weidenfeld & Nicolson; Random House). You'll get the best out of this gloriously wide-ranging and constantly stimulating three-part epic – which consists of *The Colonial Experience*, *The National Experience*, and *The Democratic Experience*, and was completed in 1973 – if you know your basic US history already, but Boorstin always seems to shed unexpected light on American culture and character.

Bill Bryson, *Made in America* (Black Swan; Avon Books). A compulsively readable history of the American language, packed with bizarre snippets, which does much to illuminate the history of the nation.

Peter Carroll and **David Noble**, *The Free and the Unfree: A New History of the USA* (Penguin). A good interpretive history of American political development, focusing on the wide gap between those who hold power and those who are disadvantaged on grounds of race, sex or class.

Robert Dallek, *Hail to the Chief* (Oxford University Press). A slim volume that examines the relative strengths and weaknesses of all US presidents in five distinct areas – vision, pragmatism, consensus, charisma and trust.

James M. Loewen, *Lies My Teacher Told Me* (Simon & Schuster, US). This critique of US high-school history textbooks also volunteers some interesting alternative narratives of its own.

Clyde A. Milner II, Carol A. O'Connor and **Martha A. Sandweiss**, *The Oxford History of the American West* (Oxford University Press). Fascinating collection of essays on Western history, covering topics ranging from myths and movies to art and religion.

George Brown Tindall and **David E. Shi**, *America: A Narrative History* (W. W. Norton & Co). The best all-round textbook, approaching 2000 pages of dense but readable narrative.

Allen Weinstein and **David Rubel**, *The Story of America* (Dorling Kindersley). This glossy volume is so beautifully illustrated you might not expect the text to be first-rate too. In fact, it provides fascinating detail and analysis of the one representative topic it chooses to cover from each of 26 eras.

Richard White, *It's Your Misfortune and None of My Own* (University of Oklahoma Press, US). Dense, authoritative and all-embracing history of the American West, which debunks the iconic status of the rugged pioneer by stressing the role of the federal government.

Howard Zinn, *A People's History of the United States* (Longman; Harperperennial Library). More a sequence of essays than a comprehensive history, but Zinn's powerful polemic makes a welcome and well-argued antidote to the bland rhetoric of many traditional histories.

Pre-colonial America

Brian Fagan, *Ancient North America* (Thames and Hudson). Archeological history of America's native peoples, from the first hunters to cross the Bering Strait up to European contact.

Tim Flannery, *The Eternal Frontier* (Vintage Books; Grove Press). An 'ecological' history of North America, very much in the tradition of Jared Diamond, that reveals how the continent's physical environment has shaped the destinies of all its inhabitants, from horses to humans.

Alvin M. Josephy, Jr (ed.), *America in 1492* (Vintage Books). A comprehensive survey of who was living how in the Americas when Columbus set sail.

Magnus Magnusson and **Herman Pálsson** (trans.), *The Vinland Sagas* (Penguin Classics; Viking Press). If you imagine stories that the Vikings reached America to be no more than myths, here's the day-to-day minutiae to convince you otherwise.

Stephen Plog, *Ancient Peoples of the Southwest* (Thames and Hudson). Much the best single-volume history of the pre-Hispanic Southwest, packed with diagrams and colour photographs.

The colonial era

Donald A. Barclay, James H. Maguire and **Peter Wild** (eds), *Into the Wilderness Dream* (University of Utah Press, US). Gripping collection of Western exploration narratives written between 1500 and 1800; thanks to any number of little-known gems, the best of many such anthologies.

Pedro de Castañeda, *The Journey of Coronado* (Dover). An invaluable historic document; the eye-witness journals of a Spaniard who accompanied Coronado into the Southwest in 1540.

John Demos, *The Unredeemed Captive* (Papermac; Vintage Books). This story of the aftermath of a combined French and Indian attack on

Deerfield, Massachusetts, in 1704 illuminates frontier life in the eighteenth century.

Jack D. Forbes, *Apache, Navajo, and Spaniard* (University of Oklahoma Press, US). A very thoroughly documented account that challenges much of the received wisdom about frontier conflicts in the Southwest during the seventeenth century.

Karen Ordahl Kupperman, *Indians and English: Facing Off in Early America* (Cornell University Press). An absorbing attempt to understand precisely what was going on during the first century of contact along the Atlantic coast between English settlers and native Algonquians.

Edmund S. Morgan, *Benjamin Franklin* (Yale University Press). Very readable biography of the intriguing polymath.

Samuel Eliot Morison, *The European Discovery of America* (o/p). A quite extraordinary resource for anyone interested in the early navigators who explored the Americas, divided into two fat volumes – *The Northern Voyages* and *The Southern Voyages* – and written by a former admiral who meticulously retraced many of the routes himself.

Alan Taylor, *American Colonies* (Penguin). Perhaps the best book on any single era of American history – a superb account of every aspect of the peopling of the continent, from remote antiquity until the Declaration of Independence.

The Revolutionary War

Benson Bobrick, *Angel in the Whirlwind* (Penguin). There's perhaps a little too much hagiography in this study of 'the Triumph of the American Revolution', but the events themselves are meticulously chronicled, from the 1750s onwards.

Edward Countryman, *The American Revolution* (Farrar, Straus & Giroux; Hill & Wang). Short but thorough history of the Revolution that takes great care to incorporate representative voices from all levels of American society.

J. Hector St-John de Crèvecoeur, *Letters from an American Farmer and Sketches of Eighteenth-Century America* (Oxford Paperbacks; Viking Press). First published in 1782, a remarkable account of the complexities of revolutionary America.

Joseph J. Ellis, *Founding Brothers* (Faber & Faber; Vintage Books). Enjoyable and informative essays on the 'revolutionary generation' that bring the characters of Washington, Jefferson, et al. to life.

Francis Jennings, *The Creation of America* (Cambridge University Press). A valuable alternative account of the Revolution, focusing in particular on the role of native peoples.

The young Republic

Joanne B. Freeman, *Affairs of Honor* (Yale University Press). A stimulating exploration of how personal honour affected the relationship of politicians like Hamilton and Jefferson in the early years of the Republic.

Reginald Horsman, *The New Republic* (Longman). A short but very serviceable survey of the United States' first quarter-century.

Roger G. Kennedy, *Mr Jefferson's Lost Cause* (Oxford University Press). Fascinating 2003 volume by one of America's foremost historians, which examines how Thomas Jefferson failed to realize his vision of America as a land of yeoman farmers, and how the rise of plantation agriculture led inexorably to civil war.

Meriwether Lewis and **William Clark**, *The Original Journals of the Lewis and Clark Expedition, 1804–1806* (Digital Scanning Inc, US). Eight volumes of meticulous jottings by the Northwest's first inland explorers, scrupulously following President Jefferson's orders to record every detail of flora, fauna and native inhabitant.

David E. Nye, *America as Second Creation* (MIT Press). Imaginative discussion of how specific technologies, from the axe to the railroad, impacted on America's development and sense of itself.

Conor Cruise O'Brien, *The Long Affair: Thomas Jefferson and the French Revolution, 1785–1800* (Pimlico; University of Chicago Press). This book challenges the notion of Jefferson as liberal icon by examining his commitment to the French Revolution and his enduring support for slavery.

Henry David Thoreau, *Walden* and *Civil Disobedience* (Penguin). A single volume containing Thoreau's two greatest works: one a transcendentalist account of a period of solitude spent at Walden Pond, the other an influential essay on the role of conscience.

John Unruh, *The Plains Across* (Pimlico; University of Illinois Press). A history of the wagon trains, drawing heavily on pioneer journals.

The Civil War

David Herbert Donald, *Lincoln* (Simon & Schuster). Perhaps the best of the many available Lincoln biographies.

Shelby Foote, *The Civil War: A Narrative* (Pimlico; Vintage Books). Epic, three-volume account containing everything you could possibly want to know about the 'War Between the States'.

U.S. Grant, *Personal Memoirs* (Penguin; Modern Library). Encouraged by Mark Twain, the Union general and subsequent president wrote his autobiography just before his death, in a (successful) bid to recoup his horrendous debts. At first the book feels oddly downbeat, but the man's down-to-earth modesty grows on you.

James M. McPherson, *Battle Cry of Freedom* (Penguin; Ballantine Books). Extremely readable history of the Civil War, which integrates and explains the complex social, economic, political and military factors in one concise volume. Highly recommended.

Geoffrey Perret, *Ulysses S. Grant* (Random House). A sympathetic and entertaining biography of America's greatest general and, arguably, worst president.

Geoffrey C. Ward, with Ric and Ken Burns, *The Civil War* (The Bodley Head; Alfred A. Knopf). Illustrated history of the Civil War, designed to accompany the TV series and using hundreds of the same photographs.

Edmund Wilson, *Patriotic Gore* (W. W. Norton & Co). Fascinating 800-page survey of the literature of the American Civil War, which in its own right serves as an immensely readable narrative of the conflict.

The Gilded Age

Sean Dennis Cashman, *America in the Gilded Age* (New York University Press). The best single-volume history of the years between the Civil War and the rise of Theodore Roosevelt.

William F. Cody, *The Life of Hon. William F. Cody, Known as Buffalo Bill* (University of Nebraska Press). The larger-than-life autobiography of one of the great characters of the Wild West. Particularly treasurable for the moment when he refers to himself more formally as 'Bison William'.

David Herbert Donald, Jean Harvey Baker and **Michael F. Holt**, *The Civil War and Reconstruction* (W. W. Norton & Co). Detailed histories of Reconstruction are few and far between; with this one, you get an exhaustive account of the Civil War thrown in as well.

Pat Garrett, *The Authentic Life of Billy, the Kid* (University of Oklahoma Press, US). 'I have known the Kid personally since and during the continuance of what was known as the Lincoln County War, up to the moment of his death, of which I was the unfortunate instrument' – irresistible Western history, straight from the horse's mouth.

J.B. Jackson, *American Space* (o/p). Engagingly written work that traces the transition of America from a rural to an urban and industrialized nation in the crucial decade immediately after the Civil War.

Luc Santé, *Low Life: Lures and Snares of Old New York* (Farrar, Straus & Giroux). A nicely written and researched look at the destitute, criminals, bent cops and immigrants in New York a century or so ago.

Joanna L. Stratton, *Pioneer Women* (Touchstone, US). Original memoirs of women – mothers, teachers, homesteaders and circuit riders – who ventured across the Plains from 1854 to 1890. Lively, superbly detailed accounts, with chapters on journeys, home-building, daily domestic life, the Church, the cowtown, temperance and suffrage.

Mark Twain, *Roughing It*, *Life on the Mississippi*, and many others (Penguin; Signet). Mark Twain was by far the funniest and most vivid chronicler of nineteenth-century America. *Roughing It*, which covers his early wanderings across the continent, all the way to Hawaii, is absolutely compelling.

Twentieth-century America

Bruce Ackerman (ed.), *Bush v Gore: The Question of Legitimacy* (Yale University Press). Legal scholars debate just what the whole 2000 election debacle really means for the future of America.

Stephen E. Ambrose and **Douglas Brinkley**, *Rise to Globalism* (Penguin). A compelling account of US foreign policy from 1938 to the present day that never pulls its punches, and always seems to have something new to say.

Harold Evans, *The American Century* (Pimlico; Alfred A. Knopf). A well-argued and well-illustrated overview of the century from 1889 to 1989.

John Kenneth Galbraith, *The Great Crash 1929* (Penguin; Mariner Books). An elegant and authoritative interpretation of the Wall Street Crash and its implications.

Peter Guralnick, *Last Train to Memphis* and *Careless Love* (Abacus; Little Brown & Co). Two-part Elvis biography that maps the rise and fall of the iconic star in a non-sensational but gripping documentary style, while also, unusually, taking him seriously as a musician.

David Halberstam, *The Fifties* (Ballantine Books). A delightfully readable yet satisfyingly comprehensive overview of the Eisenhower years.

Stanley Karnow, *Vietnam: A History* (Penguin). Comprehensive volume telling the story of the war, in part through the eyes of a range of participants.

Joe Klein, *The Natural* (Coronet Books). Klein's overview of the Clinton presidency is not quite as gripping as *Primary Colors*, his originally anonymous fictionalization of the 1992 campaign, but he still offers compelling insights into the enigma.

David McCullough, *Truman* (Simon & Schuster; Touchstone). Vast, and vastly impressive, biography that has done much to restore President Truman's reputation.

Edmund Morris, *Theodore Rex* (HarperCollins). The middle volume of a projected trilogy, this thoroughly engaging and superbly researched biography traces the energetic and controversial Roosevelt's presidential years.

Samantha Power, *A Problem From Hell* (Flamingo; Harperperennial). A ground-breaking survey of the US failure to confront genocide around the world.

Richard Reeves, *President Kennedy* (Papermac; Touchstone). A rewarding look at what actually happened in the Thousand Days of 'Camelot'.

Irwin and **Debi Unger**, *LBJ: A Life* (John Wiley, US). There are several good Johnson biographies around, but the Ungers compress the whole saga nicely into a single volume.

Martin Walker, *Makers of the American Century* (Vintage Books). A stimulating exploration of the major themes of twentieth-century US history, by means of 26 individual biographies of (not always the most obvious) Americans.

John W. Young, *America, Russia and the Cold War 1941–1998* (Longman). Perhaps not the greatest bedside reading, but an invaluable handbook of the nitty-gritty of the Cold War; who signed what when, who invaded where, it's all in here.

Native Americans

Dee Brown, *Bury My Heart at Wounded Knee* (Henry Holt). The best narrative of the impact of white settlement and expansion on Native Americans across the continent.

Angie Debo, *Geronimo* (Pimlico; University of Oklahoma Press). Gripping full-length biography of the Apache medicine man who led the last Native American uprising against the US Army.

Frederick Hoxie (ed.), *Indians in American History* (o/p). Eye-opening collection of essays focusing on the role of Native Americans in US history, presenting them as active and aware (if hopelessly outgunned) players rather than passive victims. Filled with illustrations and extensive quotes from journals and contemporary accounts of Native Americans from across the US.

James Mooney, *The Ghost Dance Religion and The Sioux Outbreak of 1890* (University of Nebraska Press). An extraordinary Bureau of Ethnology report, first published in 1890 but still available in paperback. Before the massacre at Wounded Knee had even taken place, Mooney persuaded his Washington superiors to allow him to roam the West in search of first-hand evidence, and interviewed Wovoka, the Ghost Dance prophet, in person.

David Roberts, *Once They Moved Like the Wind* (Simon & Schuster). Excellent, fast-moving history of the Apache.

Black America and the civil rights movement

James Baldwin, *Collected Essays* (Library of America, US). Excellent compendium of the most brilliant twentieth-century American prose stylist. These stunningly incisive accounts of the black experience include several works originally published as books, such as *No Name on the Street* and *The Fire Next Time*.

W.E.B. DuBois, *The Souls of Black Folk* (Dover). Seminal collection of largely autobiographical essays examining the separation of the races in American society at the beginning of the twentieth century.

Adam Fairclough, *Better Day Coming* (Penguin). The full story of the struggle for racial equality, from 1890 to 2000; the bulk of the narrative is drawn from the 1950s and 1960s, but here it's placed in a much wider context than usual.

David J. Garrow, *Bearing The Cross* (Vintage Books). A well-documented biography of Rev. Martin Luther King, Jr, that also surveys the civil rights movement as a whole.

Eugene D. Genovese, *Roll, Jordan, Roll: The World the Slaves Made* (Vintage Books). An invaluable in-depth look at how slavery actually functioned, and affected those involved.

James R. Grossman, *Land of Hope* (University of Chicago Press). Scholarly yet moving account of the exodus of Southern blacks to Northern cities, specifically Chicago, during the early twentieth century. Though it focuses on the broader social and economic issues, it also manages to bring to life the individual stories involved.

Henry Hampton and **Steve Fayer**, *Voices of Freedom* (Bantam Books). Hugely impressive oral history of the civil rights movement.

Malcolm X, with **Alex Haley**, *The Autobiography of Malcolm X* (Penguin; African American Images). Searingly honest and moving account of Malcolm's progress from street hoodlum to political leadership. Written on the hoof over a period of years, it traces the development of Malcolm X's thinking before, during and after his split from the Nation of Islam. The conclusion, when he talks about his impending assassination, is painful in the extreme.

Muhammad Ali, *The Greatest* (o/p). Powerful and entertaining autobiography of the Louisville boy who grew up to become world heavyweight boxing champion. The most memorable parts deal with his fight against the Vietnam draft and the subsequent stripping away of his world championship title.

Yuval Taylor (ed.), I *Was Born a Slave* (Payback Press, US). This two-volume set is the most comprehensive of many similar anthologies of writings by slaves, ranging from Olaudah Equíano's kidnapping in Africa and global wanderings to Frederick Douglass' eloquent denunciation of slavery and the *Confessions of Nat Turner*.

references

The following references provide publication details for those quotes used in this book which may not be widely familiar.

p.4: Samuel Eliot Morison, *The European Discovery of America*, *The Southern Voyages*, Oxford University Press, New York 1974, p.27.

p.38: Alan Taylor, *American Colonies*, Penguin, New York, 2001, p.39.

p.40: Taylor, *American Colonies*, p.128.

p.159: James McPherson, *Drawn With The Sword*, Oxford University Press, New York 1996, p.200.

p.190: Frederick Turner, *Beyond Geography*, Rutgers University Press, New Brunswick, 1983, p.282.

p.283: David Halberstam, *The Fifties*, Fawcett Columbine, New York, 1993, p.4.

p.324: James Baldwin, *No Name In The Street*, Doubleday, New Yotk, 1972, p.141.

index

index

Entries in **spot colour** represent feature boxes

a

g

I

m

S

t

u

United Nations 274, 277
United States of America, creation of
  81
Utah 139, 219
Ute 35
Utrecht, Treaty of 52

V

Valley Forge 81
Vallindigham, Clement 171
van Buren, Martin 132, 134, 135
Vandalia 68
Vargas, Don Diego de 49
Velázquez, Diego 19
Vermont 106
Verplanck's Point 84
Verrazzano, Giovanni da 20
Versailles, Treaty of 241, 242
Vesey, Denmark 124
Vespucci, Amerigo 18
Vicksburg 173
Vietnam 288, 297, 298, 303, 305,
  308, 309, 315, 317–333, 336, 347
Vikings 3, 11, 12
Villa, Pancho 237
Vincennes 84
Vinland 11
Virginia 28, 30, 36, 45, 52, 64, 67,
  70, 88, 129, 154, 161
Virginia Company 34, 38
Virginia Plan 94
Virginia Resolutions 65
von Braun, Wernher 293
Voting Rights Act 315

W

Waco 362
Waldseemüller, Martin 18
Walker, William 153
Wall Street Crash 234, 251, **252**
Wallace, George 307, 325
Wampanoag 37
War Hawks 117
War of 1812 103, 117
War of Jenkin's Ear 55
War of the Spanish Succession 49
Warhol, Andy 305, 317, 324
Warren, Earl 289
Washington, Booker T. 205, 218,
  219, 223
Washington, DC 111, 118, 305
Washington, George 53, 57, 58,
  62, 69, 74, 75, 79, 81, 82, 85, **86**,
  87–93, 96, 98, 106, 109, 110
Washington state 211
Watergate 300, 331, **332–333**,
  334–336
Watts Riot 315
Weaver, James B. 215
Webster, Daniel 128, 131, 135
Webster, Noah 126
Webster–Ashburton Treaty 135
Welles, Orson 262, 266
Wells, H. G. 224, 262
Wells, Ida B. 216
Wesley, John 54
West Florida 117
West Point 84, 87, 111, 378, 379
West Virginia 161, 175
Western Civil War of Incorporation
  204

X

Y

Z